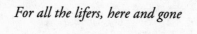

For all the lifers, here and gone

And as the smart ship grew
In stature, grace, and hue,
In shadowy silent distance grew the Iceberg too.

Alien they seem to be:
No mortal eye could see
The intimate welding of their later history.

—THOMAS HARDY,
FROM "THE CONVERGENCE OF THE TWAIN"

And there arrives a lull in the hot race
Wherein he doth for ever chase
That flying and elusive shadow, rest.
An air of coolness plays upon his face,
And an unwonted calm pervades his breast.
And then he thinks he knows
The hills where his life rose,
And the sea where it goes.

—MATTHEW ARNOLD, FROM "THE BURIED LIFE"

He was baseball.

—HOUSTON ASTROS COACH JACKIE MOORE,
ON MIKE COOLBAUGH

HEART
of the
GAME

THE BALLPARK NESTLES IN A SPACE WHERE BRIDGE AND RIVER MEET, and none of them is monumental—not the park nor the bridge nor the river nor the cities that the river runs between. In their size lies a certain charm, though to the ambitious and young such smallness can feel like a cage: The bridge serves only its function, with no cables soaring so that you can't help but take in the sky; the ballpark, with its field and stands carved well below street level, sends a message less of civic pride than of unnecessary humility, like a tall woman slouching in the hope of blending in. And after its mighty beginnings in a steep and narrow drop out of the Rocky Mountains 1,500 miles west, after its widening flood across the Great Plains, the river is weakening here as it readies to meet the mother Mississippi, decorative, a mild buffer between the two cities. The one on the other side announced its size from the start, named as it was by paddling trappers for La Petite Roche jutting out from the south bank. This one, smaller still, merited no other label but a dismissive North Little Rock, until residents from across the river began coming here to dump their unwanted canines. Then everyone started calling it Dogtown. . . .

There are two men down on the baseball field. They are small, too, by all measures of a material world, both raised in obscure towns along rivers with names like Susquehanna and Rio Yauco, both gifted but never enough to make it in the urban sprawls where one becomes famous and there's real money to be made. They'd had their chances, but long before this Sunday night the last had come and gone. The men are what the game calls "lifers," which, in its evocation of prisoners doing time, may be cartoonish but is hardly wrong. Beholden to talents they'd honed since youth, thrilled even now by moments of physical grace not replicable in any other profession, unsure how to begin the next career, they found themselves lodged in the game's minor leagues. There was no escape plan. They counted the years. Seventeen for the coach lying still on the grass. Eleven for the player on his knees, bent double, head buried in his hands.

Silence has fallen over the crowd, some 1,700 people struck as still as a forest after sudden snow. Maybe 20 seconds have passed since Tulsa Drillers utilityman Tino Sanchez swung his bat and followed the ball's flight as it curved in a line describing a scimitar blade into the rear of Mike Coolbaugh's neck. Maybe 15 seconds have passed since Tino ran up the first base line, stood alone over his first base coach, and peered into the face below. Maybe 5 seconds have passed since Tino, in one motion, stood and pivoted 180 degrees while raising his left arm to signal teammates and manager and trainer that things were bad, worse than anyone could believe, and only stopped rotating when facing the field again, as if trying to draw strength from the geometric patterns that were as familiar now as the layout of a boyhood home: the diamond-shaped basepaths, the rectangular dugout, the meticulously set lines fanning down to fences stenciled with the precise number of feet from home plate, the comforting squares and columns and numbers alight on the scoreboard—all of it interlocking into one snug and perfect whole. Still, his knees gave.

The ball lies near the first base line. It is 8:53 p.m., or maybe 8:54 or :55 now; it's impossible to say, exactly, because the timelessness of shock, the holiness attending the ultimate fear, has taken hold of every person in the ballpark. In the stands people have begun to talk again, but softly because no one knows if the coach is alive, if the game will go on, if they should stay or go. There's a paralysis of even instinct because what can your gut, slowed by cold beer and stale popcorn and a lazy night's hope for a midsummer's Double-A ballgame, tell you when seeing a man so alive suddenly not move? Phone numbers are dialed. An ambulance is called. Strangers surround Mike Coolbaugh. "No, no, no," Tino is saying to himself. "No, please. . . ."

There's but one blessing. Somehow, the moment itself has slipped past the clutch of modern experience. No television cameras captured the ball hitting the coach; no team cameras focused on Coolbaugh as he was struck or falling. Despite the prevalence of cell phone photography and portable recorders and the Internet's appetite for every recordable event, no Zapruder will surface with footage of the blow. It's as if, in that sudden erasure of noise just after, a kind hand conspired to wipe away any cheapening visuals, any reductive evidence of so public an accident, extending even to the game's official record. History is baseball's lifeblood and statistics its spine. Yet after Sanchez hit the foul ball in the top of the ninth inning, the umpires gathered and called the game over, and when it was later decided that the result was official and the game would not resume, another marker disappeared. Because the at-bat never ended, was not complete, it became a statistical non-event. Tino Sanchez's record would show a total of 2,267 career trips to the plate, but the one that matters most isn't in-

cluded; it's a phantom play, forever frozen at a 3–2 count, hazy proof that there are some baseball events that numbers can't contain.

Still: There are two men down on the field. One is unconscious. The other had looked down into that face struggling in the grass, and dropped to his knees in the universal expression of helplessness, of begging. It is a warm Sunday night and summer, but the player hears nothing now, not from the game nor the river nor the people surrounding. Silence presses down, relentless, and Tino's gasping for air and learning too fast what it means to be alone.

1

———

FULL FURNACE

Maybe, Mike Coolbaugh wondered in the free months before he joined his last team, it's that he talked too much. Analyzing every little twist in the minor league life. Picking apart all the suspect statistical cliches, all the excuses and explanations thrown down from on high. Studying professional baseball as if it were an entity that, when subjected to relentless inspection, could actually reveal itself as making some kind of sense. He knew there were logical explanations for how a man could spend 17 years in the minor leagues and make AAA All-Star teams and win awards and prove himself time and again, yet never get a clean shot at the major leagues. He knew all about injuries, bad timing, the reality that someone might be just that much better. Still, in total it was hard not to be puzzled.

"A curse on the Coolbaugh family," his father would say later about the game, and if Mike didn't go that far, on his worst days he might talk about bad luck. Really, though, mystical conspiracy wasn't his thing. His playing career ended as less a mystery than a problem, and every problem had a solution, right? So in retrospect that was it, perhaps: His attitude, his knack for worrying every angle, got on people's nerves. Maybe his failure never concerned what he did or didn't do. Maybe it was all about who he was.

And it's true: Mike hardly conformed to type. Yes, he grew up in San Antonio a star high school quarterback, tall, dark, and Texas handsome. But it's as if his brother, Scott, six years older, had absorbed the family's full share of cowboy reserve. Scott was the one who squinted as if he'd been running cattle under a blinding sun; Scott kept his own counsel and his drawled sentences clipped. Mike? He was overheated, a gabber, the kind of kid elementary school teachers moved to a desk on the other side of the room because he couldn't settle down or stop laughing. Everyone in baseball called him "Coolie," but out of uniform Mike was what his close friend and Roosevelt High School teammate Jay Maldonado calls "a nerd-o"; he carried himself with none of the king-jock arrogance. "You wouldn't think he could even run down the street, much less hit a baseball five hundred feet or slam-dunk a basketball or throw a football sixty yards," Maldonado says. "He wore glasses. He was clean-cut. He was good-looking. But his aura, his presence? If you saw him walking by, you wouldn't say, 'Whoa, who's *that* guy?'"

When a karate-obsessed peer at Roosevelt got in his face and began throwing punches, Mike's first instinct was to try to talk his way out. Nearly two decades later, when he began taking college courses, it didn't matter that the classes were held online; Mike went to the campus and introduced himself to his professors, outlined his plans, made sure they *knew* him. We normally don't meet any of our students, they said. But Mike got straight A's. "If we were driving down the street and he liked a house? He'd stop the car, get out, knock on these people's door, and say, 'Hey, how's it going? I really love this house: Would you mind if I took a look at it?' " Maldonado says. "And it wasn't for sale. But the people would say, 'Yeah, sure, come on in!' "

Baseball, of course, isn't real estate and it's certainly not academia. It's a minutely coded, testosterone-fueled universe where those who think too much and express themselves too freely, especially with the media, are viewed with suspicion. Whether Mike's theory is correct is less important than the fact that he thought it likely; his inability to "just play" marked him as different. "Very much a deep thinker, especially as far as baseball goes," says Houston Astros second baseman Chris Burke. "Mike could see the game from a lot of different angles; he introduced me to a side I'd never spent any time thinking about. It made me smarter." But it also left Mike wondering if, when all the fine-line distinctions were parsed and clubhouse chemistry weighed and roster spots filled, such a difference wasn't somehow held against him. Why not? It was as good an explanation as any.

Coolbaugh hit 258 professional home runs, played for 9 different organizations and on 19 different teams, traded 17 years of his life to play in just 44 major league games. He had been passed over for lesser talents and bigger egos and, yes, players more gifted than he could ever dream of being, and as such had seen how the game could toy with a man's soul. Yet there was a part of himself that he didn't allow any of that to touch. Mike may have been voluble, but there was nothing happy-go-lucky about him. In the clubhouse, his all-business demeanor did not invite instant camaraderie. But those who made it past that found an accessibility, an openness that verged on innocence; you can easily find a half-dozen ex-teammates who each call Mike their best friend. He smacked a ball like a caveman wielding a club, but he also wrote poetry. He sang. He designed his wife's engagement ring personally, had to wear his clothes just so; his brother-in-law would joke that Coolie had a little bit of woman inside him. When, in 2001, Mike finally got called up to the majors after 11½ years, he broke into tears in the clubhouse and didn't stop for five minutes, then welled up each time he spoke of it the rest of the day. "It's a weird game," said one teammate at the time, "that makes you do that."

But it wasn't the game and it wasn't weird. It was Mike. When he finally reached his brother with the news, Scott said, "What the heck are you crying for?" But Scott knew. That moment remains, he says, one of the happiest of his own life—and not just because he'd seen his little brother battle through season after lost season. Mike's unfiltered emotion let everyone who cared share the experience; lacking the alpha-male makeup that could keep everyone at arm's length, he invited even the family's alpha male to come close and feel it too. But Mike wasn't being generous: He needed to share the feeling. He liked being sappy. "He loved surprises," says Mary Lu Coolbaugh, Mike's mother. "He was in elementary school and they'd always ask kids to bring money in and somebody would sell them jewelry. Scott would say, 'I'm not buying anything, and walk away.' But Mike was very sentimental. He bought me a bracelet and it was a dollar eighty and he thought it was gold."

And in a sense, that was Mike's career: looking at the bright side, always seeing gold. The 433rd pick of the 1990 June draft, a 16th-round selection by the Toronto Blue Jays, Mike was sure that Scott's early success as a player, more than anything, is what got him drafted at all. He was far less accomplished than his brother coming out of high school, and it soon showed. His Rookie League season in Medicine Hat, Alberta, couldn't have gone worse: The first pitcher the 18-year-old faced was future Hall of Famer Pedro Martinez, and when Mike saw future Dodgers star Raul Mondesi blast a ball deep into the trees, he made a quick review of his own tools and thought, *I'm in over my head here.* He walked the mile from his apartment to the park and home again, hit .190, and made 33 infield errors in 50 games. His next season in St. Catharines, Ontario, proved little better. Mike began hitting a bit in 1992 but, in the first glimpse of what would become a lifelong pattern, took an inside pitch on his right thumb and shattered a knuckle. Mary Lu came north to drive him back to Texas in his '87 black Porsche coupe, and along the way they stopped so she could buy her fisherman husband, Bob, a surprise: four dozen earthworms. They took the nightcrawlers with them into the motel room. Mary Lu woke in the middle of the night to find the 10-inch worms inching along the baseboards. She screeched. Mike woke but couldn't bring himself to leave the middle of the bed, hopping and yelping as his mom wrangled them all.

The sky lightened and they packed the car and drove off toward San Antonio. Mike reclined the passenger seat and fell asleep, only to wake up hours later with nightcrawlers slithering again over his jacket and neck. He scrambled out of the car screaming. Mary Lu began to cry. The highway was empty. They jammed a load of bats on top of the worm boxes and took off, stopping only for gas, driving in a frantic slash down through the Midwest. Over the years, Mary Lu loved needling Mike for being so scared. Mike would just shudder, say "Gross!" and laugh.

The trip itself? By then they probably could've traveled the 1,700 miles blindfolded. After all, Bob and Mary Lu had grown up just a few hours east of St. Catharines, in Binghamton, New York, and all four of their kids—Scott, Lisa, Mike, and Linda—were born there. They moved to San Antonio when Mike was six, but Binghamton's endless winters and insularity fostered strong family ties and a loud skepticism that the Texas humidity could never melt; for years afterward, the family would pack up each summer and drive north to see relations, tap into the old competitive charge. The Coolbaugh clan liked their poker, and many were the nights when Mary Lu would rush to get the babies bathed and in bed so the adults could get down to the basement of Bob's parents' house to play. His mom, Bertha, was the luckiest woman in the world, they all said; she'd be clucking over her cards, and inevitably one of the men—Bob, his brother, his dad, Edward— would glance at his useless hand and fling it in a rage across the room. Arguments, games: Coolbaugh men needed always to be right and needed always to win. You learned to live with it, or you didn't.

The family had little choice but to be Yankees fans. Through the end of the 1960s, Binghamton had been home to a New York affiliate, the Binghamton Triplets, and each year the big club would come to town for an exhibition game. Babe Ruth, Lou Gehrig, Joe DiMaggio, and Mickey Mantle passed through; Whitey Ford was a Triplet in '49. During World War II, Edward worked for Remington Rand building airplane propellers; he played a nifty first base for the company team and got himself picked one year to play in an exhibition game against the Triplets. He handed down his love for the game to Bob, who starred at shortstop for Binghamton North High and at the end of his senior season heard from his coach the magic words: A Yankees scout had invited him to a tryout camp. Later, with his own two sons, people would wonder if Bob was too tough. But if he remains unsparing when it comes to judging intelligence or talent, if he constantly had to soothe Mike when he'd ask, "Are you calling me stupid?" it's important to note that at a pivotal moment the old man was no easier on himself. Bob never went to that tryout. "I just didn't feel I was that good," he says. "Young: I just felt young."

Instead, the owner of a machine shop came to school with a job offer. Bob's parents never pushed the idea of college, and a man with a trade could make a good living in a small town in the 1950s. Bob and four others signed up then and there. He was 18. He worked sheet metal, lathe work at first, but soon segued into becoming a precision tool-and-die man. He and Mary Lu married in 1964. In 1967 Bob and two partners opened DOT (Delivery On Time) Tool; they started with a few machines, hired a welder, earned enough to buy more machines. This was before people started calling the upper Midwest the Rust Belt. The world was more mechanical then, and industry paid well, provided steady work; robots hadn't taken hold in factories yet. DOT Tool made control panels for IBM, parts for an aviation trainer. Bob handled the money, figured what to charge. He studied the market, bought stocks; CDs were paying 18 to 20 percent. He fixed everything in the house himself.

Scott was ten, Mike four, when Bob brought home a used Juggs pitching machine. They had an acre and a half to play on, and Bob set up a small diamond in the backyard. When Scott began shattering windows at the rear of the house, Bob handed out gloves to Mary Lu and Lisa and Mike and had them stand guard. Mike was skinny, strong, but hardly consumed with baseball. He taught himself to roller-skate at the nearby rink in Chenango Forks, and when the family moved down to Windcrest, just outside San Antonio, Skateland management would clear the floor and ask the scrawny six-year-old to circle the place alone, as smooth as a finger on glass. Scott was broader, heavy afoot, and would find himself gasping when Mike bolted ahead on one of their runs: "Don't you beat me or I'll kick your ass!" At nine, Mike started taking guitar lessons. His Grandma Coolbaugh would visit, and in the afternoons she lay on a bed and asked him to play and sing. When he finished, she'd pay him 50 cents.

Grandma Coolbaugh was the family fan, tuning in major league games every summer night, paying Scott $10 each time he hit a home run. He couldn't get enough of watching baseball at her house in Binghamton, but she loved watching Scott play more, tracking his big years at Roosevelt High, his All-SEC years at the University of Texas, his rapid rise through the Texas Rangers minor league system. Mike was playing three sports at Roosevelt by then, inclining toward football; baseball was more Scott's game, his Grandma's game. Scott was there when she died at 78 in his parents' house in San Antonio: February 26, 1989. They found Bertha just before 7 p.m., when Linda went into the bedroom to wake her for that night's ballgame. Bob was shattered. Scott had never had anyone close to him pass, much less nearly before his eyes. "It was devastating to me, to see that," he says.

Scott never let on much, though—as always, something of the family puzzle. But he had no choice but to feel it: Even when the game served to cement the Coolbaughs together, it never provided much of an escape. From the start, baseball had insinuated itself into the family like another mouth to feed—alive, unpredictable, as liable as any brother or cousin to spark memories, laughter, tears. Road trips to see Scott play were common and crowded. Mike would start up front between Bob and Mary Lu in the rental car, but spend hours twisting himself around toward the backseat to take part in the endless Yahtzee or backgammon games that Lisa and Linda and Susan, Scott's long-time girlfriend, played as the miles whipped by. The six of them would camp out in budget hotel rooms, shuttling in one by one to hide how many were sharing the same key, emptying the ice machines to fill the coolers. Mary Lu cooked on a hotplate to save money. Nobody gained weight.

Scott hit 18 home runs in AAA Oklahoma City the summer of '89, and after a game one September night got the call from the Rangers: Pack your bags, you're going to the majors. He drove the three hours to Arlington with Susan, but didn't cry in relief, didn't gush over his journey, didn't indulge in "Can you believe this?" exclamations. Three years as a pro, and already in the majors? Scott's first reaction was the usual stoic concern about whether he would or could perform. At only one moment did he allow his shell to crack, an event so rare that the family marvels about it still.

The car was hurtling south on I-35, past Pauls Valley, Ardmore, Denton. Exits began to come faster; the Dallas lights loomed closer. He and Susan had fallen into one of those road silences, cab vibrating, tires humming. There was Scott, 23 years old and poised at the front edge of the family dream. "Do you think," he said out of nowhere, "Grandma will be able to see me play?"

By then, baseball had become Dad's pastime, too, less a sport than a task without end. Bob sold the tool-and-die company in 1977, having invested wisely enough to retire at 42, and moved the family to the warmth of San Antonio. Suddenly he had time to burn, and for a man with opinions and a mind used to crafting tools to precise dimensions, such freedom doesn't fill easily. Scott played because he enjoyed it, but Bob saw the boy's limited speed and power and knew neither love nor joy would get him very far. If you wanted to be good at something, you worked. Dad would supply the pocket money, rides to practices and games in the dusty Country Squire, a backyard batting cage with the pitching machine that he later souped up with a thick car spring and a lightened throwing arm (Mike was facing 100 mph fastballs not long after Little League). "Mike could kill that ball," Jay Maldonado says. "Myself, by the time I got started the ball was already by me. His dad told me one time: 'You know, Jay, on a scale of one to ten, you're about a half. Jump out of that cage before you ruin the carpet there.' I love the man, don't get me wrong; I love all the things he was about. But there was not a lot of room for errors or stupidity in his world."

The girls? There had been talk about a pool for Lisa and Linda, but when the cage went up that ended. The boys were forbidden to do indoor chores and Bob did the yardwork himself. He didn't push Scott and Mike so much as present them with a choice: Help yourself by practicing 100 percent, or help me pull weeds or wash the car—100 percent.

As the first son, and one whose athletic bent soon made every other sport secondary, Scott took the full furnace blast of his father's interest and energy and ideas about how baseball should be played. It took nothing to get Bob wound up talking about his hatred of Little League, the idiocies of baseball coaches always telling kids to hit grounders instead of on a line. Each boneheaded move seemed to affront Bob personally ("The defense *wants* you to hit it on the ground!

So why would you want to hit it on the ground?"), sparking thundering soliloquies, stand-up 20-minute demonstrations in the kitchen about the perils of rolling over your top hand. He was never vicious and only rarely whacked his boys' asses with a whistling yardstick, "but he was very firm when he spoke," Scott says. Which is a bit like describing a sonic boom as a noise.

"When I said, 'Scott come here' and he went the other way, he was in deep shit," Bob says. "Even with my wife, I say—and I know this sounds horrible, but in my house I feel as though I am God. When you're on the phone and I say, 'Mary Lu, come here a minute,' I don't give a shit if you're talking *to* God: Put down the phone or say you'll call back or say hold on and come see what I want. When I say something, it should be listened to."

And Scott, never one for conflict, bore up the only way he knew how: He put his head down. He got even quieter. He took it. The fact was, he lived for the game—watching it, playing it, even practice. So he did what he was told, usually: out to run a daily three-mile course at 12, no matter that he hated running like poison; digging into the batting cage, 300 to 400 cuts a day. There were times when Scott would rebel and push for a day off, and Bob would say something cutting and Scott would march off to his room to stew. Mary Lu would have to sneak him dinner. A day off? A day lost. If Scott had a date, Bob would insist he go hit the cage first: *Do what you got to do before you do what you want to do.* Or there were stumps to chop. Growing up, Bob had heard stories about major leaguers hitting the north woods in the off-season, honing their strokes by cutting timber. So he'd keep his eye out for tree trimmers in San Antonio, then haul their biggest scraps to the Coolbaugh backyard. Half the time Scott thought the exercise ridiculous. Sometimes he would even mumble, "I don't want to do this."

"Fine," Bob would reply. "Tell me and we'll stop."

But Scott couldn't. He was hooked. Soon, with his little brother's help, Scott was chopping so quickly through the stump supply that Bob had to dull the blade. "So then you'd hit it and you're barely chipping away," Scott says. "He'd have us do that two hundred times before we went to bed. There were a lot of hard times, but it created a work ethic. A lot of people didn't understand that."

After Scott got his lone scholarship offer to Cliff Gustafson's legendary program at the University of Texas in Austin, he'd bring teammates home once, maybe twice. "Camp Coolbaugh," they dubbed it, and never came back. It wasn't so easy for Scott to get away. He was the first to benefit from the family deal—though Bob and Mary Lu still drove the same battered station wagon, each kid got a car for graduating high school—but it came with strings attached. Scott brought his new red Camaro up to Austin for his sophomore year, feeling cocky. He had started fiddling with a new bat from Easton, the Black Magic, but after picking it up one day Bob had declared it top-heavy, no good. Don't use it, he told Scott. But then came a game when Scott hit a home run, rapped out a couple other hits, and decided to try out the Black Magic anyway. Bob watched from the stands, fuming. "The one thing I asked you to do," he said to Scott afterward, "and you defied me." He took the keys. Scott didn't drive that Camaro for a while.

All the discipline paid off, though: Scott played three years for the Longhorns, hit .351 and led the team to two College World Series appearances, and from there everything seemed to line up for a home-state success story. The Texas Rangers drafted him in the third round, 77th overall, and that and his resume and $40,000 signing bonus combined to give Scott Coolbaugh the most important label a minor leaguer can have: "prospect." In the outside world, the term is used casually to describe any aspiring pro player, and in theory, every kid in a team's system is studied for signs of major league potential. But the fact is, players are pigeonholed early as injury insurance or place-fillers or "organizational players," a second-class group that never gets as many chances to succeed or as many excuses to fail. Scott, though, was royalty, a Rangers third base prospect, protected from the encroaching hands of other teams by being placed on the organization's 40-man roster. He more than held his own with the Rangers after being called up for the first time in September '89: Hit American League pitching at a .275 clip for 25 games. How was Scott to know? He would never be that good again.

The next season, 1990, Scott flirted with the Mendoza Line—a .200 batting average, the barrier between mere struggle and abject failure—for 67 games, couldn't hit right-handed pitching, got sent down to the minors three times. And that was that. He'd been exposed and the Rangers admitted as much: Any trade is sign of a loss of faith. Texas shipped him to the San Diego organization that December, and Scott says, after being called up from AAA to the majors in May '91, Padres manager Greg Riddoch told him, "Son, this job's yours at third base."

But Scott lost it. He played 60 games for San Diego in '91, hit .217, and got demoted back to Triple-A Las Vegas. The following spring training, San Diego management made its intentions even clearer in February when it traded for a new infielder, Craig Worthington, then acquired star third baseman Gary Sheffield a month later. Scott barely played. He spent his days feeling more and more invisible. His father raged at the injustice. *Hadn't the owners' lockout during spring training wiped out his chance to impress in '90? Hadn't the Padres given their word? Worthington can't hit!* But none of that mattered a damn. Scott knew: When it's gone, there's no getting it back. His days as a prospect were done. "As a player?" Scott says. "That's the most hurt I ever had."

Mike, the little brother, grew up with a bit more room to maneuver. He played football, basketball, some golf and tennis as well as baseball, and that splintering of interest backed Bob off a tad. Baseball was what his dad knew best, studied closest, loved most, and Scott's own singular focus made him easy to oversee. Mike benefited, too, from the loosening of parental reins from first child to third. He was less cowed, more daring, slipping off the screen of his bedroom window when girls came to pick up him late nights, or simply rolling his parents' car down to the corner in neutral before starting the engine and taking off. Two beers was enough to get him buzzed in later years, and he liked it, but "we would go out and party and do all the wrong things and Mike would never do anything like that," says high school football teammate Billy Lee. "I never saw him drink until we were adults. I never heard him talk about a woman other than the ones we knew were his girlfriends, and while we were like, 'Hey, what did you all *do?*'—we were bragging all the time—you couldn't get that from Mike." As a high school junior, Mike drove Scott's Camaro out to Canyon Lake, lost control on the grass, and slid the rear end bang into a tree. He came home mystified: Went to Burger King, he told Bob, and—can you believe it?—came out to find someone had hit me and taken off. "Looks like you hit a tree," Bob said. Mike didn't confess that one for years.

Cornered, though, he fought back. He couldn't help himself. "Don't argue," he'd later tell new in-laws when Bob would start a harangue. "You can't win." But then you'd hear Mike mumbling, "Someday we'll win," and into the fray he'd jump. It wasn't just Bob's relentless analysis that got under his skin, though that was enough. Just as with Scott, if Mike went 3 for 4, Bob would need to know what happened on that one at-bat, always trying to keep his young tool precise, no matter that Scott and Mike soon knew far more about the game than he ever could. "How can you say that? You've never been there," Mike would demand when his dad lectured on hitting in certain situations, or how dumb he thought ballplayers were. And Bob's response couldn't have been better designed to get a rise: "I don't need to be there," he'd say, and Mary Lu would count down to the next explosion.

"My husband has his side, and his side's always right," she says. "Mike's just like him, and they'd clash like two magnets. But then they'd end up hugging each other, telling that they loved each other. Mike would come to me after and say, 'Can you believe this?' and I'd say, 'Why don't you just learn to shut your mouth?' But he couldn't."

At Roosevelt, too, Mike handled being a Coolbaugh differently than his brother. It was easier to dismiss Scott, quarterback and shortstop, reticent and surrounded by his pack of guy friends, as stuck up, but Mike's softer touch short-circuited any resentment. Stoners, blacks, band geeks, dance teamers, special-education kids, it didn't matter: "He was nice to everybody," Lee says. "Mike would play to the crowd, and whatever element he was in he'd try to adapt to it. That's why people liked him so much." He was also something of a girl-guy, not because he went from one long-stemmed girlfriend to another, but because he felt more comfortable in the company of females. Mike walked the halls with his arm around his little sister, Linda, and ate lunch with her almost daily; when his older sister, Lisa, had a sleepover he maneuvered himself onto the trampoline so he could surround himself with her friends. There's something irresistible to women about a sensitive tough guy, and with his soothing voice and challenging patter, Mike would have little problem conquering the wilds of minor league nightlife. But that was later, after he'd lost his first love.

Football was his sport. Playing quarterback for Roosevelt, being a team captain who also kicked field goals and punted, gave Mike instant relief, of course—from following Scott's baseball path, from living out his dad's baseball jones—and the constant movement, the adrenaline surge, the sense of leading a team, left him feeling something he didn't get anywhere else. "Baseball is work," he'd say. "Football is fun." Mike had talent, too, making first-team All-City and All-District in 1989 and piloting the Rough Riders to a 7–0 start, completing 75 of 135 passes for 1,018 yards and 11 touchdowns, throwing just 3 interceptions, rushing for 197 yards and 4 TDs—directly accounting for 109 of his team's 184 points. Though lacking the classic 6-foot-4, 205-pound quarterback frame, he was inundated with letters from schools nationwide, heard from recruiters at Texas, LSU, and Wisconsin, all of them talking scholarship. Would he have gotten a free ride to a Division 1-A university? Who knows? All that matters to the family is that after October 28, 1989, the phone calls and letters stopped.

That was the day Roosevelt trailed, 21–0, at halftime of a showdown against undefeated Judson. Mike had hit just one of his 14 pass attempts and thrown 2 interceptions, his receivers had dropped 4 passes, and his coach, a combustible local legend named John Ferrara, couldn't contain his rage. Scott had played for Ferrara, and he recalls the man smashing a film projector against a wall. This time, Ferrara, in mid-tirade, called out Mike for his poor play and tried firing a clipboard against a wall to emphasize the point. Instead, the clipboard slipped and struck Mike full in the face, its metal edges slicing two gashes on his forehead and the bridge of his nose. Blood and tears ran in streams down his cheeks.

Ferrara rushed to Mike, apologizing, but it was too late. When he stood up, his shirt was soaked and red. Mike was taken to the emergency room. Ferrara was fired within days, his public school career finished, and Mike's parents sued him for damages before settling out of court in 1990. Roosevelt lost that game. The season soured.

Still, Mike wanted to play. He couldn't wear a helmet, missed the next two games as the air around the team swirled with uncertainty. But with his face still bandaged from plastic surgery and a protective visor screwed onto his face mask, he came back for the first playoff game against Sam Houston at Alamo Stadium. Everyone in the Texas football community knew the story by then; his teammates couldn't stop talking about the coach, the star quarterback, and the clipboard that changed everything. But with players, with friends he'd known for years, even with his family, Mike didn't mention it. He made no pre-game or halftime speech. With a crowd of 7,613 watching, he just threw 2 touchdown passes, rushed for 85 yards and 2 more scores, and kicked 3 extra points to lead the Rough Riders to a 33–6 upset. "He wanted to move on," Billy Lee says. "I don't remember Mike saying anything about the coach or the incident at all—ever. Not even years later. It's like that game didn't even happen. I would never bring it up in front of him. That's something I would never do."

But neither silence nor that win could make the clipboard go away. Roosevelt lost its next playoff game, and the Coolbaugh family became convinced the freak event stained his resume; suddenly only small colleges like Richmond and Liberty were asking Mike to be their quarterback. Ferrara had been well regarded, and they could almost hear the whispers making the rounds: *What kind of player would elicit such a reaction? And now the family's suing?*

"People started backing off, asking, 'Is this kid trouble?'" Scott says. "Anything could be read into it. These high school coaches have power with college coaches, and anything can be said to discriminate against a player. I'm not saying that happened to my brother, but it was awful funny that teams like LSU and Texas A&M were inquiring about him and then after the incident everything dropped dead. Then they got beat and the season was over. Baseball was the next thing."

Al LaMacchia has been a scout for 52 years and in the game of baseball, he likes to say, for eight decades. He pitched 2½ seasons in the majors for the Browns and Senators, his most famous moment coming in spring training of 1945 when, irritated with his notoriously flinty Browns teammate Pete Gray, he threw the one-armed sensation a changeup for a strike that revealed to all opponents Gray's vulnerability to off-speed stuff. Two years later, a batted ball ripped into LaMacchia's throwing wrist, breaking it, and a general manager asked him to scout the Texas League while he convalesced. It has, in a sense, been his territory ever since. LaMacchia played the bushes for another decade, making it a full 16 years that he spent bombing around the minor leagues. "I was considered a guy who didn't want to give up baseball," LaMacchia says. He still is. Since starting with Cincinnati in 1956, LaMacchia has driven thousands of back roads to high school fields, sat on countless rotting bleachers, looking for the next kid who might be a star. He worked 4 years for the Philadelphia organization, 16 years for the Braves, 20 for Toronto, 5 for Tampa Bay, and 5 now for his latest stop, the Los Angeles Dodgers. "Other than actually playing?" he says at the age of 87. "There's nothing better than being a scout."

And LaMacchia has been one of the best, with his latest find, Dodgers outfielder Andre Ethier, just another beneficiary of a fierce and combative eye. By his own estimate, LaMacchia has signed some 30 ballplayers who reached the major leagues, cross-checked another 15, and saw enough in overlooked future stars like George Bell, Kelly Gruber, Jim Gott, Jim Acker, and Willie Upshaw that he was able to steal them from less discerning teams via the Rule 5 draft, the annual process in which teams raid each other for minor league talent not protected on the 40-man roster. He's also responsible for Dale Murphy, Bruce Benedict, and pitchers Dave Stieb, David Wells, Rick Mahler, and Larry McWilliams, who in 1978 was the winning pitcher in the game that halted Pete Rose's National League hitting streak at 44 games. And maybe because of his own experience—the fact that, though LaMacchia reached the majors as a wartime reliever, no team ever gave him a chance to prove himself as a starter—it wasn't the kids who frittered away their gifts, or even those whose careers were cut short by injury, who stayed with him long after they'd moved beyond his reach. It was the players who never got a genuine chance to show if they could play, the ones that organizations had sniffed and then walked away from, that LaMacchia found himself battling hardest for. And of all those, there was no one he fought for harder than Mike Coolbaugh.

"I was alone on him. That's okay: I don't give a shit who I go against," LaMacchia says softly, but quickly his voice rises to a shout. "Believe me, all Mike Coolbaugh wanted was an opportunity to prove that he could do it, and he was never given that opportunity. I differed with a lot of people on him, and I had a right to because he put numbers on the board in the minor leagues that should've given him the opportunity to play in the big leagues. That happens in this game. A lot of people said, 'Well, you signed him and you're pushing him.' *Pushing him, my ass! I'm telling you what he can do! Look and analyze him, and then see if I'm wrong.* I had tremendous arguments over that boy. Well, you can say he's from my hometown. But I liked anybody who puts his heart and soul in the game."

LaMacchia was a Blue Jays vice-president the year he first saw Mike, then a high school junior at Roosevelt. He liked Mike's above-average arm, his quick stroke. "He had tremendous *wrist*," LaMacchia says. "George Bell had that particular stroke, but he swung at more pitches. Mike had tremendous discipline at the plate." Even more, LaMacchia loved the work ethic that Bob had instilled, the aggression Mike carried over from the football field. When the recruiters stopped calling, Mike funneled all his competitive heat into baseball, hitting .356 as a senior shortstop, committing himself in a way even Scott hadn't. The University of Texas offered a baseball scholarship, but it's as if, after seeing how randomly and quickly a sport could be taken away, Mike didn't want to risk losing another. LaMacchia came to talk, said the Blue Jays would draft him late, probably wanted to play him at second or third base, but it would all work out fine, rookie ball first in some Canadian town called Medicine Hat. The whole time, Mary Lu was thinking, *Why are you doing this? Go to UT!*

"But Mike was a horse in a barn when LaMacchia came here," she says. "He wanted to go bad." Bob and Al hammered out the money at the kitchen table on a sweltering night, the Coolbaugh men in t-shirts, Mike pacing in and out of the room and scared that Bob would blow his chance by asking for too much. They finally settled on an $80,000 signing bonus, doubling Scott's take from just three years before: La-Macchia always had been a good closer. But what got him excited was that eagerness, the quality that he saw on the field and in the kitchen, the thing that no coach can teach, no amount of money can induce, and that he felt every time he crossed paths with Mike over the next five years.

"He loved the game," LaMacchia says. "I never saw a kid love the game of baseball as much as Mike Coolbaugh did."

But Bob had been right: Love could take you only so far. Mike didn't know it, but his problems began earlier in the same June draft, when Toronto selected Chris Weinke in the second round and gave him a signing bonus of $375,000. Later, of course, Weinke would leave baseball, quarterback Florida State to a national championship, and in 2000 become, at 28, the oldest player ever to win the Heisman Trophy. But in 1990, the St. Paul native was considered one of the best prep football *and* baseball players in the country, a super-sized, over-hyped, better-paid version of Mike, 6 feet 5 inches and 210 pounds of seemingly surefire All-American talent. And through him, Mike learned his first hard lesson about professional baseball: It's not always about results. Because, it turned out, Chris Weinke couldn't play—and for years that didn't matter. He hit .248 for his minor league career and was abysmal in the field, making 76 errors his first four seasons, most of them at first base. But Weinke's bonus and draft status—the public gauges of a team's ability to judge talent—had cemented him as a prospect and Mike as a roster spot, and the fact that Mike put up comparable numbers at the plate, and markedly improved in the field after his first nightmare season in Medicine Hat, wasn't enough to upgrade his status. Two years into Weinke's career, LaMacchia tried convincing fellow Toronto vice-president Bobby Mattick and others in the organization that Coolbaugh was better, but he couldn't fight the impression that the only numbers that mattered were Mike's $80,000 and Weinke's $375,000. "I was alone on him," LaMacchia says. "You see the difference? If you're a development guy, you feel it's your job to develop the guys who get the money."

It was about that time that Mike approached him during instructional league in Dunedin, Florida. "Mr. LaMacchia," he said, "why do they work with guys like Chris Weinke more than others?"

"The best way I can put it? They're non-lepers and you're a leper," LaMacchia replied. "Them kids got more money than you got, and they're determined to make them kids get the chance to play in the big leagues."

Eventually Weinke was promoted beyond his capabilities and, after two trying stints in 1995 and '96, proved a bust at AAA. By then, Mike had been moved along too, left unprotected and picked up by Texas in the '95 Rule 5 draft. "I called him a leper because he was shunned," LaMacchia says. "He fell through the cracks for us, and I thought it was wrong. I can go back and see that kid right now: His stroke was unbelievable. It irked me that the development people would walk away from this guy. *Give him the opportunity! If I'm proven wrong, I'll raise my hand and say I was wrong.* But to this day I've never said I was wrong on Mike Coolbaugh. I truly believe if he had gotten the opportunity, he would've made it in the big leagues. But he never got the chance."

But even as a leper, Mike had a few things going for him. By the time Toronto let him go, he had two role models for how to handle whatever curves the game would throw. His old high school teammate, Jay Maldonado, pitched for 2½ years in the Blue Jays organization—the two had played together in Hagerstown in 1993—but grew disgusted with the system and quit the summer before at 22. Scott, meanwhile, had lost his prospect status in San Diego, and that "turning point of my life"—the brutal demotion of a one-time high school, college, and minor league star to a bust—drained all romance from the game, hardening Mike's older brother. The Padres traded Scott in mid-season 1992 to Cincinnati, then Cincinnati released him without a major league look, then he played a mediocre season of AAA for the Orioles. Each bounce chipped a bit more off his shine, but in his head Scott had just one idea: *I'm going to prove all these people wrong.*

He almost did, too. In 1994 Scott signed on with the Cardinals and at 28 pieced together his best minor league season ever, hitting .303 with 19 homers and 75 RBI in Louisville. The call came, and suddenly he was back in the majors, three years since his last appearance. He got 15 games in, hit .190, backed up Todd Zeile and Gregg Jefferies at the corners, seemed to be just finding his legs . . . and then on August 12 the players' union went out on strike. Nine hundred and thirty-eight games, the first World Series since 1904, and any hope of Scott's major league comeback got lost in the shutdown. When his agent called that fall and said that a Japanese club, the Hanshin Tigers, wanted to sign him to a two-year, $1.2 million deal, Scott jumped at it. He and his wife, Susan, had a one-year-old son now. "You can't turn down a contract like that," Scott says. "Did it make me millions of dollars? No. Did it give me some security and the opportunity to start a family and build a house and live in a house I feel comfortable in? Yes, it did. Here I was walking away from $5,000 a month in AAA, maybe $6,500 a month for five months; I'm turning down $30,000 a year to make $600,000. I'm feeling this is a good move."

Still, in American eyes then, playing in Japan was considered a waving of the white flag. To this day, Bob believes that Scott somehow broke an unwritten rule of baseball labor etiquette by playing there during the strike, provoking a blackballing that stained Mike's career too. But Scott's take is more banal: By going to Japan, he willingly took himself out of the American loop. No scouts would travel around the globe to see him play with Hanshin. "It's probably the best thing I ever did, looking back on it," Scott says. "But in my heart? I knew I'd never play in the big leagues again."

There was one other downside: Aside from enabling him to build a new home, the big Hanshin salary also gave Scott, for the first time in his career, extra cash to play with. A former Texas Rangers teammate had introduced Coolbaugh to a financial adviser named John

Gillette Jr. during his early '90s stint in San Diego. When Gillette—a seemingly devout Christian with a picture of Jesus on his office wall—dangled the chance to invest $100,000 in a long-term investment in a SeaWorld-type development in 1995, Scott bit. Considering the far larger sums (more than $11 million total) that Gillette swindled from an assortment of pro football and baseball players at the time, Coolbaugh got off easy. In 1998 Gillette was convicted on 37 counts of grand theft and one of forgery and sentenced to ten years in state prison. He was ordered to pay restitution, and a bankruptcy court sold off Gillette's assets. But Scott got back only about $15,000. The rest of his money was gone.

He lasted less than two seasons in Japan, came home 30 years old and limping into what seemed like the end with a 58-game string in AAA Ottawa. That same year, 1996, Mike found himself busted back down to A-ball again but refused to stagnate, hitting .287 in Charlotte with a personal-best 75 RBI. The brothers would call each other over the summer of '96, Mike asking for hitting tips, Scott feeding off his enthusiasm, but more and more talking about his son, Tyler, and just-arrived daughter, Chandler, and the grind of the minors and moving the family each year. In the off-season, they went back to Texas, Scott to Colleyville, Mike to San Antonio, where that winter he was sitting at dinner at a local institution, Los Barrios Mexican Restaurant, and looked up to see a familiar face approaching. Mike stood and smiled, and Al LaMacchia wrapped him in a hug. It's usually understood that scouts lose touch with players after they sign them; their job is done. Mike hadn't seen Al in years. But LaMacchia still felt awful about what had happened in Toronto.

"Mike," he said, "you should've gotten better opportunities to play. I've always thought you can hit—and you *can* hit—but you always got caught in a numbers game."

It was, really, the perfect opening for Mike to start complaining. Texas had cut him loose; Oakland had picked him up; he could find any reason to bitch. But Coolbaugh didn't bite. "Well," he said, "I'm not going to give up."

Whenever he returned home then, Mike and Jay Maldonado had a tradition: a one-night blowout that usually ended at a strip joint. One night, one of the girls plopped herself into Jay's lap and he told her to move on; they were just two guys out having a good time. But the girl started writhing anyway, then said the lap dance was on her. And the rest of the night, from one bar to another, Maldonado couldn't stop talking about how that stripper had found him so ir-resistible. "You see that shit, Mike?" he crowed. "I still got it, dude; the girls want me." Mike smiled and ordered another beer. "Yep," he said, "guess so."

Nearly every time they spoke for the next year, Maldonado brought up that girl. When Mike came home the next winter, the two had their night out again, went to the same strip bar, saw the same stripper. She pulled the same move, but at the end blurted out that Mike had paid the tab.

"I'd expect that from me, dude," Maldonado said, both humili-ated and impressed by how Mike had been able to let the joke ride for so long. "But I never would've expected that from you."

"I wasn't going to tell you," Mike said, laughing, "until we were eighty years old."

He would be 25 soon. No one knew his swing better than Bob,

and if the two clashed over fine points, they never stopped talking and Mike never stopped listening. It wasn't rare, in mid-season, for him to sit for 30 minutes at a time on the phone and listen wordlessly to his dad's advice. "He's the guru," Mike said later. "When I'm not getting hits, I call him." That winter, he spent every day in the backyard cage, shortening his swing, trying to eliminate fly balls with a new, more compact coil. Years later, Mike would look back and realize that it had taken him those first four or five years in the bushes to learn the craft, to become a baseball player instead of an athlete playing baseball. Scott had been the family seamhead for so long, eating and sleeping the sport while Mike had simply enjoyed the competition and camaraderie. But now it had become his game, too. "Mike caught him," Bob says. "I think they turned out equal."

Or maybe Mike passed him. When Toronto cut Scott out of spring training in 1997, it seemed he had just one last option: the desperation route of independent ball, those ragtag franchises unaffiliated with any major league organization. The mere thought of it had him ready to quit. Mike wouldn't hear of it. "Hey," he said, little brother suddenly acting the older, "you always told me: 'Just keep going; you never know what can happen in this game.' Try it." Scott went off grudgingly to an independent franchise in Bridgeport, Connecticut, but before a game had been played, the White Sox came calling, in need of a third baseman in Double-A Birmingham. "And that's the year I saw him in Huntsville," Scott says. "Kind of weird how that happened."

Indeed, that summer would be the only time Scott and Mike, separated forever by the six-year age difference, would play each other as professionals. Not in the majors, like everyone had hoped; not in Texas, where it would be so convenient; but over one short stretch in the Double-A Southern League, two bushers going at it in obscurity. They met in two different series, one in early summer and one late, with the first in Huntsville proving most satisfying. Such a family showdown would've been ESPN fodder for days, of course, had it concerned baseball royalty like the Deans, the Boones, or the Griffeys, but the four-game stint in June didn't merit more than 200 words from the *Birmingham News*. "Coolbaughs Have Good Night," the headline murmured after the first game; but with Bob and Mary Lu and Scott's wife, Susan, there, it felt better than good—maybe even perfect. After all, the two sons played it nearly dead even. There was Scott, number 32 and manning third for the Birmingham Barons, and Mike, number 32 and manning third for the Huntsville Stars, Double-A affiliate for the Oakland A's. Both men picked up two hits and an RBI in the first game, and the Barons scored three in the ninth to win it 8–6. The following day, Huntsville scored four in the ninth to return the favor, and they kept trading heroics: Scott had three hits in Game 3 and homered in Game 4; Mike doubled in a run in Game 4. Each team ended up winning two apiece. Neither brother robbed a base hit or even fielded a ball from the other all series, and their one marveling moment came with Scott at third and Mike crouching there as a base runner. Barons manager Dave Huppert called for a pitching change, and during the warmup he stepped over to talk. For a few quick minutes all three allowed themselves to grin and revel in the idea: two brothers good enough to play baseball and get paid for it, with the man most responsible sitting in the stands. Later, Mary Lu would get the photos she'd taken that weekend and mount them on a massive wall hanging titled "Bama Boys," and the following winter there was a bit more spice layered into the usual shit flying back and forth. *How*

many hits you get that series against us? How many home runs you get?
"Every year we'd joke and talk: *I hit twenty-six this year; you only hit eighteen*," Scott says. "It was always a competition between us, always friendly. Something to keep us going."

By then, though, Mike didn't need much help. He found himself at last during that '97 season, became a dominating force on a Huntsville team loaded with future major leaguers like Ben Grieve and Miguel Tejada. Doubling his personal best with 30 home runs, he hit .308 and set a Southern League record of 132 RBI—the third-best such output among all affiliated minor leaguers and ahead of future stars Kevin Millar and Paul Konerko—and helped push the Stars into the championship series. In the field, Coolbaugh led all Southern League third basemen in fielding percentage, putouts, assists, and double plays. He made the Double-A All-Star game held in San Antonio that July, appearing before his hometown crowd with a league-leading 20 homers in pocket (ahead of Jacksonville's Juan Encarnacion, a 21-year-old outfielder who would make his major league debut in Detroit later that summer, who had an 11-year career in the majors ahead of him, and who, on August 31, 2007, had that career ended in St. Louis when Aaron Miles's foul ball crushed his left eye socket while he stood in the on-deck circle), came in as a midgame substitution at shortstop and made the game's best defensive play, then hit the game-clinching double that got him named the night's "Star of Stars." Best of all, the hometown girl Mike had gotten serious with, the one who didn't know much about baseball, was able to see and feel it all: the crowd cheering, the ball whizzing into the outfield, the sight of her boyfriend acclaimed by everyone, for one night at least, as the best man there.

Mike couldn't have asked for better. He finished the season satisfied, the first time that had happened since high school; he had proved himself at last. And it was all for nothing. Six weeks later, the A's gave it to him straight: He was a 25-year-old in Double-A. With Scott Brosius, Scott Spiezio, and Tony Batista on the major league level, Mark Bellhorn ahead of him in Triple-A, and teenager Eric Chavez ripping up Single-A Visalia and looking like the organization's future third baseman, Coolbaugh's brilliant season couldn't even guarantee him a spot in major league spring training. "We explained what his chances were," says Keith Lieppman, the A's director of player development. "And if you just looked around, you could tell they weren't going to be good." Mike didn't fit into the plan.

Bob raged in the kitchen: at the injustice, the fools who ran things, the hot Oakland prospects who couldn't compare. That's when it began in earnest, in the fall of 1997: the casting about for clues, the concocting of theories, the interrogation that continues even today in the unconscious hope that the guilty party might yet step forward and confess. "Another All-Star year shot in the ass," Bob says when '97 is mentioned. "He's done all those frickin' things, and yet it's like he golfed in the U.S. Open and got the top score but they didn't give him the trophy. Why not? He's done everything. Did he win the home run hitting contest by luck? Is he an All-Star year after year by luck, and not just in A, but Double-A, Triple-A? When he went to the majors he didn't do that bad. Why? That's the biggest question of Mike's life. Why?"

And Bob would go on, waiting for his son to chime in. But Mike wouldn't. Though inside he was sifting through the evidence just as furiously, he couldn't allow himself the luxury of open bitterness. "What are you going to do, Dad?" Mike said as his eighth pro season passed. "I can't control it. I just do the best I can."

Then he'd walk out into the backyard and into the cage, day after winter day, the sound of his bat crackling in the Texas afternoon. He would wait and see. He still had time.

Tino Sanchez Sr. knows exactly why he began to lose his taste for coaching. It wasn't the game—never the game. It was the kids, or their parents, or whatever it is in society or in the male psyche that makes 17-year-olds suddenly so impossible, so unreachable—those same kids who five years before hung on his every word, who breathed baseball like the purest oxygen, who could think of nothing better than to play deep into the night and then talk about it until sleep came and they could wake up and do it again. Whatever: Something changed on him, it seemed, around 1997 and Sanchez smelled that change before he saw it. One minute the head coach of Yauco's 16–18 team was getting ready for another game and the next he noticed the sickly-sweet stink of marijuana wafting about the field and found three of his boys smoking a joint; he took their uniforms and dared them to send their outraged fathers to come ask why. None ever did. The next year, one of his players oh-so-casually asked if Sanchez could hold some personal items and proceeded to hand over $5, a ring, a watch, and a .38-caliber pistol. Sanchez couldn't decide which was more horrifying, the gun or the assumption that it was no more notable than pocket change. It struck him that he should find something else to do with his time.

But truth be told, that wasn't it, not entirely. His son, Tino Jr., had been gone from Puerto Rico a year by then, was playing his second season in the Colorado Rockies organization, and baseball didn't feel the same without him. It took a while for the father to understand this, and then only glancingly, because he'd always couched his coaching duties in the bland and general societal jargon: keeping kids off the streets, giving them something to love and do. And the fact is, son or not, Tino Sr. would often go over to Yauco's big old ballfield at Ovidio "Millino" Rodriguez Park and hit ground balls for hours to any boy willing to eat that dust. Tino Sr. was a baseball fan, had been ever since, at 11, he had flown up from Puerto Rico to visit family in the Bronx and rode the subway to Yankee Stadium and felt the hum of 50,000 sweaty people—the biggest crowd he'd ever seen!—pushing through the turnstiles. He sat in the upper deck with his uncle Julio in the buttery summer evening light, heard the announcer's clipped introduction of Mickey Mantle, and *Dios Mio*, he was hooked. From then on, of course, it was the old New York story: baseball and the Yankees forever for Tino Sanchez Sr. Few events in this world could match the first-time impact of that historic ballpark on a boy.

He wasn't much of a player himself. That was okay. Wedged up in the hills along the southern coast of Puerto Rico, Yauco was a company town, built around the harvesting and selling of coffee. Tino Sr.'s father drove trucks and hauled sugarcane for one of the biggest growers, Llinas; his mother was a secretary there and kept the books in an office and demanded her three children attack the world with their brains. Tino did that. Tino studied hard, got his degree in accounting. But he also made sure to get over to Ponce and Mayaguez for

Winter League games, took in the Puerto Rican players who returned home after the major league season to play all over the island. He saw the great Roberto Clemente with the Caguas team a few years before the plane crash. He went to college, got a master's degree in finance. He married a strong woman named Rosa Julia, had a daughter, moved to San Juan. Then came Tino Jr. in 1979 and the family moved back to Yauco because he could afford a house there. Then Tino Jr. discovered baseball, and his father fell in love all over again.

The second time, with his son, hit him even harder than the first. Because now Tino Sr. didn't just watch games; now he got *involved*. Because Tinito—Little Tino, as everyone called him—was a superb athlete, fast, with a good arm, and if a coach is tutoring his son it's one thing, but if a coach finds himself with a son who loves the game as much as he does and turns out to be the best player on every team, well, that only gins up the potion. Despite its population (50,000), Yauco is one of Puerto Rico's better youth baseball towns, its beloved Cafeteros annually taking on the best kids in 77 other baseball-mad towns and cities and more than holding their own. Tinito won his first island championship as an 8-year-old "Coqui" (the town paid for a team trip to Disney World as a reward), and then won three more—at the 11–12, 13-, and 15-year-old levels, earning the right to represent the whole island in tournaments in the Dominican Republic; Taylor, Michigan; and Monterrey, Mexico. For the last two, Tino Sr., who had studied the game and put in the years coaching younger kids, was made the head coach, and by then he'd long established the coach's-son rule: You'll work harder than everyone, daily. If practice was Tuesday and Thursday, then Monday and Wednesday and Friday were reserved for Tino and his Tinito to spend on running, individual hitting, drills. When Tinito was 13, Tino insisted his son start hitting lefty every other at-bat, to make himself even more dangerous. Mantle was a switch-hitter, after all.

But it was never a battle. Tinito loved it, wanted almost all his father could give. The family was all about music, too, with Tino Sr. on the trombone, daughter, Hilda Rosa, on the saxophone, and Tinito playing an even better trombone than his dad. From the fifth grade on, the boy played, became part of Luis Muñoz Marin High School's 150-man marching band, practiced each day for seven years. Damn, but it was creative and cool working together on the biggest team you ever saw (all those hearts and lungs and instruments working together like one big musical machine) without baseball's deadly competition, and, yes, you met plenty more girls, too—all of it fun in a way sports couldn't be. Come Christmastime, a few dozen of them would grab their instruments and some bottles and load up cars to roam Yauco's streets in the annual *parranda*, a roaming late-night ambush on slumbering homeowners who, by tradition, must throw open their doors to the clamoring half-tanked party crowding the front door. Still, Tino Jr. quit the band by 11th grade: He'd had to make the choice. "Baseball drove me crazy," Tinito says, "and, you know, Puerto Rico is all about baseball." He never played the trombone again.

Instead, he had the vision of Juan Gonzalez and the Alomar brothers, Roberto and Sandy Jr., and Carlos Baerga and Ruben Sierra all making big marks in the majors, all of them singing a *parranda* in his dreams. Tinito was 16 when his father installed a batting cage in the backyard, bought one of those dual-wheeled Bulldog pitching machines, the kind that can loop in curves and knuckleballs as well as fastballs, and he'd happily spend hours hacking away. But Tino Sr.

insisted he had to do more: As a catcher and center fielder, as a leader, he needed to *think* the game, too.

That was a harder sell. Tino Sr. would come back from Winter League games with videotapes of pre-game practice to show the boy how the pros worked. He bought all the bibles—Ted Williams's *The Science of Hitting,* Tony Gwynn's *The Art of Hitting,* Dusty Baker's *You Can Teach Hitting*—and spent hours painstakingly translating the English into Spanish, page by page, scribbling down the words and then typing them into the computer for Tinito to study. His wife called him crazy. Tinito always said thank-you when his father handed him the pages, the videos. But he never read a word or watched a minute. That all felt too much like the trombone's dull downside, studying the sheet music, practicing scales. Didn't he always hit the ball hard and clean? His teams won, didn't they? Tinito just wanted to play.

Okay, Tino Sr. figured, *I'll give the boy his head there.* But no relenting on the basics: seriousness, respect, standing by what you say and believe. *Don't make me look bad,* Tino Sr. warned his son. He had told Tinito to never expect favorable treatment, and when the 17-year-old got into a fight with a teammate, Martin Sanchez, Tino banished them both from practice for a week. When they came back, he made Tinito and Martin run a full lap around the ballpark together, holding hands while their teammates hooted. "He was just another player," Tino Sr. says.

But he wasn't, of course, and Tino Sr. had a plan. Yauco is some two hours from San Juan, too far off the beaten track for the big league scouts who liked to stay up in the capital, so he decided to bring his son to them. Late in 1996, he arranged for Tinito to play for a San Juan team, the Raiders, organized by Latin American superscout Luis Rosa, who had discovered the likes of Benito Santiago, Ivan Rodriguez, the Alomar brothers, and Gonzalez: practices twice a week, games every weekend. Tino Sr. outfitted a van with a bed and a TV and the three of them made the drive night after night, month after month, Tino Sr. behind the wheel while his wife and Tinito slept, rolling into the driveway at 3 a.m and still getting up for his accounting job at Stor-ageTek a few hours later. Or, just as often, Tino would pepper Tinito with questions about the game just passed. "We had our controversies, because he always wants to push me, push me," Tino Jr. says. "Some-times we'd be driving four hours across Puerto Rico and if I'd gone 0 for 4, it'd be a long drive. He'd want to talk about mechanics and why did I go 0 for 4? I just wanted to sleep, and he'd want to talk. But I appreciated it. It wasn't in a bad way, no cursing, no bad words—but a lot of repetitions. I appreciated his character, his responsibility. I am what he made of me."

Everything, it seemed, was in service to the idea of baseball—pro baseball. Tinito ran track in high school, a 200- and 400-meter star, but that was just for filling time between seasons, keeping his wind. When he didn't have ballgames, his dad was driving him all over the island to tryout camps, workouts for scouts—running a 60-yard dash, throwing, hitting. Small colleges in the U.S. wrote letters asking Tino to come play baseball; he received a scholarship offer from Western Kentucky. But that was a backup, and they all knew it. Tinito turned 18 in February '97, his senior year, and Tino Sr. wouldn't openly pres-sure him toward school or pro ball; he didn't want the responsibility for any future regrets. But he also knew that if Tinito got anything close to a decent offer, he was gone.

Father and son had one final run together. This was also in February, after Tino Sr. had booted the malcontents off Yauco's 16–18 team. With Tinito catching and hitting in the number three spot, the Cafeteros bulled their way through the Puerto Rican playoffs, underdogs giving everyone a scare. After finishing fourth in its section in the regular season—losing so badly each time they played the first-place Ponce Lions that the opposing manager joked before the first game of their sectional semifinal, "Tino, you can't beat me in anything, not even eating"—Yauco beat Ponce in four games in the semifinal and made it all the way to the island finals in San Juan.

And here's the weird thing: Though the Cafeteros got swept in the best-of-five series by Guaynabo, though they lost all three heartbreakers after leading with two outs in the final inning, in a way that was Tino's favorite season with his son, the last and best. Together they had shut up that manager from Ponce. Together they had excelled and suffered. "It was a *challenge*," Tino Sr. says, laughing. "We lose, but that was a great experience with him."

In the spring, Jorge Posada Sr., father of the Yankees star catcher and scout for the Colorado Rockies, started calling. He had watched every weekend in San Juan. The Rockies chose Tinito in the 11th round of the June 1997 draft, the 342nd player taken overall. The Sanchez family didn't bother with an agent, let the team set the terms: A $25,000 signing bonus and a $20,000 scholarship, plus a $7,500 make-good bonus—if Tinito ever spent three months in Double-A, he'd get $1,000; if he spent three months in AAA, he'd get $1,500;

and if he spent three months in the majors he'd receive the remaining $5,000. Tinito would receive $800 a month in salary his first year. "Your decision," Tino Sr. said again. His son signed.

It took a while to sink in: Posada's connection to the Yankees bringing the whole thing full circle, the fact that his boy was on his way, maybe, to the big leagues. It took, in fact, until Tino Sr. saw his son the following November, when Tinito came back from rookie ball to play Winter League in Puerto Rico for the first time, like Clemente and all the others who came home from the States. Tinito was playing for the Arecibo Lions, batting right-handed, and years later Tino Sr. could still see that hit, his boy's first as a returning pro, crashing off the wall in left field. That's when he knew he and his wife had actually done it: They'd gotten their son there, close enough to the dream so the boy could maybe see the rest of the way clear. Now there was no turning back. Now they were fully invested, a baseball family for sure—the kind that, when you ask the mother years later how important the game is, Rosa Julia will look at you half-puzzled and without hesitation say, "It's everything."

2

—

THE ROOTS

A BALLPLAYER? *NO, NO,* MANDY PAVLOVSKY THOUGHT. *THAT'S the last thing I need.* Here she was, just getting over a serious boyfriend, still student-teaching to finish up her degree at University of Texas–San Antonio, 21 years old: What would she want with a guy who's never around, who's got girls hanging all over him on the road, who probably thinks he's God's gift . . .

"What kind of car are we looking for?" Mandy asked. It was September 1996. She was driving to Crabby Jack's, a San Antonio seafood and beer joint, with her roommate Lisa and a girl she'd met at school, Linda Coolbaugh. The two other women had cajoled her into this . . . what? A blind date, technically, but with each passing mile another layer of romance sloughed off, leaving behind the usual dread. By the time they arrived, she figured on an obligatory meet-and-greet with Linda's older brother: hello, goodbye, a free night wasted. *Maybe he's some kind of loser, needing his own sister to set him up. . . .*

"A Porsche," Linda said.

Oh, God. "I can't do this," Mandy said.

She would've just stayed in the car the rest of the night, too, if not for the signal they'd devised. Linda and Lisa wouldn't leave. If the night went disastrously, Mandy would slap Mike demonstrably on the leg and say, "Well, I've got to get up for work tomorrow!" and the girls would swoop in for the rescue. But when he arrived, Mike didn't come off like some cocky jock. Not that, with movie-star hair and a 6-foot-2, 200-pound frame nicely filling out his Guess jeans, he didn't look the part; in truth Mandy felt instantly that, looks-wise, he was out of her league. But she found him shyer, more serious, more opinionated than she expected. And he wasn't trying to win her over—not conventionally, anyhow. The guy wouldn't loosen up, not once, despite the chicken strips and beer—and of course she took that personally. Mandy didn't know then that people always thought Mike was mad the first time they saw him, that he couldn't just flash what he called "a pasted-on smile." Was she the only one who was going to make an effort here? *How do I even talk to him, if he's just going to sit there?*

Still, something kept her from giving the signal. From the moment Mike stepped out of his car, Mandy felt her stomach flopping, and she needed to figure out what that meant. They played pool, and Mandy couldn't have been worse, scratching the cue ball in ever more inventive ways. Then all four went to a club called Park Place with dancing and karaoke—but nobody sang. Then Nine Inch Nails' "Closer," with its chorus about primal sex ("My whole existence is flawed/You get me closer to God"), started playing, and she dragged Mike out to the dance floor and soon they were mashed together, making out like every other half-buzzed couple. At some point Lisa and Linda made their way to where Mike and Mandy were swaying. "Are you sure you don't need us to drive you home?" they said.

"No," Mandy said, grinning.

"We'll stay a bit," Mike said.

But after Mike took her home, glanced around at her apartment, and left without asking for a phone number, Mandy figured that was that. On paper, she wasn't his type. Mike had always been with tall, athletic, dark-haired girls—and spoke often of how much he wanted tall, athletic kids—and Mandy was short and light and blissfully clueless about sports. In high school, she had visited San Antonio from her home in Fort Hood once, had gone to a Roosevelt practice because her friend had a mad crush on the star quarterback there. When she later moved to town to attend the University of Texas, a boyfriend talked constantly about being at Roosevelt with one particularly gifted baseball talent. But Mandy had no idea who Mike Coolbaugh was. It didn't help, either, that she had broken one of Bob's cardinal rules for dating that first night: If the girl doesn't unlock your car door after you open hers, she's no good. And the fact that she didn't rush out to get a teaching job after college, kept on waiting tables, rubbed Mike wrong, too. Mandy seemed to lack ambition, didn't want to grow up. He kept telling her: "I leave in March, I can't guarantee anything, I'm not looking for a relationship." But he kept calling.

"So," Mandy says, "I played the friend card. If that was going to keep him around until he knew he was interested in me, I was okay with it."

She had fallen hard. Mandy was used to dates who asked for a ride and finagled her into paying the tab, boys who made themselves scarce after she said how much she wanted to get married and have kids. She had never been with a man who opened doors, had pocket money but didn't lord it over anyone, knew what he wanted and lived it every moment. All that winter of 1996–97 they'd go to movies, have dinner, hang out each night, and then go home and talk on the phone for hours. She'd never realized you could *know* a man like that. She took Mike to the airport for spring training with the A's, and he kissed her and blurted a benign "I'll keep in touch." Her heart sank all the way home. *I bet this is the end*, she thought, right up until the phone rang that night and it was Mike, checking in.

And all that summer, as Mike ripped up one pitcher after another for Huntsville, the conversation went on. He couldn't help himself: There was something about Mandy's face—open, fun, mischievous—that told him she'd be a great mother, and something in her rich, earthy laugh, her utter disregard for material goods, that marked her as a striking contrast to the ballpark honeys who buzzed around every minor leaguer. Mandy had a quality that was less innocent than oblivious; she seemed so unconcerned about what it took to survive in "the real world" that it struck Mike as hilariously sweet. And if she wasn't ambitious, she also lacked the mercenary impulse that so often walks hand-in-hand with ambition. She drove a battered, paint-chipped old Buick Skylark for years, parking it away from other cars as if it were some freshly minted roadster. When Mike put it to her on their fourth date, "Come on, how much money would it take to make you happy?" Mandy answered as if envisioning a lottery score.

"If I could just get my bank account over $1,000," she said, "I would be ecstatic."

Mandy was, in fact, nearly tailor-made to be a minor league wife. Her father, Col. John Pavlovsky, had been a 30-year Army officer, carting his wife, Anne, and their four kids around the world. Born in Nuremberg, Germany, raised in Annapolis and Ft. Leavenworth and back in Neu-Ulm, Germany, and, finally, in Fort Hood in Texas, Mandy knew how to make friends fast, pack quickly, and make do with second-rate accommodations. Stay in the home of a minor league booster? Sure. Never know what school your kids will matriculate in from year to year? No problem. A minor league rookie made $750 a month for five months then; when Mandy met Mike, in his seventh year, the minor league minimum for a player of his tenure was $2,000 a month—$10,000 for the year, before taxes. When Mike got home from his date that night, he called a few friends. "I think I found the girl I'm going to marry," he said, laughing, "because she has no concept of money. She's not going to need much."

By the end of the '97 season, after watching Mike belt home runs and win the MVP award at the All-Star game in San Antonio, after a season of yearning long-distance night after night and knowing he felt that too, Mandy couldn't have been happier. *You stood by me and waited,* Mike wrote in November after that season, for her 23rd birthday, the words bursting off the page like skyrockets. *That's something I haven't found in a woman. It's hard to be involved with a baseball player. . . . You're the first person I've ever trusted being away from and that means a lot to me. . . . Happy Birthday Amanda. I hope to spend all of mine with you. Love you—Mike*

It's easy for the world to ignore baseball's minor league system; that it's so ignorable, in fact, is one of its enduring attractions. From a fan's perspective, the Rookie League teams scattered from Florida to Oregon, the AA franchises sprinkled throughout the South and West, the AAA stalwarts dotting the Pacific Coast, through the Ohio River

Valley, and along the Great Lakes, have managed to remain a tonic to the manic flood of big-city sports, Armageddon championships—Super Bowl! NCAA Tournament! Olympics!—and the know-it-all posturing of Internet blather. Go to a ballpark in Memphis, Midland, or Asheville and no one, not even the players themselves, will expect you to know anything, much less everything, about the teams taking the field. The crowds are tiny, the prices low, the pace languorous. You may well, as baseball fans like to boast, see some wrinkle in the game you've never seen before. You may even see a spectacular catch you'll remember the rest of your life. But the feeling you walk away with is usually the same, almost always the opposite of pro or big-time college games plumped thick with the juice of clever sneaker commercials and endless analysis: blissful disregard. Peanut shells crunch under your feet. Humidity lies on your skin like a tarp. The score doesn't matter much, and may well be forgotten by the time you roll out of the parking lot. Your kid carries his team cup, or the wristbands they gave away, and you wonder how hot it must feel wearing the mascot's fuzzy getup. You think about work on the way home. It was a night out, a step or two up from a carnival. Fun.

And that's all true, to a point. Minor league baseball also sells itself as a place where major league dreams are born, the place to see stars before they get too big and leave, and as a marketing play it's the only one to make. You always want to flatter your audience, and it's never bad to reinforce the collective hope that, like those ballplayers scrambling around the field, we're all just punching our tickets here; we all can move up and out of this small town someday; we all have roots but are capable of leaving them behind. The truth wouldn't sell nearly as well: too scary, too depressing. The fact is, from the players' perspective, there's nothing casual or forgettable about any game in the minors. Every pitch and every play is, to at least one man there, loaded with significance. The pressure to perform is crushingly heavy, the financial cushion nonexistent, the line between haves and have-nots vividly pronounced. Maybe two or three of the players you saw have a chance of playing in the major leagues. The rest, no matter how they perform, are learning—maybe even tonight—that this year or next year or the year after, they'll be going back to their own home-towns and humdrum jobs for good.

Still, for those who survive them—and sometimes even more im-portantly, for those who don't—the minors is where everything about the game is taught: not just the time and place to hit the cutoff man or translate the signal for a hit-and-run, but the secret language, the hidden codes, the way to walk, trot, run, and speak the way DiMag-gio, Mays, Aaron, and Feller learned to walk, trot, run, and speak. Baseball has always had its rebels, and for the likes of Bill Veeck and Jim Bouton and Mark Fidrych, baseball's culture has always allowed itself a modicum of tolerance. But on the whole it's a conservative world, with hidebound mores and a near mystical regard for what is generally called "the game"—a term that stands less for rules and scoring than for a way of looking at life. Players learn plenty in the minors, but the biggest lesson is always the one they didn't, as onetime superstars, ever expect: how to lose, how to fail, how to get kicked in the teeth and pretend to come up smiling; how, in the great baseball paradox, to learn to give yourself to "the game" even as you feel it op-erating contrary to all you've been taught, even as it rewards those who don't "respect the game" or give themselves up for the team. Because baseball does that, too, especially in the minors: It teaches a man how to endure being crushed and then stand up and declare himself in love with that crusher for life.

"I went from a can't-miss hotshot to a 'miss' to an everyday player who started in the World Series to the twenty-fifth guy on the team to a guy who had to go back to the minors and battle my way back to the big leagues," says Colorado Rockies manager Clint Hurdle. "And one thing I try and hold on to here, and I let my people know: I've still got minor league blood in my veins, and if I lose it I need to get out. Because that's the roots of who we are and what we do.

"Time passes, memory fades. You get to be big, your name gets thrown around, you get stuff. The more money you make, the more free stuff you get: It's crazy. But in the minor leagues you're scratching, you're clawing, you're biting, nothing's given to you—other than a signing bonus, if you're even fortunate enough to get one. Then it's just go out and play, man, and do your talking on the field. And it's so important to me that our major league staff and major league players don't lose sight of where they've come from, and what it took to get here. There's a humility that's special about great players and great teams and great deeds, and that humility starts at the minor league level when you get thrown into that melting pot. No matter where you came from or how big a player you were, now you've got to measure up. Now you're facing players globally, there's no age divisions—so the humility that needs to be put into play and learned is special. We need to be focused, we've got to have fun while we're doing it—but it's got to be laden with humility."

If not? Then "the game" asserts itself. It doesn't matter where baseball is played, or how high or low in the system a player has been slotted. If he crosses the line between humility and ego, there's going to be trouble. In the winter of 1997, with the A's infield glut forcing him to cast about for another organization, Mike kept sharp by playing third base for the Lara Cardinals in Venezuela's Winter League, joining Miguel Cairo, Luis Sojo, Mark Whiten, Brian Hunter, and Scott Pose in the feisty town of Barquisimeto. The Cardinals dominated the two-month season, rolled into the championship series with Caracas and split the first four games, then faced Venezuelan star Ugueth Urbina in Game 5. Urbina, an Expos pitcher and notorious hothead—who, a decade later, would be dealt a 14-year sentence for attempting to murder five farmworkers on his property with a machete and gasoline—felt very good about his fastball that night, so good that (despite the fact that he was losing at the time) he began mocking the Cardinals batters by giving the universal sign for fastball used from pitcher to catcher during warm-ups—a waved glove before his windup—*during the game: Here comes the heat, coño, just try and hit it.* That kind of flamboyant gamesmanship—de rigueur in, say, pro basketball—is, in baseball, akin to torching an American flag at the Lincoln Memorial, and everyone in the irate Cardinals' dugout gathered at the dugout's top step. The already keyed-up Barquisimeto crowd grew only more lathered up with each pitched insult; the patrol dogs held by riot police strained at their leashes. After Urbina fired the ball behind the heads of two Lara batters, "all hell broke loose," Pose says.

The Cardinals bolted out of the dugout. Whiten chased Urbina into center field. Both teams started brawling. As he ran across the diamond, Pose noticed a flurry out of the corner of his eye: one of his teammates getting dragged into the Caracas dugout. It was Coolbaugh. Pose raced over, jumped down the stairs, and found lover-not-a-fighter Mike with his back to the wall, surrounded by three Caracas players—his blood up, eyes flashing, jaw set. The Caracas men tried moving in, but Mike kept throwing roundhouses and connecting, holding them off. Pose finally dragged him out, and when order was restored some 45 minutes later, found that he, Mike, and every other American on the roster had been ejected.

In the clubhouse, nobody could recall ever being part of such a scene. But what the hell: Barquisimeto won and a message had been sent. In its way, the whole affair had been one adrenaline-rush delight. "I don't even know," Mike said, shrugging and grinning at the same time, "how I ended up in there."

He could say the same thing about the minors. Mike would still tell reporters that, in his mind, he'd always been a football player first; but for the flight of John Ferrara's clipboard, he'd figured on being a pretty good college quarterback somewhere. But now in the winter of 1998, it was clear that baseball had him locked in its bewildering grip. He was heading into his ninth year as a professional, and coming off the biggest season of his career, and it all added up to . . . what? After the sixth season, a minor leaguer becomes a free agent, which for most everyday players means an annual search for the organization present-ing the best chance for upward mobility—or at least the 500 at-bats that can demonstrate your value to next year's team. Mike had a vari-ety of tics—puffing air up over his face from an extended bottom lip, like the cartoon character Popeye; jerking a leg so suddenly and hard that once he snapped off part of the dashboard in a car—that eased in the off-season. The Coolbaugh family didn't need budding trees to tell them spring was coming: In the weeks before baseball began again, Mike's tics would get so bad that his sisters feared riding in a car with him behind the wheel. Now he was heading off to '98 spring training with his fourth organization, the Colorado Rockies. He had gotten a better deal than what the A's could've given him; he would, in fact, have a spot on the 40-man roster, a chance to show his wares to Colorado's top brass in major league spring training. But beyond that, nothing was guaranteed.

The lone piece of stability in his life lay in bed in San Antonio, asleep still as he began his drive to the team's spring home in Tucson, Arizona. He and Mandy had spent all winter together in San Antonio after his return from Venezuela, but she was still new to the quirky rhythms of a ballplayer's life. When Mandy woke, there was a note under her pillow:

> *This is a crazy time of year. You might think I don't want to stay because of my anxiousness to leave. This has been my life for a long time and half of me cannot wait—this is the year, right?! But, the other half will miss everything about you. My friends have always talked about what kind of wife they would want. My answer was, and still is, a great mother for my children. That never really had full meaning. I think I understand now. My mom has the gift to really care 100% about her family no matter what the case—sports, school, hobbies, dating. She really loves being a mother. You feel her love every day. That's how I know you're the one. You're the only person in the world I've ever felt love me. I know you will make a beautiful wife and loving mother and I am so happy you're going to go through this life with me. Whether it shows or not, I am always grateful we're*

together. My goal has always been to make it to the big leagues
but now I have someone to share that dream with. You deserve
the best and I will do my very best to give it to you. I want to
make all your dreams come true. I love you!!! Sleep tight and see
me in your dreams. Until tomorrow night, good night good-
lookin'.

I love you Gorgeous,
"Chief"

Mike finally broke into AAA for the first time that '98 season, hitting .277 in 108 games with 16 home runs and 75 RBI for the Colorado
Springs SkySox, mulling how to take that final step to the majors. He
understood that, at 26, this would likely be his last shot at establish-
ing himself as a prospect. His bounce from organization to organization had put a self-fulfilling stench on him that smacked too much of
the way colleges had backed away after the clipboard incident. Yes, all
agreed, Coolie could hit for power and field a clean third base. *But why
did all these teams let him go?* He couldn't get a straight answer himself,
and trying to parse the crooked-road thinking of team executives was a
maddening, if irresistible, exercise. More experienced minds had tried
and failed; one of them was sitting in the opposite dugout when the
SkySox played their one series that season against the Iowa Cubs.

Alan Zinter, Iowa's 30-year-old first baseman, had been the Mets'
first-round pick in 1989, the 24th player selected overall. Now ten seasons later, he was playing out his fifth straight season in AAA, the
epitome of what's known as a "AAAA" talent—a tweener stuck between the top level of the minors and the majors, a player who, all
agreed, was plenty good but missing some vital quality that would

land him a major league spot. For years, Zinter's effort to penetrate the game's opaque logic, its arcane rules for advancement, proved all-consuming. "It should've been the best time in my life," he says. "But from '89 to '96, I was trying to figure stuff out, trying to control, trying to please—and nothing was working for me. You look at stats and teams, stats on the scoreboard, stats in the locker room—and that just drives you nuts." And then there was the issue of trying to make—and understand what it took to make and stay on—an organization's 40-man roster, the player's ultimate signifier that he is valued and being watched and protected.

With 25 players on the major league roster, that leaves 15 prospects, and "they're all scattered throughout the minor leagues, depending on how deep an organization is," Zinter says. "A lot of times, there's guys in A-ball, pitchers who are not physically or mentally ready for the big leagues but they're considered top prospects. They're in A-ball but they're on the forty-man roster; they get to go to [major league] spring training. Then there are the guys in Double-A who are becoming prospects, who are put on the roster after having shown the organization how good they've become over the years and they need to be protected. Otherwise there's the Rule 5 draft in December where other organizations can draft the guys that are off the forty-man roster."

But that's hardly the end of it. "Then they also slot guys in the Triple-A rosters," Zinter says. "You'll have the major league roster—forty guys—and then the Triple-A roster. Take, for example, one guy we had with the Diamondbacks, Dan Uggla. He's a superstar now with the Florida Marlins, but the year prior to being Rookie of the Year with them, he was left off the forty-man roster of the Diamondbacks, and he had played that year at Double-A. So the Diamondbacks did not or could not consider him a prospect on the forty-man roster. They tried to sneak him through by putting him on the Triple-A roster—meaning that, if a club picks him up they'd have to keep him in the big leagues for one year or give him back. So they tried that, and the Marlins took a chance and look what happened. It usually doesn't, but it could."

Zinter is speaking now from the perspective of a decade later, in 2008, after he'd retired at the age of 39. But nine more seasons in pro baseball brought him only a bit closer to understanding every loophole and machination at work whenever a player's future is being decided. "You think you understand the system but something else always comes up: This guy has run out of options, and that guy *has* to make the team; this kid has to be protected, that kid *can't* be protected," he says with a sigh. "So many scenarios where you're saying, 'What in the world?' I *still* don't know what's going on."

Mike lasted that one season with the Rockies, protected on their 40-man roster until, suddenly, he wasn't. Squeezed out again, he got picked up by the Yankees and sent to their Triple-A club in Columbus, Ohio. He played two seasons there, driving in runs with metronomic regularity, playing every position but pitcher, catcher, and center field, hitting 23 homers in 117 games in 2000. He and Mandy had gotten married on January 22, and in July, when the Yankees acquired outfielder Mike Frank, who in 1998 had been elevated to the majors faster than any Reds position player in the franchise's modern age, Coolbaugh was the first to approach him on the team bus.

"Hey, my wife left, she's a teacher, went to go back to school,"

Mike said. "I have an empty room. You want to stay with me the rest of the year?"

It made sense. Frank had been a phenom, the kind of prospect Mike never had a chance to be, but after 28 struggling games with the Reds in '98 his stock had plummeted. "I went from prospect to bust probably faster than anybody," Frank says. "I played six years, five of which were in Triple-A. Ninety-nine percent of the people who play pro ball were fans at one point, but you play that many years in Triple-A, it takes that feeling out of the game. In the lower minors, you always have the sense *If I play better, I'll move up.* But when you get into Triple-A it's almost like you're in an airplane circling the runway. You can hit .210 and get called up because you're on the roster and someone got hurt, or you can hit .390 and they put you on the phantom disabled list. It happens to everybody—and if you're there long enough, it happens multiple times—and you lose that feeling. For me it was hard: I started to blame the game for the way I was treated. My wife and I started talking about having a family and I didn't want to get to a point where I didn't want to take my son—who I didn't even have yet—to a game because I'm so bitter at the game. It's not baseball's fault."

Frank paused. "Not that Mike was that way," he said. "He never complained about it. I never one time knew him to have an ounce of jealousy or anger or resentment towards someone. Ever. If you got called up and he told you he was rooting for you? He meant it."

That's not to say Mike didn't get annoyed by the hidden politics, or rail against the game's conventional wisdom. He hit .276 and .271 during his two seasons in Columbus, and it made him fume to hear executives and scouts pronounce: "If you hit .300 in the minors, you can hit .300 in the majors. But if you hit .270 in the minors, you can't move up and hit .270." Why? No one had a real answer, but Coolbaugh kept feeling like he was stuck in a box that, no matter how much he splintered it with his bat, got rebuilt before he could set up to swing again. He would buttonhole another teammate on that Columbus team, outfielder Kerry Robinson, and the two would vent their frustration over the growing realization that, even if you do exactly as you're told, even if you produce season after season, it may make no difference at all.

"One day in the big leagues," Mike told Robinson then. "That's all I want: one day."

But every time he heard that, Robinson just shook his head. He had had two stints in the majors with Tampa Bay and Cincinnati by then, just 11 games. But it was enough to know.

"You get one day? You'll want more," Robinson told him. "You'll see."

Now he was heading into his 12th year of pro ball, and there was no avoiding the label. Mike was a AAAA player, yes, but something worse, too, something even harder to put a finger on: He was hard-luck. He was Mr. Just Missed. In August 2000, Coolbaugh had been a surprise pick for the 29-man preliminary roster of the U.S.A.'s 2000 Olympic team, and he looked upon it as a chance to start fresh, impress baseball people on a new stage, maybe be part of a huge upset and come home with a gold medal. "The highlight of my career," Mike called it at the time, and he almost had it right: The U.S. did topple mighty Cuba in the 2000 Olympic final to win the gold. But he wasn't there. In mid-September, just before the team left for Sydney, Mike had been one of four players cut. A month later, the Yankees released him. "It's like," Mike told his sister Lisa, "I've got this bad cloud following me."

Maybe Mike's big brother was just trying to be nice, then. Maybe Scott was giving back some of the encouragement he always got from his little brother. But after Mike signed in November with the Brewers organization for $11,000 a month, Scott insisted, "This is going to be your year." He had never said that before.

And for a time, there was no good reason to think 2001 would be. Mike started off well enough in AAA Indianapolis, made the AAA All-Star team and hit a home run in the All-Star game, finished among the International League's top five in doubles. But he wasn't hitting homers or driving in runs at that eye-popping pace; he'd had better seasons with Columbus in 2000, Colorado Springs in '98, Huntsville in '97; he'd had moments when he mistakenly figured the next call into the manager's office meant a plane ticket to the bigs. But Mike wasn't thinking that on Saturday, July 14, after he'd recorded 1,215 minor league games and 4,371 minor league at-bats; he wasn't thinking that when he started, bat in hand, out of the dugout at Bulls Athletic Park in Durham, North Carolina, to take batting practice and Indianapolis manager Wendell Kim stopped him.

"I don't think that's a good idea," Kim said. "It wouldn't be good for you to get hurt just before you go to Milwaukee."

"What?" Mike said.

"You're going to the big leagues."

Mike warned Kim not to joke. He looked over at Indianapolis

trainer Paul Anderson, who was grinning and nodding his head. "Yep," Anderson said. "You got called up."

"Better get packed," Kim said. "You're going to be late for your plane."

Mike rushed into the clubhouse, mind whirling. His teammates' congratulations were wonderful to hear—how many times had he been on the other side?—but he was desperate to make some calls. His parents and sisters and Mandy had all been in Indianapolis for the AAA All-Star game but had since scattered: his wife to Chicago to visit a sister, his family to upstate New York to visit relatives on a lake. Mandy and he had one cell phone between them; Mike had given it to her so she'd have it in case of emergency. But when he dialed Mandy, she didn't recognize the number of the incoming call and let it slide to voice mail. It was 4:54 p.m. Mike heard the recording, the beep, and started talking.

Then Mike tried his parents, but their cell phones couldn't get service at the lake. He called Scott: His brother's cell phone was off, too. Mike packed his bags, his gloves, his equipment, went to the airport, and reached his agent finally—the only person he could reach that whole day with the news. When Mandy finally checked her voice mail later that night, walking down Chicago's Wacker Drive, she heard the thickness in his voice and instantly started crying, there on the street. "Hey, uh, baby . . . I got called up," Mike's message began, and for a few seconds he sounded almost cool about it. "I got called up, baby. I'm going to the big leagues." Then the voice began cracking. "I can't breathe. I couldn't stop crying for about five minutes. I love . . ." Mike paused, sniffled; his voice rose and wavered. "I love you. I wish you had your phone on. You're the first one I called. Call me back, okay? Bye."

But by then Mike was on his way to Milwaukee, and Mandy didn't know how to reach him. The next morning, she drove up from Chicago and, unsure where he was staying, went to the Brewers home field, Miller Park, just as the 1 p.m. game was about to start.

Mike had been there for hours. Unsure when to check in, he had had a cab drop him at the park at 7 a.m. When he had knocked on the service entrance door, the startled guard informed him that no one from the team would arrive until 11. Mike's cab was driving away. He had nowhere to go. So the guard had given him a tour: up and down the concourses in a golf cart, out to the perfect field, into the silent and empty clubhouse. Mike found his locker, with a Brewers jersey hanging in it: number 14, with COOLBAUGH stitched with care across the back. The first time he saw Mandy, she was smiling at him from the stands.

The next day, Mike tracked down his sister Lisa's husband, David, who had the number of the lake house in Oxford, New York. Linda answered the phone. Mike asked to speak to his mother. Within seconds Mary Lu was crying and yelling, "Mike got called up!" She and Bob and their daughters had just gotten to the lake, but she told Mike to get tickets anyway: They would load up the Lincoln and be in Wisconsin for the next game. The four of them took turns driving all that Monday night, 826 miles from Oxford to Milwaukee in one fell swoop along the rump of the Great Lakes, trying to tune in that night's Milwaukee–White Sox contest. Reception restored, Mary Lu kept punching at her cell phone as exits whisked past, listening, over and over, to Mike's message from the day he got the news.

They didn't hear him get his first at-bat then, pinch-hitting in the sixth inning for Milwaukee's Will Cunnane. Mike hadn't played for three days; the bat felt light, his body felt good. White Sox reliever Jon Garland waited on the mound. *Get a pitch to hit and swing,* Mike thought. *If you don't get a hit, you don't, but go up swinging. Enjoy yourself.* But he took the first two pitches, got the count to 2–1, guessed right on a fastball, and rapped a clean single to left field for his first-ever major league hit. Mike found himself so pumped, trying to run so fast to first, that he stumbled making the turn.

The next morning, at 6 a.m., Mike got a call at his hotel. His family had arrived. Later, before the game, he told a reporter, "My dad's here today. I'm going to have a good game."

He grounded out to second his first at-bat. In his second time up, again against Garland, Mike worked the count to 2–2.

Some 40,332 fans packed Miller Park that day, their hum filling the air. Lisa was sitting in the stands with Mandy and Linda and her parents, giving David in Texas a pitch-by-pitch account by cell phone. In the batter's box, Mike heard only silence.

Down in Indianapolis, 244 miles away, a dozen of his former teammates on the AAA Indians, the men who'd seen him cry so openly just days before, stopped cold to watch the clubhouse TV.

Garland threw a changeup. Mike swung and the ball sailed just over the left field fence, so close to the line that Mike was racing past third before he realized it was a home run. The Indianapolis clubhouse erupted in a flurry of cheering, backslaps, fists flung skyward. Lisa and Linda and Mary Lu hugged and shouted and cried, nearly two decades' worth of care and worry and frustration spilling out. Mandy screamed with the thrill of her man proving the world wrong and a future looking brighter. Even Bob got choked up. After Mike rounded the bases and his new teammates greeted him with high-fives and hugs, his dad bolted from his seat to wander the concourse in search of a hot dog. He found himself transfixed by the replay on the monitors.

"I can't stop watching the video of that hit," he said when he returned. "Mike's swing is perfect. It's the most beautiful thing I have ever seen."

A teammate presented Mike with the ball he'd hit. The home run validated every day, every year gone. "I just felt like, *Hey, I can play here*," Mike said a week later. "It's really not all that different. You just have to get your pitch. Maybe you won't get as many pitches to hit, but if you get your pitch and put a good swing on it, it's pretty much the same deal. That was the best feeling, going around the bases knowing that I had done it. I had hit the home run."

He was sitting on a stool at Miller Park. A film crew had been following various Indianapolis players all season for a documentary called *A Player to Be Named Later*, and now a camera was rolling and producer Bart Stephens was asking how it felt to make it after all those years.

"Relief," Mike said. "I think if I would've been called up four years ago, it would've been more of an awe, like, 'Wow, I'm in the big leagues'—maybe a little more nervous. Because I wasn't as sure of myself four or five years ago. I felt like I could play but I just didn't really feel like I should be there, I *should* get my shot. But the last couple years, I've felt like I've really done what I should do to get here and it just didn't work out—and now that I'm here I feel more like, 'Whew! I did get here. I did get my shot.' I just feel relaxed.

"I don't know why. I almost feel less pressure because this is the big leagues. I felt like, in the minor leagues, you have to do *something* to get here: *You have to do it, you have to do it, you have to do it*. And you try to do too much. Here, being a pinch-hitter off the bench, kind of the extra guy, I don't feel like it's me that has to get the job done. You know what I mean? In Triple-A when you're batting fourth, fifth, you feel: *I've got to get the job done, I've got to get it going, I've got to get to the big leagues, I'm twenty-nine, I haven't been there, I have family to think about.* I think there's more pressure in figuring out what's going to happen next year. But when you're here? I feel if I'm going to be nervous, I'm going to ruin a shot—and luckily I haven't been so far. For me it's been a storybook year. Everything has just *worked.*"

The words kept coming then; he couldn't help himself. All of it— his brother's prediction, the timing that placed infielder Tyler Houston on the disabled list just after the AAA All-Star game, the fact that his wife and family were near enough to make it to Milwaukee to see his first hit and home run—made Mike almost giddy. He started to giggle, and watching the footage you wouldn't be shocked if, at any one moment, Coolbaugh pinched himself. Now he was going to give it everything and let the chips fall, he said: If he's not good enough, he's not. But if he is? "Hip, hip, hurrah: I'm in the big leagues," Mike said.

"Some guys don't understand what I'm saying when I say that, but to me it makes sense. I don't know if a lot of things I say make sense to other people, but it makes sense to me right now and I just feel *good.* Come to the field, and you just feel *good.* You look around and there's forty thousand people and, you know, you think about this game: How perfect is it? Ninety feet is, like, the perfect distance from home to first; the guy is just out and if you bobble it he's safe. The pitcher's mound? If it was any closer, it would be too hard [on hitters]; if it was any farther back, the pitchers would get killed. It's just a perfect game, and up here you appreciate all that. I didn't really appreciate that in the minors. I just felt like *I've got to do what I got to do to get here*—and that's all that mattered. Now that I'm here, I appreciate everything that I've gone through."

For his last question, Mike was asked if he had envisioned it taking 12 years. And he spoke then about how he hadn't grown up thinking he'd be in the major leagues, how football was his first love. He spoke of how "horrible" a player he was his first four or five years in the minors and how his confidence was wracked daily by the suspicion that he'd never be good enough. But then he grew into his body. He began to figure baseball out. He began to perform better than players he once stood in awe of. And now he had gone where few baseball players ever had.

"I made a good choice," Mike said. Going to college, playing football or baseball there, that would've been nice, he said, "but I can't say I made the wrong move now."

BY THE SPRING OF 2001, Tino Sanchez had hit a wall. He was just 22 years old, but all the factors that age ballplayers before their time— the injuries and slumps that feed off each other and reduce confidence to rubble, the little signs reinforcing the nagging notion that, no, you're not ever going to make it—had taken their toll. His attitude had soured. The Rockies were close to releasing him, and he might not have even cared. He was mulling retirement anyway.

Tino didn't start out that way; few do. He played rookie ball in the Rockies organization his first two years in Arizona, Mesa and then

Tucson, and couldn't believe his good fortune: A uniform! Money in my pocket! Girls in the stands and after the games, all of them thinking what he's thinking: Maybe this Tino will be the one to make it. Everyone back home knew he was up in the States, making his way. One of his high school teammates, the wonderfully named Perfecto Gaud, had been taken in the same '97 draft by the Blue Jays but gave up after toiling two years in some far-off Canadian town called Medicine Hat. Homesickness had driven Perfecto back to Yauco for good, but Tino had different wiring. Tino was ready to go. "I was not even thinking," he says. "You don't think anything at that age, because you don't *know* anything. I was just so excited."

He had talent, too: A good arm, quick release, decent speed, the ability to switch-hit. "Very usable tools," says Marc Gustafson, the Rockies director of player development. "But nothing to blow you away." Rookie ball is a volatile environment, as much about transitioning as it is about performance. Far from home for the first time, barely out of high school, players get mashed in a competitive cauldron in some second-tier town, big shots suddenly relegated to obscurity. Some are poor, some aren't; all are immature. There's little travel. You stay in the same musty hotel, day after day for ten weeks, 74 to 76 games, one of a testosterone-fueled crew of teenagers killing the dead hours between games, fending off boredom and easy trouble. In the summer of '98, while Mark McGwire and Sammy Sosa captivated the nation with their home run chase, Sanchez and teammate Rene Reyes found themselves captivated by the Holiday Inn's oh-so-tempting fire alarm. Finally one June night Tino wedged a bat into the lever and Reyes smacked it down. The two tried running, but how were they to know the elevators would shut down? The cops glimpsed them long enough to figure they were ballplayers, and notified the Rockies.

The next morning, Tucson manager P. J. Carey got the news. The 54-year-old Carey, now a minor league field coordinator with the Los Angeles Dodgers, is one of those baseball figures who helped mold the game in relative obscurity. With the exception of a one-year stint as Don Baylor's bullpen coach for the 1997 Rockies, for more than three decades Carey was the entry point for thousands of young players, bouncing occasionally up the minor league ladder but mostly managing rookie clubs in the Philadelphia, Seattle, Cincinnati, and Colorado organizations. In one sense, Carey was a classic baseball type: He'd spent five years playing in the Philadelphia organization, never good enough to break into the majors and seguing naturally into the next-best thing.

"Thirty major league organizations, each of them have six minor league affiliates, and you've got three coaches on each of those teams. Figure the math," says Clint Hurdle. "How many of those guys are former stars? Not many. They're lifers. They're guys who played the game, love it, they want to teach and stay connected to the game. The thing I'll hear from time to time is, 'Well, they can't do anything else.' No. They don't *want* to do anything else. They're looking to help, to teach, to enjoy, to complement, to be involved—to still feel that adrenaline you used to get when you played and did something well, or the sting when you didn't. Now as a coach, you're the conduit to the player. You still have a thread to the game when you see your guys play well, and when they don't do well you feel the sting a father feels. You know how they feel, because you've been there."

But unlike many lifers, Carey refused to encrust himself with the usual gruff cynicism. Renowned for honesty and a gentle touch, he found his calling in the bushes, a way to teach the hit-and-run while serving an ideal. "I've always looked at professional baseball this way: Where in the world do you ever bring so many different people together to accomplish the same goal?" he says. "It's a great equalizer; that's why it demands the respect it does. The game brings people from all types of environments—different religions, races, languages—and we put those kids on the same field to get along, to become good teammates and to teach them to improve their skills so that someday maybe they'll walk on a major league field. If there's a dream that's more worth pursuing in the world, I don't know what it is. To have a chance to instruct and manage kids in that environment is a privilege."

But Carey wasn't just a superb teacher. Despite his spotty Spanish, his softest spot may have been for the Latinos in his charge. When they couldn't afford to abide by the Colorado dress code, he was known to pay for their collared shirts out of his own pocket. He and his wife, Katherine, opened their home to countless players needing a home-cooked meal and made sure that low-paid staffers had a place to go for Thanksgiving and Christmas. "P. J.'s been a father to a lot of us, me included," says Gustafson, who broke in with Carey as a trainer in rookie ball in 1993. "I get chills even talking about him, because he means so much to me and to players for the same reasons. He cared for you not because you played baseball, but because of who you were and what you did off the field. A tremendous person."

He's no pushover, though. When Carey met with the players that morning about the fire alarm, he lit into them hard. It was a talented bunch—future All-Star Matt Holliday, future major league talents Jorge Sosa and Juan Uribe—but they hadn't jelled yet as a team, and now a few players were making them all—and by extension, the Colorado organization—look bad. Carey demanded that the guilty parties step forward. They didn't. None of their teammates said a word. Infuriating Carey even more, Sosa kept falling asleep during the manager's harangue. Carey announced: You'll all run until someone talks. And so they filed out and ran for 45 minutes, around and around the four-field complex below Tucson's Hi Corbett Field, gasping and sweating and mute beneath the relentless Arizona sun. Finally Sanchez and Reyes came forward together, admitting their guilt but refusing Carey's demand to know who specifically pulled the lever. "Someday you're going to tell me," Carey said.

"But nobody gave it up, which I still admire them for," he says. "And after that whole ordeal, we had an 11 o'clock game and it was the slowest-moving game I'd ever seen. We only lost fourteen games that whole season; I don't know if we won that game or not. But I'll never forget sitting there watching: If the ball was hit to the right or left of anyone, they could barely move to go get it."

Tino had a great summer in '98: led the team in doubles, hit .318, played a smart and strong center field. It didn't matter that he could barely speak English; Tucson had plenty of Mexicans and rookie ball is filled with Dominicans and the rest of baseball's endless Latino wave. Besides, he was moving up, he was sure of it: After playing like that, then having a strong spring training in '99, Colorado would surely promote him. Wasn't it time for him to play a full season—140 minor league games—and get on the major league track with the Rockies Single-A team? Instead, Sanchez found himself heading for his third short-season stint, this time in Portland, Oregon. It was like that cliched movie moment when the seemingly sweet boyfriend abuses his wife for the first time. Baseball slapped Tino, drew first blood, and he didn't even know why.

Gauging his outfield competition, Tino sounded out a few coaches and decided to convert to catcher. At first that provided the Colorado brass with a small revelation. "He amazed people with his release and arm strength throwing to second base," Carey says. "No one had realized he had that." But in Portland, Tino struggled to keep his average above .170; near the end of the season a rogue foul tip fractured his left knee, and he underwent surgery. Yet Sanchez remained a valuable cog. His outfield experience and ability to play first and third base allowed a team to save money by carrying him as their extra outfielder, infielder, and catcher. Colorado promoted him finally to its Single-A club, the Asheville Tourists, for the 2000 season. Four years in, he had finally gotten some purchase: a full season to show what he could do.

And he blew it. It didn't help matters that the Rockies had thrown a golden boy in his path, Jeff Winchester of Metairie, Louisiana— high school All-American, first-round draft pick in '98, bearer of a $537,000 signing bonus and all the advantages that come along with it. Though a defensive liability, though not nearly as quick with the throw to second base, Winchester was the catcher Colorado wanted to look at that summer, and Tino found himself stewing on the bench, playing every third or fourth day, gaining none of the continuity necessary to show what he could do. Baseball is a game of days, strung together one by one until they reveal a projectable pattern. Lacking consistent time at the plate, on the field, players can almost feel their skills slipping away. Sitting there, useless, they have too much time to study the game and all its secret angles. They think too much. Sometimes, they get dangerous.

Because now, in his fourth year of baseball, Tino came to know something. Or thought he did, anyway: He was being screwed. Latino players often whispered about how white players won the tie when it came to filling out the last spots on a roster. Sure, there were plenty of Latino stars in the heart of nearly every major league lineup, but it's impossible to keep *them* down. But at the margins? That's where the Latino player seemed to get thrown overboard. As he began to truly struggle, Tino began to like that theory. It allowed him to blame the manager, the coaches, the organization, for the fact that he wasn't producing yet again in Asheville, that his demeanor stank, that he'd gotten a bit too heavy, that by July he could barely stand the sight of his teammates. He wasn't alone, of course; late July is when the season seems to stretch forever, when slumps seem unbreakable, when the sight of the same broken, ugly toenails in the same grimy shower shoes in the same bathroom stall next to yours, day in and day out, stretches nerves to the snapping point.

But Tino was beyond the usual grouchiness, pitying himself, hitting .251 in just 58 games, favoring a tender knee. He had no car. He walked the dull half-mile every day from his apartment to McCormick Field. He didn't know how to work. He didn't study pitchers or read his dad's books on hitting. He didn't play much and when he did, he lacked intensity because he had no idea how to get better. Years later, Tino was sitting next to Stu Cole, his manager in Tulsa, watching an infielder butcher a routine play. Cole didn't even yell, just smiled and shrugged and said, "It's not his fault." Meaning: Why bother? In Asheville in 2000, Tino sensed that he'd become that guy, the one the organization had soured on, the one drowning in his own limitations. He feared that he'd found his level—low A-ball or worse—and hated himself for that and for the dream he'd indulged for too long. He wanted out.

It didn't help that the Tourists were battling for eighth place that summer. Or that Tino's manager was a first-year Lombardi wannabe named Joe Mikulik, who as a minor leaguer wore wristbands bearing the words "Never Surrender" and who, in 2006, would become a You-Tube sensation when, during a game in Lexington, Kentucky, he tore out second base and hurled it across the field, flung a handful of bats onto the grass, and poured water on home plate in a tirade against the umpires. All in all, 2000 was a miserable season in Asheville. But no manager would've reacted calmly to what happened one July night.

Tino was standing in the dugout, in front of the Tourists' bench, watching the game. Sitting directly behind him was outfielder Melvin Rosario, a fellow Puerto Rican born, in fact, just a year before Tino in the same San Juan district of Rio Piedras. The two had been sniping at each other for a month, and finally Tino heard the word "motherfucker" uttered low, in that familiar annoying voice, and all of it—his frustrations, his failure—boiled over. He balled his right fist, pivoted, and swung. Rosario ducked it, but Tino landed a quick left before teammates yanked them apart. Mikulik's face went scarlet and he started screaming. It figured: Tino's best hit of the season, and he felt anything but good.

"I was about to cry," Tino says.

3

CIRCLING

Details change, but not the story line. Stay in the minors long enough, and all paranoia becomes justified. *I got screwed* is one of the game's mantras, as common—if not as public—a baseball trope as boy-plays-catch-with-dad. It starts innocently enough: A kid starts his career, maybe sporting a hefty bonus but usually not, and he's the best athlete his town ever saw. But now he's in this machine, this *system*, and it's large and both intensely personal and impersonal—men walking around naked, their daily work published for all the world to see—and suddenly he feels like one of a thousand crabs in a bucket, trying to claw his way up and out, fate decided by management whim or something called "the numbers game," and all while the manager and coaches keep saying, "No, keep pushing. You're doing everything right." And of course the kid has an ego or he never would have been the best his town ever saw, so he tells himself: *It can't be me. It's that I got hurt at the wrong time. Or the GM or the manager doesn't like me. Or that the bonus boys get the breaks.* "Everybody has a war story," Scott Coolbaugh says. "'What if . . . this or that. I should've been . . . this or that.'" Scott's a coach now, has been coaching or managing nearly every year since his playing days ended, and like most baseball men he can barely keep the annoyance out of his voice when the subject comes up. What's the point? War stories—no matter how true—are an excuse. Which makes it worse, somehow, that his brother might end up being the most pitiable war story of all.

After that home run in Milwaukee, Mike appeared in 37 more games for the Brewers, hit .200 and one more homer. He had one other sweet moment, in a game against St. Louis, when he reached second base and the action paused for a pitching change, and Coolbaugh saw his old teammate, Kerry Robinson from Columbus days, trotting in from the outfield to talk.

"You got your one day in the big leagues—you happy now?" Robinson asked.

"Yeah," Mike said. "But you're right. I want more."

That was during Robinson's first long stint with a major league team; he had no sense of the line he had just crossed. Leaving your position to talk to an opponent during a game? When Robinson dropped back into the dugout after the third out, the Cardinals vets lit into him: "Are you fucking kidding me? What are you doing coming in?!"

"I got a pretty bad ripping," Robinson says. "I didn't understand at the time that you weren't supposed to do that. But it was a special time. That was my buddy. I knew he was happy and whatever ripping I took was absolutely worth it. I could've waited until after the game, but it was important to do it then. When you know somebody's life story and what they've done to get to the major league level, I just thought, *Besides sending me down, whatever you guys say to me doesn't matter.*"

Still, Mike couldn't relax. He was used mostly as a pinch-hitter the rest of that year, hard enough duty when you're a secure major leaguer. But it's even tougher "when you're a bubble guy," says Alan Zinter, who in his 14th year of pro ball finally got called up to the Astros in 2002, where, like Coolbaugh in Milwaukee, he appeared in 39 games and hit just .136. "You start reading, 'How Long For Alan?' and quotes like, 'We don't know how long he's going to be here.' So, yeah, now I was on the roster—but I hadn't felt this pressure for the last eight years because before then, I was just playing. Now I'm thinking, *I've got to perform so I can stay here.* Unless you're getting a guaranteed contract, you never get comfortable there. Because you never know how long it's going to last."

Milwaukee released Mike in October 2001. But far from being depressed, he felt rejuvenated. He had done it; he had actually made it to the major leagues. Yes, it was sweet to sleep in plush hotel rooms, fly first-class, fiddle with the bump to a $320,000 salary, to get a sniff of that major league life. But even better, he was sure now that he could hit that pitching, given a regular diet of games, a spot in a major league lineup. He just needed to find the right club. "That's what kept him going," Scott says. "He got a taste of it, and then he didn't want it to end."

Mike went to 2002 spring training with St. Louis, 29 years old and in his prime. He ravaged Grapefruit League pitching, hit .365 in 27 games with 3 homers and 8 RBI. What more could they ask? "Our best player in spring training," says Robinson, an outfielder with St. Louis that year. "He was so hot, it was ridiculous. Everybody thought he'd be on the team."

Al LaMacchia buttonholed Cardinals manager Tony La Russa late that spring. "Tony, don't walk away from this kid," he said. "He can help you. He can come off the bench, he can hit, he can play several positions in the infield and the outfield."

"Right now," La Russa said, "he's got my club made."

But when it came time to make a decision, the Cards couldn't resist the idea of Eduardo Perez, son of a Hall of Famer, an eight-year major leaguer just back from Japan, and—most important—a better option to back up first as well as third base. Perez had hit nearly 100 points lower than Mike that spring (and to this day is still shocked that he won the job), but it didn't matter. He gave La Russa that extra bit of comfort with his bench, a known quantity who had played in St. Louis and hit well two seasons before. It was one of those close calls, based more on feel than on any number. "La Russa is really loyal. If you were on the team before, you were already a leg up with Tony," Robinson says. "And he wasn't big on stats; it was the way you went about things. There was a year when I made the team out of spring training when So Taguchi deserved to make it more than me. But in that situation? It was wrong. Mike deserved to be on the team, period. Everybody has this misconception that, if you go to big league spring training, you have a chance to make the team. What they don't realize is that twenty-four spots are already picked and maybe one new person has a chance to make it. Mike ran into that, right there."

When he saw the manager calling to him that March day in 2002, Mike began to jog away. "You're not going to catch me," he said, laughing outside and groaning within. "This is not going to happen."

But it did. Mike begged for an explanation, or at least a detailing of the gaps in his game that he could work on. "But I couldn't even get an answer from them because I don't think they even had one," he told Scott soon after. "I can't believe it. I've done everything. Eddie didn't have a good spring and there's nothing I did wrong." Of all his disappointments, this one cut deepest. Here was the truth of Mike's career made brutally plain: Baseball had no plans for him, no matter how hard he worked, no matter how impressive he might be. He was an organizational player. Filler.

He reported to the Cardinals AAA club in Memphis but didn't have time to sulk. Mandy was just about due with their first child, a boy, and late in April went into labor. Mike boarded a plane for home, scribbling a song for the occasion on a piece of spiral notebook paper.

When I close my eyes at night
I dream about our life
I see a little place
Deep inside my mind

The baby's fast asleep
The day's work is far behind
We're laughing on the porch
Deep inside my mind

I wish that you just weren't so far away
I miss you more and more every single day
And if I could I'd be back home tonight
Instead I have to see you deep inside my mind

Remember this for all my love is true
I couldn't be the same being without you

And even though we are so far apart
You'll always be with me deep inside my heart

I can't wait to be back by your side
The real you's so much better
Than deep inside my mind

Mike went back to Memphis, turned 30, and went on to hit 29 AAA home runs. St. Louis called him back up for one five-game stint in June and July, and Mandy flew in with Joey, just eight weeks old. Mike called his sister Lisa, the family photographer, and begged her to come too; who knew how long he'd be there? He wanted pictures, lots of them: Dad in the big leagues with his boy. He got permission, before one game, to get on the field early and Lisa snapped away and the best was one of Mike holding Joey and staring off into the outfield, the huge and empty stands. Later, Mike blew it up and hung it on a wall and called it "Field of Dreams."

In his final outing Mike went out with a bang: playing third and starting two double plays, going 1 for 4 with a sacrifice, picking up his one major league hit that year, a single, in his final at-bat off reliever Jesse Orosco. "It was terrible," says Robinson of the moment he learned that Mike had been sent back down to AAA. "But we figured he'd be back, because he'd tore it up in the minors and people get hurt all the time. We just thought, 'Mike will be back. No big deal.'"

But he wouldn't be back, ever. Coolbaugh didn't know that, of course. Players are rarely judged on short stints; the game is all about production over time. Mike loved to sit and try to pick the game apart: Analyzing baseball and the way its talent was distributed was one way of controlling, if just for a chat in front of his locker, a world over which he had no control. It's a minor league conceit that any player who produces at AAA can do so in the majors, so there he was back in Memphis again, finishing out his best season yet in AAA and gaming out the numbers: If I'm hitting 30 home runs in 400 at-bats in a 5-month minor league season, what could I do with 6 months and 500 at-bats in the majors? Doesn't it follow that I'll hit 25 to 30 home runs there?

Just give me a chance. It's the lifer's motto, and as necessary as oxygen, because once he stops believing, it's over. That's why, though a spasm of jealousy runs through all lifers each time one of their own breaks onto a major league roster, they're still desperately rooting for him to stick. And when someone like pitcher Travis Driskill not only gets called up by the Baltimore Orioles but then does what he did in the summer of '02, it provides ammunition for every other "AAAA player" still arguing his case in Memphis and every other second-tier town. Driskill got his opportunity that season, and then he did more. He carried the flag. For a short time, anyway, he showed what a lifer can do.

Ten months older than Coolbaugh and raised just an hour north in Austin, Travis Driskill had spent a decade simmering in AAA burgs like Buffalo and New Orleans before the Orioles organization signed him the previous winter. Then came the Four-A dream: injuries at the major league level, a phone call, a plane ticket out of Rochester, and suddenly he was walking, 30 years old, into the Orioles' bullpen at Camden Yards midway through a May loss. "You guys have room for one more?" Driskill asked.

Of course, Driskill could have been like Mike in the summer of

'02, sent down after five games. For a while, he served strictly as Balti-more's mop-up man, eating relief innings in one-sided losses or wins, desperate not to give management any excuse to demote. In one of his early appearances against Cleveland, slugger Jim Thome hammered the ball square into Driskill's back, in the soft flesh just above his kid-neys. "He smoked it," Driskill says. "The ball went to third base and Tony Batista threw him out at first; I got an assist. But here's why I stayed in the game: I'm a thirty-year-old rookie. Have the trainer pull me? There's no way I was coming out. If I was peeing blood and spit-ting up blood, I was staying in just to prove that I could.

"I finished the inning, but they took me out and a couple days later we're finishing the series with Cleveland and I get this bad feeling that I'm not making the trip. I'm like, 'Oh, man, am I going back to Triple A? Am I ever going to get back up to the big leagues?' Two days later, [Baltimore pitcher] Scott Erickson came up with a sore ham-string and I pitched five innings in relief and thought 'I should be good now.' And I was."

Then Driskill picked up a win in relief against the A's, and after that came a juggling of the Orioles rotation and an emergency start that no one figured for permanent. Except that Driskill picked off the masterly Ichiro Suzuki at first base, four-hit the Mariners over six innings, and got his second major league win. Then he seven-hit the Yankees, struck out Derek Jeter three times in New York, and ran his record to 6–1 heading into the All-Star Break. He eventually came down to earth, finished the year 8–8 with a 4.95 ERA, but his story was irresistible and Driskill said quotable things and laughed at himself and the media recited his Crash Davis bona fides all the way into September.

It didn't last. No one really expected it to. Driskill had often said that he'd always wanted to throw just one pitch in the majors, just to get in the record books, and he would never again be as good as he was in the summer of '02. The following year with Baltimore he never started, made 20 appearances and went 3–5, with his best moment, oddly enough, coming when he surrendered the 10,000th home run in Fenway Park history.

"Wrigley Field, Tiger Stadium, Yankee Stadium . . . and there's one other. Hey, I'm one of five guys in history to give up a ten-thousandth home run," Driskill says, and he's chuckling at first so it sounds as if he's joking. He's not. "Roger Clemens and Cy Young and all those guys? They're one of twenty-seven or thirty guys to win three hundred games. I'm one of *five*," he says. "You've got to find your place in history."

Mike's place? He knew it the moment he and Mandy married. He knew it even more the moment Joey arrived: April 27, 2002. Coolbaugh didn't bring the clubhouse home with him, at least not the major league version where players drop their dirty laundry on the floor and milling strangers with cameras and pens hang on their every word. He didn't treat Mandy like an accessory, a dolled-up announcement of success, and anyone who saw them together couldn't help but be struck by their closeness. "As an outsider, I don't know anybody who wouldn't envy what they had," says Katie Pavlovsky, Mandy's sister. "I would take the seven and a half years of marriage and the years they dated before that over any other option. It was that strong and powerful. But what struck me even more? I never met anybody who wanted kids as much as he did."

Mandy insists: They had tense moments like any two adults living in close proximity, but never an argument that degenerated into nastiness. "He just did everything right," she says. "He was the one who made sure we got to church every Sunday, who made sure the kids prayed before every meal, who tucked them in at night. He would leave me surprises everywhere. If he left before me for the season he would leave handwritten notes, but he would hide them under pillows, in shorts, drawers, suitcases, a book I was reading. He would call every night, no matter how late it was, just to tell me he loved me. He would leave notes in the car, too; I'd find them in the consoles: 'I miss you every day that we're apart.' When we had our kids he wrote two songs describing our life. I was in labor, and he sat in the hospital and took out a notepad and wrote them down and would sing them to me. He sang all the time."

But family created new pressures. The baseball options were dwindling. The Cardinals released Coolbaugh after the '02 season, then the Phillies signed and released him just before 2003 spring training. Desperate, he went the foreign route for the first time, heading to South Korea to play for his 16th team, the Doosan Bears. *I can't believe I signed with a Korean team*, Mike scribbled in a notebook in the Honolulu airport that February, on his way to spring training. *I realize sitting here that it's time to find out if I can make it in the game financially or not. I'm not exactly getting a full time job in the majors. Having been successful at AAA for five years now, I can't go back again. If I do well in Korea I can make some real money. If I fail, well then I wouldn't have made it in the U.S., and at least I'll know I had the chance. In the end, that's all a good player wants. A real shot. A go-out-there-and-play-every-day kind of shot.*

Mandy and Joey stayed with him in Honolulu for five weeks, leaving for the mainland when Mike went on to Korea. *Her mom is really sick*, Mike wrote. *She has been for three years now and it doesn't look good. I want them to come with me so bad. But it's probably for the best. I'm gonna miss Joey's life for six months. Walking, talking. He's gonna forget who I am. Mandy's having our second baby, I'm gonna miss it. I'm gonna miss them.*

But a .215 batting average, a back injury, and an allergic reaction to penicillin ended that foray after four months. With Jake due in September and Mandy's mother declining fast with breast cancer, Mike knew the family needed a jolt of stability. The Astros, meanwhile, needed a utilityman in their system. Mike swallowed hard and that July went back to AA for the first time in six years, living—in an arrangement typical for minor leaguers—rent-free in the home of a local team booster named Nikole Smith and her son; Mike bought groceries to pitch in. And though he was now another step removed from the majors, Round Rock, outside of Austin, was actually perfect: Mike signed the papers on a house, an 1,800-square-foot fixer-upper in San Antonio for $122,000, at the end of the month. Now Mandy and the kids would have a real home, with both sets of grandparents nearby. He'd be playing just 80 miles away.

That mattered. Mandy and Joey drove up for every home stand. Scott lived outside Dallas in Colleyville, and Mike kept at him, always looking for an excuse to get the cousins and uncles and in-laws under one roof. "He never talked about, 'Who'd you sign with this year?'" Scott says. "He talked about how he wanted the families together all the time. It was always 'Let's get the kids together.'" And the kids would chatter and run and somehow the two brothers would always end up at the kitchen table, playing cards, talking about how Joey was doing in T-ball and Scott's son, Tyler, was doing with his select team, giggling at guys they knew, stories from the road and the game, bad hotels, punishing bus rides, all the funny, cruel stuff that only another ballplayer could understand.

Mike was, as one in-law put it, the family "glue." He wasn't a peacemaker, nor was he all sweetness; there were times when, Mary Lu says, "he could bitch up a storm." But Mike had to have a hand in everything, from planning Thanksgiving and Christmas to dirty diapers to the furniture. He didn't trust the store-bought cribs and changing tables, so he built both by hand—complete with a pull-out drawer and delicate inlays—from scratch. He installed the catcher's mitt light in the boys' room. The battle with cancer had drained Mandy's mom, but Anne had always been a devout Christian; that combination of struggle and certainty intrigued him. Mike would visit Anne alone sometimes, sit and read her Bible. Once he brought her a cross with the Lord's Prayer engraved upon it, never even telling Mandy. He'd call his own mother constantly, inviting her to lunch, shopping, the playground with the boys. He wasn't looking to score points. He liked the action. Mike would wait until Mandy went out of town to visit family, then paint the bathroom the color she liked, or install that crown molding she'd always admired. "He would always surprise me. He always put me before him," she says. He couldn't be with her long without touching her, holding her hand, kissing and hugging her. They'd go to bed and he'd want to make sure none of the day's petty annoyances lingered. "I want to live every day without regrets," Mike would say. "I don't want us to hold anything back."

Joey's first word was "ball." Mike reveled in that, and not just because he wanted the boys to grow up in baseball. It hurt whenever a team rejected him and he had to start over again, and there were times when he wondered why he was spending all his energy and time chasing a boy's game. "There's got to be a reason I'm still playing," he'd say. "Something good has to come out of all this." But the way Joey, especially, took to the game gave a partial answer, enough so Mike could actually feel some control: in at least one small way, baseball was working for him now. "His game became more about playing for his kids," Mandy says. "They loved being at the games and running the bases after and going into the locker rooms; they lived for that. He played more for them in the end than for anybody else. He had gotten to the point: *If I don't make the [major league] team out of spring training it's not going to bother me. I'm playing for my family now.*"

A few weeks after Mike signed with Round Rock, Bob and Mary Lu and Mandy and the kids drove up from San Antonio for a treat: Scott and Mike were playing each other for the first time in six years. Scott's wife, Susan, came in from Colleyville. But this baseball reunion felt different from the last one in Alabama. Back then Mike was having his monster season, seemingly on track for stardom, and Scott's playing career was nearing its end. Now in a role reversal of sorts, Scott was the hot young thing—a 37-year-old manager in his first year with the AA El Paso Diablos—while Mike, the 31-year-old veteran player, was trying to carve out a place on a Double-A team. The two men couldn't compete directly at Dell Diamond, not like they did when both played third base and faced off for two series in Huntsville and Birmingham in 1997. This time, Scott could even allow himself to wish for Mike to play well . . . so long as El Paso won.

The series could've been a mother's nightmare. Instead, the games again unrolled with Solomonic symmetry: Round Rock and El Paso split the four-game series. Mike pounded the Diablos pitching for 7 hits in 17 at-bats, including a game-winning homer in the opener— doing a little *too* well, if Scott had any say—but Scott landed as good a punch as a manager can. The next night Mike ripped another solo shot in the seventh inning, and Scott had had enough. When his little brother came to the plate in the tenth inning, Round Rock had the go-ahead run at second base with Mike at the plate, batting right-handed with a left-hander on deck. El Paso had a lefty going on the mound, but few managers would put a base runner on to gain a lefty-lefty matchup. Then again, few managers would have watched that right-hander as a 13-year-old take 200 swings at a stump with a dulled ax blade. Scott called for the intentional walk.

"I was not," Scott says, "going to let my brother beat me."

Watching from the stands, most of the family understood: Who wanted to see the cards fly across the table? But to Bob it made no sense. *Boy, Scott, you're putting yourself in a hole here*, he thought. *Why would you do it? That's the dumbest friggin' move going.*

Mike never even looked over at his brother as he dropped the bat, jogged to first. The batter after Mike, Anthony Acevedo, grounded out to end the inning. The Diablos held on to win, 7–5. "Because it worked," Bob says, "no one could say anything."

It had only been four years since he played, but Scott could already sense a subtle shift in the minor league landscape. The aging player was sticking around longer. Whether the reason was expansion, base-ball's fading relevance among young athletes, or an impatience with the sport's traditional learning curve, organizations were now pushing phenoms to the majors faster. Meanwhile, an ongoing minor league stadium building boom had goosed attendance and improved working conditions, while salaries kept creeping upward. A veteran like Mike could make anywhere from $50,000 to $80,000 playing in AAA. Once considered finished at 30, more AAAA players found themselves less disposable, and more willing to hang on into their mid-thirties instead of embarking on a new career. Why not? Mike could still hit: His 7 homers and 29 RBI in 147 at-bats for Round Rock in 2003 were proof enough that he hadn't lost bat speed. If the majors seemed increasingly distant, there were still jobs to be had. Baseball could pay the mortgage, feed his family. A man could do worse.

At home, it seemed as if Mike embraced that notion. When he was assigned to the Astros' AAA roster in New Orleans out of spring training in 2004, neither Mandy nor his sons saw him snarl in disap-pointment. She kept waiting for some sign of frustration. "If it had been me, I would've quit," Mandy says. "I often wondered if he was just holding all this in. I took it harder because I wondered if one day he was just going to blow up. But he never did."

Only in that den of ego, hope, and fear—the clubhouse—did Mike let it show. His father's cynical streak was only fueled by his sons' just-missed careers, and if Mike often disagreed with the man and vowed to raise his kids less stringently, a variation of that darkness still ran through him like a current. He wasn't a sunny, "Let's play two!" type. When Mike got a bad hand in a clubhouse poker game, he'd slip into a funk for three or four hands, silently grumbling at the fates that wouldn't cut him a break. If some callow phenom or prospect with lesser numbers got the nod while he continued to toil in the Texas League, it inflamed his sense of injustice, tickling every bitter nerve he'd inherited and tried to control. Second baseman Chris Burke, a teammate from 2003 to 2005, called Mike "a lovable grouch" because you could see his cynicism warring with a lighter sense of perspective. Half the fun of being around Mike was watching him fall into a foul mood and then pull himself out.

"Ahh, I'm just a bitter old fart," Mike would say at the end of some rant. "Listen to me complain. Like I've got it bad."

It's a truism of minor league ball that anyone who plays it a long time must be a team guy, short on complaints and good for clubhouse chemistry. By definition no lifer, no one-time star who has lost his "prospect" status to become an "organizational player" or "a roster spot" will carry a me-first attitude. That type is tolerated only as long as he demonstrates jaw-dropping potential; a mediocre jerk, though, soon finds himself out of baseball for good. Mike would quietly corner people he trusted, like Round Rock manager Jackie Moore, to vent and ask the rhetorical *What else do I need to do here?* Moore, of course, knew the song. Hell, he *was* the song: As a player he'd had one short major league stint in 11 years and hit .094. As a coach he'd shuttled around the game for three decades before his lone major league managing chance in Oakland, where he lost more than he won and was all but forgotten when replaced by Tony La Russa. But Moore never complained, not publicly anyway, and he saw himself in Mike. "He was always so close, one break away, but he never took that disappointment into the clubhouse or on the field," Moore says. "Once he left my office he put his game face on and didn't disrupt the clubhouse. No *I didn't get the break* or *I got screwed*. That was a large part of his value. He was the older player you'd want your younger prospects to be around and learn from."

Mike started off the 2004 season slowly, then fell into a full-blown slump. One night in Omaha, after he struck out three times, the New Orleans players looked out the windows of their bus to see Coolbaugh walking along the road back to the hotel, ten miles alone. "He's got his head down and he's talking to himself," Burke says. "Here he is, with a thousand games in his career and he couldn't handle the fact that he was in a bad rut. But he ended up with thirty home runs that year in New Orleans—just an amazing turnaround."

It wasn't easy. Mike was the big bat in the lineup, known for hitting 25 to 30 bombs a year, and pitchers nibbled around his strike zone every time. He hated when the count went full, 3–2, knowing full well that no self-respecting pitcher would give him much to hit, and knowing he'd be expected to squeeze out something regardless. Really, a hitter could ask for no greater sign of respect, but it only made Mike boil. He could count on younger players hanging a curveball, or getting macho and thinking they could fire the ball past him, but experienced pitchers knew better. And when Coolbaugh would dig in against a fellow AAAA type, the at-bat assumed even more resonance. He faced Travis Driskill for the first time in 1999, when he was in AAA Columbus and Driskill was in Buffalo, and he'd kept track of Driskill's sweet ride in the majors in 2002. Each man had a mental book on the other, adding yet another layer to the pitcher-batter duel, the game within the game. Fans might not notice, but these moments—facing someone who'd been up there like you, a player with just as much mileage on his bones—are when lifers get closest to the bigs again.

"Those are the matchups I wanted," Driskill says. "Getting one of those young kids coming up? They're talented, but I know more about the game than they do at that point in their careers. I can *do* things to them. But with Mike, it was a chess match. It was, *All right, I got you out this way; can I do it again? Or are you not going to let me?* Our brains got to work."

Late in that 2004 season, Driskill, released the previous fall by Baltimore and back in AAA with Colorado Springs, began an at-bat against Mike with a couple split-finger fastballs, the kind that drop like a rock off a table instead of drilling straight into a catcher's mitt. He was no fool; his fastball had lost some pop. But Driskill could also feel Coolbaugh, eager to hit that 30 home run mark, getting more and more frustrated. So he kept them coming: four, five, seven split-fingers in a row. Driskill can't recall how Mike got out that at-bat, but he won't ever forget Mike screaming as he trudged back to the dugout, "Just throw me a fastball!" Which, to a pitcher, is like hearing beautiful music.

"Hitters all say, 'Challenge me, challenge me,'" Driskill says, chuckling. "Well, challenge yourself by not swinging at a bad pitch."

Just throw me a fastball. Such a close echo on the lifer's motto was hardly accidental. Baseball's first dividing line, the one separating the casual player from the serious, is the curveball, of course, and Mike had passed that long ago. But he never got comfortable with the game's serpentine dimensions, the byzantine politics and hidden motives that became manifest in the nibbling off-speed pitches, the dancing sliders that so resisted his need to hit the damn thing solid. Mike relished those one-on-one battles, and with 258 professional home runs won more than his share. But philosophically he liked the world and its challenges to come at him straight down the middle.

The following spring, Driskill showed up in Astros spring training; now he was Mike's teammate. Still, in an intra-squad game, that lifers' face-off, the game within the game within the game, went on. This time, Driskill threw Mike nothing but fastballs, even with two strikes, even as the foul balls skittered and the pitch count rose to ten. He knew Mike was just waiting on his splitter, timing off just a hair, and knew it for sure when Mike popped out. And for the rest of the season, whenever he'd hear Mike complaining about some pitcher not giving him any fastballs, Driskill would say, "You remember: I gave you fastballs in spring training!" and Mike would nod and laugh hard. Their wives had become friends.

He had had yet another good spring, hitting .304. Nothing changed. When Astros manager Phil Garner and then general manager Tim Purpura sat him down in Garner's office in Kissimmee, Florida, and told Mike he'd be going down to AAA again, Mike couldn't help himself. He slumped in his chair. Morgan Ensberg still had a lock on third base in Houston; it had been that way for three years. Each time this had happened before, he'd asked the coaches and GMs what he could improve on, and no one really had an answer. Now he had a different question. He would turn 33 in June, and he needed to know.

"Should I bag this?" he said. "Should I give it up?"

Garner and Purpura said no. They needed him. "You've got power," the two men said. "You play good defense, Mike, you've got skills, you're smart. Of course not." So Coolbaugh left the office, went to his locker, cleared out his bats and spikes and family photos. He packed his bags. He moved over to the minor league side of Astros camp and, as Purpura says, "did his job."

He did more than that. Mike snapped out of his funk. "I'm not going to let them beat me," Mike told Scott, and from then on everything he did went into proving it. He set himself one last mission: just one more September up there, one last short ride in the majors. Mike had always been a little surprised by his call-up by Milwaukee in 2001; he'd had better seasons before and since without going to The Show. This time, he wanted to get that call and deserve it, and it only helped that all the elements seemed to conspire to make 2005 his best season yet.

The Round Rock Express had moved up to become Houston's AAA franchise, so the families were only an hour away. Mandy and the boys moved into booster Nikole Smith's house for home stands and came to the park every night. Joey and Jake had free run of the ballpark, as always, and Mike kept an eye on them even during games. Beyond that, nothing could distract him. Mike would crank a song in the clubhouse before games, Mercy Me's "I Can Only Imagine," and if its Christian lyrics bothered any teammates, it didn't stick. The booming title, repeated over and over, could strike a chord with even the staunchest atheist because it verbalized every minor leaguer's daily bread—the fantasizing about what it would be like to be in that great rarefied place, one day, with all the stars. Mike won Defensive Player of the Month honors in July, and with his 27th homer on August 18 drove in his 101st run, his biggest RBI haul since Huntsville in '97. More important, he was healthy, tallying more at-bats than he'd seen in 11 years. "He just *knew* he was going to have that call-up," Mandy says, "and at that point that's all he wanted."

He wasn't alone. Coolbaugh had long passed the point of being a faceless number in the Houston organization. Night in and night out that summer, Purpura would receive the voice-mail reports—*Coolie went 3 for 4, played good defense*—and found his usual detachment fraying. Like media and fans, even the cold-eyed analysts can't help but want the lifer to get his due. "You pull for those guys," Purpura says. "It's not like you want someone to get hurt on your team, but every night you'd think, 'Man, I wish I had a spot for this guy.'"

By then, no one believed Mike was a hidden star. His weaknesses were well catalogued. Both his thumbs had been broken by pitches—the first during his second year in St. Catharines and the last time during the previous winter ball season in Venezuela. He kept that one secret, though, even to the point of paying for treatment out of his own pocket, and for good reason. Mike knew that more than most players, he literally couldn't afford to be seen as fragile because any injury, especially to his hands, was a vivid reminder of his technical flaws. He was a smart hitter, quick to pick up tendencies, and if a pitcher got lazy and threw the same pitch twice, Mike could make him pay. But his inability to avoid the ball is as good an indicator as any of "the book"—the opponent's scouting report on each hitter's tendencies and strengths—on him as a hitter. Coolbaugh was what's known as a "diver," the kind who digs in close to the plate and feasts on outside pitches, so opposing pitchers constantly attacked him with high, inside fastballs, backing him off and trying to capitalize on the hole in his swing. "The one pitch he had trouble with—and that's the one pitch everybody throws you first to see if you can hit it," Scott says. "Playing in Triple-A as long as he did, there were enough veteran pitchers who'd been in the major leagues who knew how to attack a hitter's weakness. But fact of the matter is, pitchers can't throw inside for strikes too many times. Those injuries were a case of Triple-A pitchers trying to exploit his weaknesses. They came in hard a lot."

Baseball is a results game—you either do or you don't—and its practitioners have no choice but to see their peers and themselves clearly. Mike was a Triple-A player for seven years for a reason: He was a Triple-A talent. Former major league managers like Jackie Moore and Greg Riddoch insist he could've produced on the major league level, but Coolbaugh had deficiencies that major leaguers know how to fill or protect day after day, and even those who loved him couldn't help but see them. "Hey, I was that guy too," Driskill says. "To be honest, he could not have been an everyday player up there, I don't think: He didn't hit a well-located fastball well enough. Not that that's an easy thing to do—Chipper Jones doesn't hit a well-located fastball all the time either. But I think Mike would've been exposed had he gotten to play all the time up there. If he had gotten the chance, he might've been able to make the adjustments. He was professional enough to put forth the effort to do it; he wouldn't have been stubborn. But from what I saw I don't think he would've been a great major league hitter or even a guy you would consider a good major league hitter. He could've come off the bench, and he had game-breaking power; he would've given you quality at-bats and he would've been nothing less than professional. He could've provided a good service."

"Mike would cheat on the inside fastball and become vulnerable to the outside breaking ball; the combination of that, with the swing he had, wasn't going to give him an opportunity to be an everyday [major league] guy," Scott says. "But a pinch-hitter? He would've done a good job with that."

A good service. A good job. Maybe that's all that awaited Mike Coolbaugh if he indeed made it to the major leagues. Never stardom. Competence at best. Maybe he knew that, in the moments when he had to be honest with himself. Maybe he kept pushing because he'd never gone to college and he had one, then two, then three mouths to feed, and baseball was all he knew so he had to play it out until it was done. Still, it's true, Coolbaugh never got his clean shot at that pinch-hitting spot or any other, and never got enough big league games to prove the book wrong. Those who wouldn't give it to him understood: He was good enough, yes, but always in organizations where someone was a bit better. But that didn't mean that the baseball men didn't know they could've been wrong, in the sense that they could be wrong about anyone. The mystery of talent, reacting to the ultimate pressure and the best competition, remains as deep as ever. "The opportunities just never came for him at the right time, in the right circumstance," Purpura says. "Honestly? He had talent. There just wasn't the opening. And you never know what a guy's going to do at the big league level until he gets an opportunity to show you."

Now, though, it looked like Mike's chance had come. The first-place Astros were gunning for the wild-card spot and needed all available veteran firepower. Purpura says—and Mike was told—that the team had every intention of calling him up the first week of September. But on the August day after Coolbaugh launched his 27th homer, on a warm and clear Friday night in Nashville, he took an inside pitch from reliever Jeff Bennet on the back of his left hand, breaking a bone. "Devastating," Mandy says.

Chris Burke, Mike's teammate and close friend for three years, had already been called up by the Astros in June and had embarked on a stellar rookie season, a 25-year-old second baseman hitting his stride. Mike stayed with the Express, coaching first base with a soft cast on his hand, but within two weeks he was swinging a bat again—just in case. A local doctor cleared him to play. His hand felt good.

He couldn't keep his frustration from surfacing now: The Astros kept saying they wanted to give him a call-up. He was swinging, hitting. He had given them everything, was coming off the best season of his life. The odds of them playing him—or any other call-up—were very rare anyway. Why not throw him this one bone?

Round Rock was playing in Albuquerque when the players got the news: The Astros had recalled five players, Driskill included. The Express players were holding a fantasy football draft party that night, and looking forward to the major league meal money coming his way, Driskill supplied the food and the beer. His phone buzzed with calls from names he hadn't heard from in years, guys from rookie ball who had long been out of the game. Mike congratulated him, was polite when given the explanation by the Houston brass: Sorry, our doctors advised against it. But inside? It felt like a spit in the face. Another year gone. "There was not a doubt in my mind that he would've been called up," Moore says. "Baseball gods, whatever: Probably one of the best years he ever had and on the verge of going up and he breaks his hand. It just told the story of his whole career."

And the season wasn't even over. "Watch," Mike told Mandy. "They're going to go to the World Series."

Driskill spent a month with the Astros, pitched just one scoreless inning and struck out two. Once 15 games under .500 in May, Houston came back to win the National League wild-card berth on the season's last day. Thus began, yes, an improbable run into the 2005 World Series, 14 post-season games in which anyone could get injured, and unlikely heroes always surfaced; it's tempting to wonder how things would've turned out if Mike had been healthy. "Who knows what could have happened?" Purpura says.

Instead, Mike was at home in San Antonio. He planted himself in front of the television for each game, and when Game 4 of the Division Series against the Atlanta Braves turned into a 5-hour-and-50-minute epic, he sat there cheering. Down 6–1 in the eighth, the Astros tied the game 6–6 in the ninth to electrify Houston's Minute Maid Park. For the next 8½ innings, no one scored, Roger Clemens pitched in relief for only the second time in his career, and by the 18th inning every exhausted baseball fan knew they were witnessing a classic, the longest playoff game in major league history. Few would've picked Burke, a 10th-inning sub-stitute with just 5 home runs and 26 RBI, to end the series when he stepped in against Atlanta's Joey Devine at the bottom of the 18th.

But Mike knew. He turned to Mandy. "Chris Burke is going to hit a home run here," he said. "He's going to finish this game."

Burke swung. The ball sailed over the left field wall, and Mike stood and roared as his buddy rounded the bases and the Houston crowd screamed and cried and announcers yammered on and on. Mike watched it playing out on the screen, all these men he knew so happy now, living out that storybook ending in a city not far away. And he could only imagine.

BASEBALL, LIKE POLICE WORK OR POLITICS, has its Hollywood version: A man builds a diamond in a cornfield, a minor league lifer can't give up his mitt, Robert Redford returns after being gutshot by some mysterious dame. In 1999 Kevin Costner, whose stardom was all but built on America's appetite for baseball movies, came back one more time in a film that cut to the thematic chase in the title: *For Love*

of the Game. Why bother with subtlety? Baseball has always peddled treacle: The game is about fathers and sons, or clean-cheeked family fun, or an idyllic past when small-town neighbors looked after each other. Unlike any other sport, its core appeal is sentimental—and strong enough to withstand labor disputes, the designated hitter, or even years of steroid revelations. In 2007, the year the game's greatest slugger and greatest pitcher—Barry Bonds and Roger Clemens—seemed to betray its halcyon ideals when they were all but unmasked as users of performance-enhancing drugs, major league baseball set an all-time league-wide attendance record. Fans love baseball, and if the success of *The Natural* or *Bull Durham* is any measure, they love the idea of being in love with it even more.

But players don't see the game that way. To them it is, indeed, the same impossibly beautiful woman the fan sees shimmering from afar. But they actually live with this woman, and she's a succubus: moody, mean, and about as sentimental as a mob assassin.

"When a player says someone loves baseball, it's not this warm-and-fuzzy *Field of Dreams* love of baseball," Chris Burke says. "You've got to understand: Every day we go out in front of forty thousand people and look like idiots. You see great players go 0 for 25, hit .150 for a month, leave the bases loaded two times in a row. There's stuff all the time that makes you come out of the game saying, *I hate this game.* When a player says someone 'loves the game,' it's more a description of a person's dedication to try to do as well as he can in the game. It's a love-hate relationship that most players hold for baseball, and frustrating as it is, you want to conquer it."

Failure is the baseball constant. As the saying goes, fail to hit seven out of ten times and you're a star. But major leaguers have the compensations of posh facilities and massive salaries to soften the sting. As hard as the game itself remains, nearly all material concerns are removed at the top. "It's easy to love this game when you're making $1 million every two weeks," Tino Sanchez says. But the professional world below the majors is different. Everyone there wants to get out. Minor league baseball is the dusty road to the castle, and after a while the road wears everyone down. The castle? People want to stay there forever.

Minor league clubhouses feel nothing like the luxury dens of New York or Detroit, but it's as much a matter of mind-set as it is furniture. In the bigs—not to mention sports like football, basketball, and hockey—once final cuts are finished, the team gets down to the process of winning. But minor league baseball is an endless winnowing process. Cast for months into a confined space where people are promoted, demoted, traded, and released every day, where today's teammate is tomorrow's memory, players literally live with rejection. No one can truly relax; even the most secure prospects sense the insidious thrum of fear. "You can feel the tension in the locker rooms. The teams get quieter as the games approach, thinking, 'Who's going to get released?'" says Alan Zinter. "There's just that silence, that quiet pressure; guys' eyes are looking back and forth. It's that anxiety, that internal anxiety of performing, the fear of failure, all the stuff you have to learn to control to look tough out there."

After a loss, a bush league clubhouse resembles a wake: hushed tones, young men with their heads bowed, fingers snaking through their hair. "You go hitless three games, you want to kill yourself," Tino says. "You think your career is over." And after a win, a 3-for-4 day, a two-hit outing? The place feels like a wedding: smiles, straight backs, brave talk about the future. To be whipsawed between the two is a daily ordeal, corrosive to the soul and all too public.

"There's so much hope involved," says Rockies manager Clint Hurdle, who as a player and coach has worked at every level of the minors. "You need to find a way to circumvent your emotions. You think it's all about *the day*—and it is, in a sense—but it's all about washing that day away at the end. That's how you find your comfort zone and can become the best player you can be. But down there, more often than not for most guys it's day-to-day and it's up or it's down—a lot of spiked emotions. There's only a small percentage of guys who can play the game on the minor league level on a nice, even keel."

If the system were pure, if everyone involved believed that, indeed, only the best rise to the top, maybe such stress would be easier to endure. But there's also a pervasive feeling in the minors—as much a part of baseball as bats and balls—that the game is rigged. As much as players are told that numbers—their statistics—don't lie, everyone knows that the wholly subjective feelings of scouts and general managers, shaded by the often-unshakable labels they put on players, dictate who will rise, fall, or stagnate until it becomes clear it's time to quit. Players know that certain names will be given chance after chance to succeed, and that those players are the ones whose most crucial numbers—their large signing bonuses—make it necessary for front-office types to keep supporting them, come hell or low performance, if only to justify paying out that huge number in the first place. It's no wonder that a clubhouse can often seem like the most sour room on earth; a world where men are told daily that performance is all and shown daily that performance can count for nothing will make a cynic out of any saint. And not many ballplayers are saints to begin with.

Those who stay in, who become coaches and managers and scouts themselves, can't be blamed for their caution; they can't love the game purely because they've seen all its dirt. It's only after someone shouts, "Play ball!" that they remember why they loved baseball at all.

"It's kind of like getting married to that woman when you were real young, going through the hard times and good times and you find a way to make it work," Scott Coolbaugh says of the lifer's relationship with the game. "You've always got that peaceful ground where you can come to grips with it, and that's when you step between the lines or when you step into the coaching box and you say, 'You know what? All the bullshit that I've gone through, all the pain that I've suffered, is worth it.' But then after the game you're back being pissed off again."

Because there's always some new good reason. In 2000 Tino Sanchez was playing for a Winter League team in Bayamón, Puerto Rico, with a friend, Jerry Amador, a Mariners' fourth-round pick, 19 years old and coming off his first pro season. The Bayamón brass told the young outfielder that he'd be activated onto the roster, and for three weeks Amador trailed the team across the island, driving two hours before and after every game, waiting for his shot. It never came. Finally, during the second game of a doubleheader, a teammate, then–Texas Rangers star Ruben Sierra, motioned for Amador to get ready: He was pulling himself out of the lineup. Sierra told the manager to put Jerry in.

"I can't do that," manager Carmelo Martinez replied. "He's not active."

"And he never was," Tino says. "That's embarrassing. That's no respect for baseball, no respect for the kid. The kid is traveling with the team to the games, he's ready, he's happy, he thinks that at any moment he can be playing. But the manager lied. The manager told him he was active but he wasn't. Amador's dad wanted to kill the manager. Amador left the field. He left the stadium. He retired three years after that."

That phrase, *respect for baseball*, surfaces often with Tino today. It wasn't the kind of thing he'd say during his struggle in Asheville, but since their 1998 season together, P. J. Carey had taken Tino's measure during every spring training. He was sure he'd come around. "As much as the kids show you what they need, they always show you signs of that character to come," Carey says. "Tino always had it. He just didn't know it."

When he floated into Rockies spring training in '01, sour attitude in place, Tino had little idea how close he was to being flushed. One morning, when Rockies coach Dave Collins was passing Field 2 at the Hi Corbett complex, he noticed an intern putting eight players through a conditioning drill. Seven were running hard. The intern tried goading Tino on; Tino ignored him. Collins stopped. He called Tino over and introduced himself. As a player, Collins had one great tool—speed—yet he played 16 years in the major leagues because he knew that wasn't enough; the gift that made him a high school star never clouded his thinking. Following the lead of teammate Pete Rose, from 1975 to 1990 Collins became a paragon of intensity, compensating for his average arm and power by working out to exhaustion and making himself useful. He learned how to play every outfield position and first base. He hit .272 for his career and stole 395 bases. To see some 22-year-old A-baller dogging it? Collins found the idea insulting. He let it rip.

"I played sixteen years in the major leagues," he rasped at Tino. "I went on strike three times for you, so that when you make it to the major leagues you can make all the money that we never made. All we ask of you guys? Respect the game, and be a pro out here all the time. Part of being a pro is being coachable and giving your best effort. You think that's a good trade-off—what you're getting and what you gave here today?"

Tino blinked. "You'll never see me again on the field with a bad attitude," he said.

The next morning Collins was dressing in front of his locker when Sanchez found him again. "Hey, Dave," he said. "I just wanted to say hi."

Collins eyed Tino all spring training. When, in March, it came time to assign players throughout the system, the vote on Tino Sanchez was nearly unanimous: Not worth the trouble. Release him. But Collins, off to coach the organization's Salem, Virginia, affiliate in the Carolina League, held up his hand. "I want this kid," he said. "I think he's a winner. It's in there. And more important, he can help our team win." The vibe in the room: You want him that much? He's all yours, Dave.

At first, many of the Salem Avalanche players hated playing for Collins. The roster was stocked with prospects, but the manager was a stickler for process. Within days everyone was complaining about his boot-camp ways. Collins made them all take batting practice and infield practice every day, including Sunday. Collins made them sprint after every game. Collins coddled no one, especially Tino, bracing him with blunt breakdowns of his game and personality, drilling him with the need to put the team's interests before his own. "You're not talented enough and you really can't improve what you've got," Collins told him, "but change your outlook and you can play in the majors." Collins meant it, too. He sensed that once a manager gained Tino's trust, once the player knew you cared about him, he would give you everything. Collins also had the arrogance to believe that, aside from making ballplayers, he had a mission to make them men.

So that season, Collins loaded Tino with responsibility. He had been tagged as an organizational player—one of the replaceables, one of those whose washout would hurt no scout's reputation. And yet Collins made him feel as vital as future major leaguers Matt Holliday, Garrett Atkins, Clint Barmes, and Aaron Cook. Tino played nearly every position in the field: first, third, every outfield spot, catcher. Tino pinch-hit, left-handed and right-, or got inserted to catch late when Collins needed him to keep base runners at bay. Sometimes he'd start, sometimes he wouldn't, and he rarely came to the ballpark knowing which it would be. In a sense, Tino had perhaps the toughest job on the team: Come into a game with less talent, continuity, and time to prepare than your teammates—and then bail them out. Just as important, come into the clubhouse the day after getting three hits, find yourself back on the bench nevertheless, and carry on without bitching. Your role? You have no defined role. The only constant in the situation is you, committed to producing no matter what.

On paper it didn't look like much, a utility guy doing his job, and Tino hit just .233 with 26 RBI in 91 games. But his was a subtle value, not instantly visible to stat-freaks or those dazzled by the long ball. "He delivered for us everywhere," Collins says. "He would get maybe one or two at-bats a game, and this is how it would be: *Tino, you're pinch-hitting next inning. You'll be hitting off their closer, who's their best pitcher, you've been sitting there for eight innings, and you'll be leading off. Get ready.* Or I'd put him in the sixth inning against a guy who was pitching well because I wanted to keep him sharp. He never got that consistent opportunity to get his form back, but you know what? He was hitting .220 in the newspaper, but it was like he was hitting over .300 because he'd hit the ball hard for an out. He hit more balls hard for outs than any kid on our team. That's why stats are misleading: This kid had a lot of bad luck getting balls to fall for him. And when I did give him the opportunity to play, he took advantage. All of his hits seemed like big hits. He was always asked to come into a game to help us win—and he seemed to always do something to help us win. It was amazing."

Two months in, before a batting practice one June day in Salem, Collins gathered the team in. "You see Tino Sanchez? Tino was about to get released in spring training"—the first time Sanchez knew how close to the edge he'd been. "And now," Collins continued, "he's one of the top prospects in the organization." Tino didn't know that, either.

It was the smallest of gestures, a few words tossed into the air on a minor league ballfield. But it meant plenty, good and bad, because Tino had the gratifying understanding at last that he could contribute, that he did matter, that he understood the game and was just good enough to make it work to his advantage. But believing in Collins and Collins's idea of him also shut down all the childhood options of stardom and fame. Yes, Dave said he could get to the majors still, but only this way, as a cog, a clean-up guy. Everyone eventually accepts that they will not grow up to be president or play center field in Yankee Stadium, and one perk of being a pro ballplayer is that the moment gets delayed far longer than it does for the average man. But when it comes, the truth of it cuts deeper and takes longer to heal. Though Tino was Collins's good soldier that season, he had his withdrawal spasms, times when he'd pout or snap. Collins would jump him each time, always with the same thought: *I'm not going to let you slide back into being a mediocre person.* A month after his moment on the grass, Tino walked into the manager's office feeling low, and Collins said, "You think you'll ever come in here just once to tell me about someone else's problem?"

Tino got up to walk out, stopped, and turned. Collins waited at his desk for the explosion. "Dave," Tino said, "I'll never forget what you said right now. Thank you."

The Avalanche won the Carolina League championship that year, the only team in the organization to compete for or win a title. Collins's influence still hangs on Tino: It's no mistake that when asked for his best performance, he doesn't recall going 3 for 4 or making some astonishing catch. Tino talks about the season's final game, the one that would decide the title series against Wilmington.

Collins's team had barely broken .500 for the season but won its first-round playoff series as a wild card, then battled the favored Blue Rocks to a deciding Game 5. On the mound for Wilmington: Jimmy Gobble, the best left-hander in the Carolina League. Collins countered by starting a fading prospect named Ryan Price, who had battled with his head and arm all season, throwing a league-record 45 wild pitches and performing so erratically that at one point Colorado officials tried to deactivate him before Collins backed them down. A couple hours before the game, Collins made out the lineup card and called Tino in. "You're catching tonight," he said. "You know why?

Because you're the guy I trust most to get Price through this game." The implication: You fail? We lose.

It was Monday, September 10, 2001. Some 3,500 fans crammed the stands. Tino made his last warmup throw down to second base. In the dugout Collins turned to his pitching coach, Bob McClure. "Look at that," Collins said. "There's a pitcher pitching in the championship game who's not even supposed to be on the mound, and the next important position on the field—catcher—is a guy who is supposed to be at home right now."

Tino kept telling Price, "Don't think about mistakes; don't think at all. Throw the ball. Get rid of it and let's see what happens." Price was far from perfect, giving up 4 runs over 6 innings. But the Avalanche scored 6 to win Salem's first championship in 14 years, and the crowd stayed late. Everyone in Memorial Stadium sang "We Are the Champions."

"That was his best," Tino says. "I helped him out with the thousands of balls he threw in the dirt, and now it was do or die, and I was in the zone, handling him and getting the balls both." He smiles. "Yeah: I remember that game."

Collins went on to coach in Milwaukee and then Colorado in the years after Salem, then went back to minor league managing for the Los Angeles Dodgers. Few jobs are both as intense and as transient as baseball; it's never odd for that familiar face to be with a different organization come spring. In the winter of 2008, 56 years old, Collins left baseball for the first time in three decades, maybe for good. He still counted the title won by that 70–68, Single-A ball team as one of the great thrills of his career—right up there with going to the playoffs with the Reds himself in 1979—and credited Tino's growth not only as a key reason but as one of its more gratifying twists. "He was remarkable, not only as a player for us that year but as a person," Collins says. "I really admire Tino. I have the greatest respect for him."

Still, connections get frayed, phone numbers lost. Tino went back to Puerto Rico after that fall. The two never spoke again. This is a shame. Because after speaking for a while about his former player, it becomes clear that for Collins, "respect" and "admiration" aren't strong enough words for what he's trying to convey.

"I assume you're going to talk to Tino?" Dave Collins says, just before hanging up. "When you do, will you tell Tino that I love him?"

In 2002 Colorado promoted Sanchez to its Double-A club in Zebulon, North Carolina, the Carolina Mudcats of the Southern League, where he and Rene Reyes reunited with P. J. Carey. Like a classic Marine drill instructor, Collins had snapped Tino to wide-eyed attention. But it was Carey who instilled in him baseball's code. The Mudcats manager had learned it himself in the Phillies organization from his mentor Larry Rojas, a former Olympic sprinter with a thick Cuban accent, and carried it throughout a life bouncing through America's minor league towns: Always be honest with the player; always set a standard; always let him know you care. In 1978 Rojas was managing and Carey coaching a Rookie League team in Helena, Montana, when they first saw a second base prospect named Ryne Sandberg. Nearly 30 years later, though he lasted only four years in the Phillies organization and made his name with the Chicago Cubs, Sandberg invited Rojas and Carey to his Hall of Fame induction in Cooperstown, New York.

In his speech, Sandberg thanked both men, who "taught me to respect the game above all else." Then he explained what that means. "You never, ever disrespect your opponent or your teammates or your organization or your manager and never, ever your uniform," Sandberg said that day in July 2005. "Make a great play? Act like you've done it before. Get a big hit? Look for the third base coach and get ready to run the bases. Hit a home run? Put your head down, drop the bat, run around the bases because the name on the front is a lot more important than the name on the back." Sandberg used the word "respect" 19 times in his speech. Carey had a copy printed up and hung it on a wall in his Tucson home.

Tino calls Carey "my second dad," and he's not exaggerating. Every household needs a defining presence, a father figure, or the kids will indulge their worst impulses. Baseball was Tino's home away from home, the place where he had come to define himself. In Carey he rubbed up against a man who short-circuited his bitterness, who taught the one way to fight off the cynicism so easily absorbed in the minor leagues—the understandable cynicism that nonetheless must be avoided to survive. Players can never help but be mystified by the sight of less productive, less serious players being elevated above them or by a numbers game that cuts out many good enough to play; it's only human to rail against such decisions. But Carey's way is the embracing of a paradox: Baseball owes you nothing. Respect the game even when—especially when—it doesn't respect you. Work harder when no one is watching, help the very teammate who is passing you by, honor the jersey when you want to tear it off your back.

Tino was primed to hear that in 2002. By then, his English had so improved that he found his easiest crutch—suspected bias against

Latinos—splintering. "The truth of the matter is, you can be whatever you are," he says. "If you're white and you're good, you'll play in the major leagues; same with Latinos. When you're down, you start looking for excuses: *Why didn't I get called up?* But then I met people, spent time, learned the language—which opens another window, because if you can't communicate with your pitcher or partner, you don't know what he's all about. When you start speaking better English, it gets easier. You start understanding the culture of America."

With Carey in 2002, Tino had perhaps his best overall season, hitting .283 with 16 doubles. He'd arrive at the park before his teammates each day, take extra hitting, ask Carey for tips on defense. Carey remembers him in a batting tunnel at 1 p.m. in Sevierville, Tennessee, six hours before game time, sweating like a stevedore. It was a breakthrough. Every time Carey would look into Tino's eyes, "he'd give me a look, like, "I'm getting it, aren't I?'" Carey says. And that's all there is for the minor league coach. The only payoff was in Carey finally knowing: Tino's going to become as good as he can be in this game.

Sanchez wasn't posting huge numbers. It wasn't about that. "Anytime he played, he gave his heart, gave up everything he had to compete as well as he could," Carey says. "He not only competed with his average talent and contributed to the ball club winning; he became that guy that younger players looked to for advice. A lot of times everyone looks to that big bopper, but Tino was very outgoing and he really grew up. The guy who pulled that fire alarm? That's not who players are going to look to for leadership. But he became the guy players go to."

At one point that season, Tino and Reyes walked into the dugout and Carey called them over. "All right," he demanded, "which one of you pulled that alarm back in Tucson?" Tino looked at Reyes, Reyes looked at Tino, and at the same time they pointed at each other and said, "He did!" All three men broke up laughing. They laugh about it still.

The Mudcats won the first-half championship that season. The team had a little party to celebrate, and Tino brought a girl and liquor flowed and soon Tino was dancing with Carey's wife, Katherine, and P. J. was dancing with the girl, two couples doing a little salsa in Zebulon, North Carolina. It was funny and sweet, a small moment, but it felt like something bigger. Tino was twenty-three, and Carey watched him smiling and so polite. *He deserves this*, Carey thought. *He deserves this dance.*

Now that he'd gotten a taste—of progress, of winning, of feeling that his team depended on him—Tino wanted to keep it going. Collins and P. J. had staked their reputations on him, and he didn't want to let them down. He heard and saw what other players in the minors—"a big percentage," Tino says—were doing to get an edge: steroids, HGH (human growth hormone), the amphetamines known as "greenies," "so many things to make you improve the level of your game," Tino says. "I know for a fact that a lot of people did it during my career."

Estimates vary, but no one denies that—contrary to José Canseco's pinpointing of a bathroom stall in the Oakland clubhouse—the minor leagues were the true testing ground for performance-enhancing drugs. In a world where the competition is so fierce, the insecurity so deep, it's inevitable that the search for an edge would lead to the closest syringe or pill. Mike Frank, Mike Coolbaugh's teammate in Columbus in 2000 and Memphis in '02, says that drug use and rumors of drug use had gotten so pervasive that he would joke about writing a tell-all called *Everyone's on the Juice* and that players would sidle up to him and say, "I don't want to be in your book." He also remembers one player, later named publicly as a user, telling him in 2000, "'Frank, you get on the juice, you'll make $5 million a year. If you don't, you'll be out of baseball in two years.'

"Sure enough," Frank says, "two years later, I was done."

Curiously, condemnation from so-called clean peers is rare. Beyond the usual code of baseball *omerta*, even those who didn't partake understand the temptation. They all live under the same relentless pressure to perform. "I knew guys that did it—anything and everything," Travis Driskill says. "It didn't bother me. If someone wanted to do that, go for it—make the money. I know that's probably not the right thing to say, but that's why we do anything. We play baseball to make the money. We love the game, but we're in it for the money; if there's better money to be made in an easier way, we'd all be doing it. And if anybody was to do it, it would be a guy like me who spent nine years in the minors before he got his first shot. Would it be the difference-maker in me getting called up?"

With every player at once a watchdog, a critic, and a competitor for spots, with so much empty time begging to be filled with gossip, no one could avoid suspicion. "It was nice," says Alan Zinter, "because people thought I was doing it." Zinter isn't being sarcastic. He broke into the minors in 1989, right at the start of the Steroid Era, and attributes much of his two-decade tenure in the bushes to rigorous workouts and a lucky avoidance of injury. When people would say to him, "You've got to be on something," Zinter says, "I'd say, 'Thank you for the compliment.' You think I did it? I appreciate that because of the way I hit the ball and the way I look. I'll take any test, blood test; I would love to take a test for the last twenty years. I have nothing to hide.

"I wanted to make it on my hard work, what my dad taught me and all the love I had for the game. So I didn't drink, I didn't smoke, I've never taken a greenie, and I can look myself in the mirror and say, 'I made it.' I played my whole career in the Steroid Era, and saw a lot of guys go by me. That's their choice. Did it frustrate me? Yeah. I knew what was going on, but I never said, 'This guy's cheating. It's not fair.' It made me work harder. Now seeing these guys coming out and getting it off their conscience and apologizing—it makes me feel a little better. I did it the right way. I made it, and even though it was for just a short time, I was able to get there in an era where all these guys were doing this."

After 2000, minor league baseball had a far stricter drug enforcement policy than the majors, but during the 2001 and 2002 seasons Tino felt pressure to use anyway. But it wasn't the weight of competition, the feeling that he needed a chemical edge just to keep up with peers using performance enhancers, that got him using too. It wasn't even that he could make more money if he got to the next level and would be damned if he didn't do everything possible to get there. His motivation was far simpler: "Curiosity," Tino says. "Because when I started using it, I was young, I was healthy, I was full of energy. Everybody was using it, so why not? At that young age—when I was twenty-two, twenty-three—you get used to it, your system adapts. And then when you don't use it? It's all psychology. You really think that you can't play. You really think that you're not going to hit the ball."

Sanchez insists that he never used steroids or HGH, but he did consider it. Instead he took the more traditional route, the most wide-spread minor league drug: greenies, the stimulant used for decades throughout baseball, tacitly approved of as a way to fight off the rigors of overnight bus rides, day games after night games, the fatigue that sets in come August after three months straight of straining a body to its limit. For years clubhouses had two coffeepots, leaded and un-leaded, one spiked with greenies (so named because the original Dex-edrine came in tablets that hue). "Greenies were everywhere," Zinter says. "In 1997, when I was in big league camp in Seattle, a pitcher from the Dominican said, 'If you're going to play a long time and you're going to be good, you're going to have to use greenies.'" A player who tried to compete without such a boost was considered "naked," with the implication clear: He was going onto the field unarmed, weakened, a fool. Later, straight amphetamines were largely replaced by ephedra, an over-the-counter weight-loss supplement that produced the same result and, because it was legal, became as popular in some quarters as chewing gum. But the "greenies" name stuck.

Mike's parents, as well as Scott and Mandy, say that Mike never used any kind of performance enhancer as far as they could tell—which, as anyone in contact with human beings, much less athletes, knows, is not very far. "If you ever saw him," Frank says about Mike's hardly chiseled frame, "you knew Mike never used steroids." Still, Scott says, Mike felt the same pressure to use—especially near the end of his career—that he himself felt years before. "No question: Mike was a smaller kid, he was six foot one but he was always a thinner guy. He'd see these guys who were bigger, stronger, and it did frus-trate him," Scott says. "It's something that always ran across the mind:

Is this the time of my life where I need to take this to get over the hump?" But two highly personal factors would have made Mike think twice. First—though Bob says, "I wouldn't hold it against Michael, but I would've said, 'Do you understand what you're doing?' "—Mike was convinced his father would never forgive him. "That's probably the one thing that kept him from doing it," Scott says. "I know deep in his heart that if he felt comfortable with it or got encouraged by anybody that it'd be okay, he probably would've done it just like everybody else. But the way he was raised, he just wasn't going to go down that road."

Second, Mike knew Mandy's entire ambition centered on family, kids; whenever the subject arose at home, she didn't wait to hear Mike's opinion. "I'd better not see you do it," she told him. "Because if I ever have a baby with a handicap I'll never let you live it down." So it was that the only time Mandy heard Mike talk about it was after games, when he complained about the urine samples he was asked to produce—sometimes two or three at a time. He knew he was a textbook suspect—aging, frustrated slugger, in need of money, wondering if three more homers a season could make a difference. But all Bob and Scott and Mandy heard were his unproven suspicions that team personnel were taking his clean samples and substituting them for those of dirty teammates. Bad enough that he had to constantly feel others were getting the shot he deserved. Now he had to help them cheat, too? "Are they taking my urine and giving it to guys they know are doing it?" Mike would say repeatedly. "I'm not even called up. Why else would they be taking mine?"

Some players have tried to make a distinction between the muscle-boosting effects of steroids or HGH and greenies, and Tino says he never noticed an increase in his power. But pop a few before batting practice and then just before game time, and "inside you feel you're Superman," he says. "I never did cocaine, but I guess it's kind of the same, because a lot of people got very aggressive."

Tino says he limited his use to only when he was fully exhausted. He didn't want to get caught, and he didn't like the aftereffects; stimulants wear down the body even as they rev it up. It's a ballplayer's paradox: The very drug you take to combat weariness actually compounds the problem. "It was destroying," he says. "It destroys your system. You can't go to sleep after games, you can't eat because your system is so hyper. You have to drink either beer to calm down or a liter of milk to go to sleep."

The problem, though, is that it's easy to believe greenies work. After his big season in '02, Tino got his reward: The Rockies brought him to 2003 major league spring training in Tucson for the first time as a non-roster invitee. He was 24, officially a prospect and electrified by the realization: *This is it. I'm in the show.* That he, like most invitees, was earmarked for eventual demotion was beside the point. Maybe he'd get red-hot and some big-leaguer would snap a femur and . . . you never know, right?

So he got a bit cocky. The Rockies routinely took extra batting practice after games, but something about that rubbed Tino wrong. It felt very un-baseball, against the code, like what ballplayers still call "eyewash"—doing something not because it's right, but because it looks good and the lingering fans will ooh and ahh. Tino always took his extra hitting before games, as P. J. had taught him. One afternoon during the post-game session, he and his old partner in crime, Reyes, headed to deep right field with bats in hand. They began shagging balls not with gloves but with bats, respecting the game with a little disrespect, hitting the balls on a bounce or two back to "the pocket"— the protective screen set up on the grass behind second base, where a few unknown Rockies were gathering the balls bouncing in from all points. "Hey," Tino told Reyes. "Watch my pop."

He launched a high fly toward the pocket: very nice. The ball hit its parabolic peak and began to drop, and Tino and Reyes looked at each other.

"No way," Tino said.

"That's hit pretty good," Reyes said.

"That ball is carrying . . . it's going to get there. . . . Shit, there's someone . . ."

The ball hit the screen on the fly and ricocheted square into the face of Rockies first-year manager Clint Hurdle, whose spiked gray hair and permaflushed cheeks suggest a temper rarely held in check. Hurdle staggered back but didn't fall. "I John Wayne'd it," he says. "But I answered as if somebody punched me in the face."

"Motherfucker!" Hurdle screamed. Tino jogged as slowly as possible toward second base, head down. The fire alarm? The fight with Rosario? Neither could compare with this.

"I wanted to dig my own grave," he says. "I knew my career was over. Two days later I got sent down to Triple-A."

Not long after, Sanchez was back in Double-A, this time with the Tulsa Drillers. It wasn't purgatory, really; the team was stacked with some top prospects—Holliday, Jorge Piedra, Brad Hawpe, J. D. Closser. Tino started off slow after pulling a muscle in his groin, then hit .287 the last 49 games but finished at .233 with 35 RBI. "If I had put up some good numbers?" he says, shrugging. "That was the chance right there."

From then on, Tino knew. He began looking at the minors as his destination, the place to make a living. It's a kind of surrender when that realization hits, but he made a point to advise younger players on their hitting, their attitude, started thinking about being a coach himself. He became a free agent, got signed by St. Louis in January 2004, and was released four months later. He spent the next season and a half with the Bridgeport (Connecticut) Bluefish of the Atlantic League, a collection of teams unaffiliated with a major league baseball organization—and not subject to the affiliated minors' drug-testing program. By then, the sheen on performance enhancers had dulled some; the death of Baltimore pitcher Steve Bechler on February 17, 2003, from heat stroke, with his ingestion of ephedra listed as a contributing factor, sounded an alarm through the bushes. "I don't know if it made me play any better," Driskill says of ephedra, which he used until baseball banned it in the minors a week later. "Sometimes it made me feel I was more energetic, so if that's a performance enhancer, I did do it. But when Steve Bechler died, it goes out the window. It wasn't worth it."

Tino, though, wasn't deterred. In 2004 he hit .290, found himself using greenies more frequently. Then the Colorado Rockies re-signed him midway through 2005, and Tino had to stop cold turkey. "I got caught," he says. One of his tests came up positive in Tulsa. The first-strike punishment, if it can be called that, was increased testing and a round of counseling. He says he never used greenies again.

"I didn't want to do it, and they put in this drug-test policy so that you don't often see people carrying a lot of greenies; you couldn't find them easy, these greenies," he says. "Then I had probably my best years without it. Then I knew that you don't need that."

Tino hit .235 for the Drillers in '05, .325 for Bridgeport and Tulsa in '06. Ever since he'd hit Hurdle in the face, the two hadn't spoken. Tino veered off in the opposite direction whenever he saw the man coming. But early in spring training in 2006, one of Hurdle's coaches talked with Tino and insisted he tell his side. Tino wasn't sure. What would Hurdle say? But he did it, stood before the team and coaching staff in Tucson with stomach fluttering and described the fly ball, the ricochet, his long walk toward Hurdle at second base. The other coaches howled, but Tino only relaxed when he saw that face, the one reddened by rage three years before, chuckling too.

"We are human beings," Hurdle said when Tino finished. "And we forgive."

4

—

DADDY DID IT

THE HOUSTON ASTROS' WILD-CARD RUN INTO THE 2005
World Series, despite a subsequent sweep by the Chicago White Sox,
all but ensured that Mike Coolbaugh's time with the club was done.
He had had three seasons with the organization and, despite impressive stats in 2005—27 homers, 101 RBI—had no way to fudge the
most obvious one: In June he would turn 34. Astros third baseman
Morgan Ensberg was coming off an MVP-caliber season; Houston
management smelled the chance to compete for a championship;
the numbers were squeezing Mike once again. Purpura's advice for
such cases was always the same: Go. Find a second-division club, one
without a lot of talent, because that's the only place you'll get a real
opportunity. "Kansas City, I thought, was a good fit for him," Purpura says.

The Royals, perhaps the prime example of the once-storied franchise that still hadn't figured how to compete with the big-market
teams, were mired in an endless rebuilding campaign. Mike signed
with Kansas City in November 2005, projected as a starting third

baseman for its Triple-A affiliate in Omaha. He ventured to 2006 spring training with no illusions, a non-roster invitee hoping at best to shuttle over the season from Triple-A to the majors, maybe play well enough to get the September call-up he missed the year before. The Royals shared a four-year-old training facility with the Texas Rangers in the town of Surprise, Arizona. He drove in alone. Mandy stayed home in San Antonio to pack the family's belongings, and Mike began hunting for an apartment.

On Tuesday, February 28, the Royals held their first game, a split-squad affair designed to get the winter kinks out, with even the most hardened coaches and players made jumpy by the vibe of a new season. Mike walked to the plate for his first at-bat. Watching was George Brett, a Hall of Fame third baseman and one of baseball's most famous faces when the Coolbaugh boys were growing up and learning the game. Brett had come to camp as an extra coach, to give the youngsters a link to the Royals' glorious and ever more distant past. On the mound was Denny Bautista, a 25-year-old right-hander with a 95 mph fastball, eager to show he'd overcome a year of shoulder pain.

Mike stepped in, the second batter of the day. His left elbow was padded; a hand guard protected the area where he'd had his hand cracked the previous August. Bautista fired his first pitch, a slider. Mike recoiled, but not fast or far enough, and the ball found one of the few unarmored spots, his left wrist, drilling in and breaking the ulna. Normal prognosis for a 22-year-old prospect: out six to eight weeks. But for an aging slugger?

Four batters later, Royals outfielder Shane Costa caught hold of a Bautista pitch and lasered it foul into the dugout. Players scattered.

Brett, slowed by his 52 years, had no time to react. The ball struck just left of his crotch, high in the inner left thigh, leaving behind a searing bruise. Concern, nervous laughter, jokes: the usual macho jockeying when a guy's sexual organs become, even briefly, the center of attention. *Hey, legend! A couple inches to the right and you're singing soprano!*

Mike called home from the clubhouse. The instant Mandy heard his voice, she felt a twang of fear. It was too early. Mike never called in the middle of the day. "You're not going to believe this," he said. "My wrist is broken. I'm done for the season."

She wanted to cry, but it was almost funny now. "I just didn't get out of the way," Mike told a reporter with the *Kansas City Star*. "It's something I've had trouble with in the past. Obviously I need to work on it a little more." Then, in the understatement of a lifetime, he added, "It's just freak things. Luck isn't running my way."

Mike gave his roommate, Kerry Robinson, his buddy from Columbus and St. Louis, the keys to his car ("Don't worry about the insurance; I've got that," he said. "Just drive it and be safe.") and flew home to recuperate. He felt the end looming. He was too old, and a season-long gap in his resume would make him radioactive to clubs hesitant to take a chance. The last few years he'd chewed on the idea of coaching, but now he had to get serious. Mike began putting out feelers, sizing up teams. In May, the Royals came in to play at Round Rock, and he loaded up Joey and drove the 80 miles north to show his face to Jackie Moore and his old teammates again, to let the Express staff see him and file him away for next year. He saw Kerry Robinson, mired in worry about his play. "He was always positive for me," Robinson says. " 'You'll be all right, dude; you're going to make it, you've got talent.' All the time, when I was down the guy kept me up. Even when he should've been down." Travis Driskill was back down with the Express again, and Alan Zinter, who had toiled 14 years in the minors before getting his first shot with the Astros in 2002, had washed up there as a 38-year-old first baseman. Mike walked into their clubhouse before the game, and for a while it was like a lifers' convention.

"We were just laughing," Zinter says. Mike shook hands all around, wrist still wrapped and tender, telling everyone it wasn't yet 100 percent. "He talked to everyone there, telling his stories. I thought the world of him. If you're a good guy, you're going to be well liked. He was very well liked." Mike took Joey onto the field, and played catch and felt divided: happy to be back but different, too, already like an outsider.

But his season wasn't over. The wrist healed, and Coolbaugh decided to play out the string. He went back in late June, hit .333 in six rehabilitation games with the Royals' Rookie League team in Arizona, and flew to Omaha on July 2. By then the third base job was locked up, and Mike filled in mostly at designated hitter and first base. But he carried on, sharpening his swing, quicker to laugh in the clubhouse, though his slow start had him so nervous that each day he thought he'd be released. "But there was no joking when it comes to baseball, because that was his life passion," says pitcher Ryan Braun, who got bumped up from AA to Omaha in mid-season. Even more, Braun kept noticing how Mike always had his sons with him, running around the clubhouse before and after games. "He was a ballplayer, but more a family guy who happened to play baseball," Braun says. "For me he was the correct example. He had his life *together*. You could ask him questions in any area of life, and he just cared, you know?"

During one game after his return, Coolbaugh was sitting in the dugout when he saw his pitcher, 21-year-old Leo Nunez, give up a hit, then gesture in frustration when one of his infielders made an error on the ball. It's one of baseball's cardinal sins: Never show up a teammate. Mike confronted the kid in the dugout, Nunez erupted, and the two teammates had to be separated. "He wasn't doing well, our team was horrible, but he was on the bench paying attention, trying to teach a young guy how to play the game to get to the major league level," Robinson says. "That's Mike: Respecting the game. Doing it the right way. That's what he was about."

Mike got himself on a little run by the end of the month, hitting 2 homers and driving in 7 RBI in one 10-game stint, but the team was bad and getting worse, heading for a franchise-worst 53–91 record. He finished out hitting .223, his lowest average ever in the minors. When the Royals posted their September call-ups, Mike wasn't on the list. Braun was, 26 years old and eminently resentable. "There can be animosity at the Triple-A level, those players not getting back into the major leagues. I understand it; it's in the best people, too," Braun says. "But you couldn't see it on Mike's face."

Instead, he played clubhouse poker. He got into a manic four-way videogame competition with some teammates; night after night back at the team hotel, battling on the console for supremacy in that year's Madden NFL videogame, talking constantly about the upcoming fantasy league season. Any competition would do: All season Mike and Robinson and infielder Fernando Cortez had giggled through this endless little verbal face-off called I'm The Unluckiest Guy Alive. Each man would lay out his hard-luck stories, trying to win the title as the saddest sack, and the others would howl in response, all their failures reversed for a moment into black-humored virtues. Finally Cortez came up with an unbeatable tale of woe and Mike cried uncle. "You're right," he said. "You are unluckier than me. I'm white, I've got a good-looking wife, and I've got boys." And the other two men, one black and one Latino, laughed and laughed.

Coolbaugh went 0 for 3, with a walk, in the final game of the season. It was September 4, Omaha hosting the Iowa Cubs at Rosenblatt Stadium. Mike, at designated hitter, hit cleanup. A crowd of 5,286 rattled around a park capable of holding 24,000. The Royals trailed 4–2 with two out and men on first and third in the eighth inning. Mike dug in. Someone named Brandon Emanuel fired a slider on a 2–2 count. Coolbaugh drove the bat through the zone, too late, fooled for strike three. For a few lingering seconds—as the ump called him out, as he turned and walked to the dugout with the words ringing, with that pitch replaying in his head, as the young Cubs ran in from the field and his equally young teammates jogged to their positions for the ninth inning—Mike still thought and ached like a player. That would pass, though. His career was done.

Houston? Houston seemed logical. Hell, Houston was perfect. It was an organization close to home, had farm teams in Corpus Christi and Austin, and if they didn't owe him anything, the people in charge certainly *knew* Mike Coolbaugh. Hadn't he had some of his best years with the Astros organization, been the ultimate good soldier? They knew how he'd driven himself to a certain excellence despite a growing suspicion that it would probably come to nothing. He could feel how bad they felt about that untimely injury in '05. When he went up to Houston's Minute Maid Park that September, got introduced before a game along with the rest of the club's minor league MVPs, Purpura had whispered to him, "I thought you were going to be here a lot sooner, under different circumstances." The two men laughed then, that rueful *What the fuck can you do?* kind of chuckle. But they knew it wasn't funny. "It was sad," Purpura says.

And then even after that, after Houston hadn't called him up that season though Mike insisted his hand was fully healed, even after he'd missed out on a month's worth of a major league salary and watched the Astros' series run from afar, didn't he still go to Round Rock's annual baseball banquet that winter as their Player of the Year and leave all lingering bitterness outside and stand up at the podium and thank everyone anyway? More than that: Didn't he stand up there, eyes welling and voice growing huskier by the word, and rave about how the organization treated his wife and kids, about how much his relationship with Jackie Moore meant to him? People from the Express front office were stunned by the sight: Mike had always been so stern come game time, all business. Now the room was thick with emotion. Now Moore was pointing back at Mike from his table, lifer saluting lifer. "I remember it because of all the tears in my eyes," Moore says, and he starts crying all over again in the retelling. "It's tough to talk about it, but . . . that's something I'll always remember."

So when he got home from Omaha in September, Mike began pulling every string he had to the Astros front office. He tapped Jackie at Round Rock. He dialed up assistant general manager Ricky Bennett, let him know: I'd like to get started in coaching, wherever you can use me. In the meantime, it had always gnawed at him that he'd never gone to college, and not because he missed out on being a football hero. Mike knew the world for its unforgiving, competitive snarl, and he didn't want his boys to point to him and be able to say, "But Daddy didn't go. . . ." He signed up for online business courses at San Antonio Community College for the spring. He took note of shuttered restaurants, wondering if he could make a go with his own. A Subway sandwich shop, maybe, downtown near the college: Kids there have no place to eat. It's a potential gold mine. . . .

Eventually, though, he always came back to the game. Mike started typing up notes about his playing career, 15 pages' worth, thought about putting together a book. Always irked by the lack of baseball facilities in San Antonio, he traded phone calls with a local councilman about opening a select-team field nearby, a place where he could pass on to kids all he'd learned. He began scouting for a likely plot of land.

Winter came, with no word on the coaching front, with no team calling for him to come play again. It was tough enough making that decision on his end, but to find that the baseball world agreed? Could all that time have added up to nothing more than . . . silence? "I put in so many good years," he told Mandy. "I wish I could at least have the respect that I was a good player."

He would be 35 come June, and that number had always bothered him: the milestone. For most men, 40 looms as the shadow line between youth and old age, but athletes are different. Only near the end does the trade-off become obvious: They get to be boys longer than the rest of us, but the midlife crisis comes sooner. The stress of providing didn't help. For the first time in their decade together, Mandy and

Mike had their first deep disagreement: She wanted another baby, a girl, and was pressing hard. But with all the uncertainty, Mike resisted. Besides, as a ballplayer he'd had a close-up view of the alpha-male on the prowl; he didn't know if he could take worrying over a daughter. All things considered, weren't two boys enough?

Mandy figured it for a battle she couldn't win. She all but gave in, forgetting that in their time together Mike had always put her first. They celebrated their seventh anniversary on January 22, 2007, and a week later made love. "That one did it," Mike said right after. "You're pregnant." Her doctor later called this impossible, but Mike had known with Joey and Jake, too, the exact instant the boys had been conceived. This time, though, his calm shocked her. "I thought we had decided we weren't going to have three," she said.

"But I know you want this," he said. Money trouble, the sure loss of sleep in a trying time—it bore down on him, but not enough. She had a flash then, one of those moments where words mattered less than the deed: Her man loved her. "And it's your girl, too," he said. "I guarantee it."

Then a job opened up. The Astros were looking for a bench coach for one of their rookie teams, and on February 20 Mike flew down to the Astros' spring training site in Kissimmee, Florida, to interview. Mandy took a pregnancy test while he was gone, and the test strip came up positive. Suddenly, the winter's dull freeze seemed to thaw; the Coolbaughs were on the *move* again. He came home sure that Houston wanted him, said they'd all but promised him the job; he knew Jackie Moore was pushing hard for him inside. He'd just have to take a physical exam; surely they'd be in touch within a day or two. When Mike walked in that night, Mandy had her news spelled out in rhinestones on a maternity T-shirt she'd kept hidden for three years: "Daddy Did It."

One day, two, then three passed. *Here it is*, he thought, every time the phone rang. But Houston didn't call.

The boys felt spring coming, Joey especially. This was the time of year when the rhythm of the house changed. The four-year-old couldn't really remember Mom packing them up for New Orleans in 2004, or Austin in 2005, but it was February in Texas now and the breeze smelled different and it was warmer out and he knew: Baseball's coming. Daddy's getting a new uniform. But nothing was happening this time, and that didn't seem right. "When are we going to leave?" Joey asked, and Jake picked up the refrain. "Who are you going to play for this year? What colors do we need to get? What gear?" Some Saturdays Mike would take the boys to Baseball Express, a store down off Jones Maltsberger Road, let them wrestle their way into shirts, try on gloves, play dress-up for a couple hours. They had their favorite players, always based upon whoever was wearing a jersey with a number that matched their age: 2 or 3 or 4. Mike wore number 32 or 29 usually; too big for them. "They don't want to play me," he'd say. "It's always someone else."

He didn't have an answer about the new team, and at times that even felt okay. They went to church each Sunday. He threw them hundreds of pitches in the front yard—always overhand, because Joey didn't want to be treated like a kid. During the week he'd take them over to Windcrest Field and Mary Lu would meet them down there, grinning at the rerun of those weekends from 20 years before: Mike and the girls shagging balls, Bob throwing, Scott lashing ball after ball. Afterward they'd end up at McDonald's, chatting over burgers and fries. Mike loved the freedom, all this new time to play with. And maybe it was as it should be: Life was one cycle after another, and here was just another one to get used to. He didn't have a job or health insurance. Mandy felt so unsettled that she didn't want to tell even family about the new baby yet. Mike was different: Everywhere they went, he would grin and tell cashiers, waitresses, strangers in the park that a third was on the way.

He took the boys and Mary Lu to the rodeo at the beginning of the month, played arcade games, and won them a huge stuffed dog named Barker. "Barker is here to protect," Mike told them all spring. "He won't let anything happen to you." Country singer Alan Jackson performed, and the women walking by kept saying how sweet it was: a grown man bringing his mom and sons to a concert. Mike especially loved one of Jackson's songs, "Remember When," and loved that he could sing it, too, sliding his fine baritone in under Jackson's slow killer drawl:

> *Remember when the sound of little feet*
> *Was the music*
> *We danced to week to week*
> *Brought back the love, we found trust*
> *Vowed we'd never give it up*
> *Remember when*
>
> *Remember when thirty seemed so old*
> *Now lookin' back it's just a steppin' stone*

To where we are,
Where we've been
Said we'd do it all again
Remember when

Remember when we said when we turned gray
When the children grow up and move away
We won't be sad, we'll be glad
For all the life we've had
And we'll remember when

EVERY MAN OR WOMAN, especially those with the slightest athletic inclination, wants to be a hero. That's the childhood appeal of sports, the hook that sets in a kid's gut when he sees Joe Carter or Kirk Gibson or Bobby Thomson circling the ninth-inning bases, confetti and screams filling the sky. Time and ability weed out most of us, and for many who manage to stay in the game the chances narrow too; football linemen and bench-warming centers get relegated to the psychic sidelines. They learn their roles. They know they'll never throw the last-second pass, hit the winning basket. Baseball may be less like that than any sport, though. Everyone in the lineup gets his hacks. Anyone can make a difference. Even a lifer, a light-hitting utilityman career buried ten years deep in the minors and on his way out . . .

On Memorial Day, May 29, 2006, Tino Sanchez had his day. It doesn't matter now—and it certainly didn't then—that it didn't come in New York or Los Angeles before 45,000 fans. It doesn't matter that it happened in a small park in the scrubby Connecticut town of Bridgeport, or that he was playing for an independent minor league team named the Bluefish. What matters is that, for one day, Tino got to feel like Ruth and Clemente, got to feel *feared*. He would hit just 29 home runs in his 11-year career; three different times he had hit just 2 all season. Yet here it was, bottom of the ninth, two out against the Lancaster Barnstormers and Bridgeport down by one. Tino, hitting left-handed, launched a solo home run to send the game into extra innings. That was nice.

But then, in the bottom of the 14th he strode to the plate again, the score tied. Tino switched to righty, and for one instant all his dad's advice and lectures and questions kicked in; didn't the man push him to learn how to switch-hit? Tino drove the first pitch over the fence to give the Bluefish the 5–4 win. Fewer than a hundred major leaguers have ever hit home runs from both sides of the plate in the same game. Eddie Murray did it 11 times for the all-time record; Mickey Mantle all but invented the genre when he did it 10 times during baseball's golden age. So now Tino watched the ball sail—just a bit, not enough to disrespect anyone—and now he circled the bases carrying that supreme walk-off satisfaction: He'd ended it. The game was his. For one afternoon, one obscure moment, he was Mantle. The crowd cheered and stomped. His teammates mobbed him at home plate. He had given ten years to get that feeling. It almost seemed like a fair trade.

Could Tino have risen higher? Maybe. What's often left out of any player equation, especially regarding the marginal talents, is the voice of an angel—someone in the organization willing to stick out his neck and defend the player's case. Under Collins in Salem, Tino "knew he had somebody that believed in him and he flourished," Collins says. "I really believed he would play in the big leagues. People in the Colorado organization kept saying they didn't see him being able to make it, but I said, 'He's not going to be an everyday player in the big leagues. The role he's doing with me? That's his role. He's *showing* you what he can do really well. Play him every day and he won't play well.' But that's what happened to him anyway: They tried to make him a kid who could play one position. His value was as a switch-hitter who could pinch-hit, play in a lot of different positions—and that's when he played well. That's where he got the most out of his talent."

Since high school, Tino had been friends with a Yauco girl named Maria Santiago de los Angeles, whom everyone called "Angie" and who ran track too. Angie kept her eye on him from the start and stayed close whenever he came home. Before Tino left for the '06 season they fell in love, and when he came back in the fall things became even more intense. On December 7, 2006, Angie discovered she was pregnant. She drove to the clinic where Tino was getting treatment for some routine aches, and told him. "I was a little shocked," he says. "But at the same time I was getting old, and I wanted to have a baby for a long time." They moved in together, taking over the upstairs of his mother's home. Life after baseball began to rush at Tino like a sudden wind.

He had always served as his own agent, and in truth wasn't a particularly good one. But when the Rockies called to discuss a contract for the '07 season and offered the same money as the year before, Tino tried a little hardball. "This is going to be my eleventh year," Tino said to Marc Gustafson's assistant, John Weil. "I'm not asking a lot, but can you treat me a little better?"

A few days later, Gustafson was walking on the beach in Hawaii, coffee in hand, when his cell phone rang.

"Can you give me a little more?" Tino said.

"How about $500?" Gustafson said. That would mean a monthly salary of $4,500 in AA, $5,500 if Tino made it to AAA, a formula for 2007 that would work out to $23,500. He had never made more.

"Okay," Tino said. "Let's go."

5

—

WHAT YOU DON'T SEE

SOMETIME AROUND THE FIRST DAY OF FEBRUARY 2007, WITH
pitchers and catchers about to report to his 29th spring training with
the team, Cleveland Indians vice-president Bob DiBiasio picked up
the ringing phone in his office at Jacobs Field. "You've got to get down
here," said Jim Goldwire of the team's operations department. "You
won't believe what we just found."

DiBiasio rode an elevator down to the stadium ground floor, clubhouse level, and walked to a storage room that's known officially as
"the promotional warehouse" but is, in all actuality, a rarely visited
dumping ground for miscellaneous ballpark items that no one could
quite throw away: boxes and bats and baseball caps, empty file cabi-
nets, bobblehead dolls and other begrimed giveaways from years past.
DiBiasio walked in, and Goldwire and the head of the mailroom,
Steve Walters, led him to one of the homely piles. They shoved aside a
bunch of C.C. Sabathia hand puppets, brushed the dirt off the top of
a wooden crate, and removed the top. And there—browned dark by
the oxidizing air, nearly unreadable, huge—it was.

"You've got to be kidding," DiBiasio said.

After he joined the club in 1979, DiBiasio had gotten occasional calls from old-timers looking for a bronze plaque dedicated to former Indians shortstop Ray Chapman, pressing him about an object that he wasn't sure ever existed. The raspy voices described it hanging in League Park in the 1920s, then in Cleveland Municipal Stadium in the years just after the Indians moved there in 1946. DiBiasio asked around. Nobody in the Cleveland Indians organization, including Hall of Fame pitcher Bob Feller, who pitched there from 1936 to '56, could remember the piece at all. "I've never seen it, we've looked, no one can find it, we don't know what you're talking about," DiBiasio would say. Eventually the calls stopped.

DiBiasio stared. Now, after more than 50 years lost, Ray Chapman was found again. The timing couldn't have been better: Walters had actually dug the plaque out months before, but with the team opening its long-planned history exhibit called Heritage Park in two months, he figured it was time the team brass knew. Decades of moldering under an escalator in Municipal Stadium, then in the storage room in Jacobs Field since its opening in 1993, had left the 4-foot-by-3-foot, 245-pound plaque a mess; you couldn't even see the 2-foot-long bat, with the glove dangling off, that dominated its right flank, nor the epitaph embossed along the bottom: "He Lives In The Hearts Of All Who Knew Him." But there was no question about what needed to be done. And in the ensuing weeks, as Jim Folk, the Indians executive in charge of ballpark operations, took on the task of getting the bronze restored in time, and Bob Knazek, the man in charge of constructing Heritage Park, arranged to have it fork-lifted into a truck, and the workers who sandblasted and painted and polished and highlighted the letters and applied the protective clear-coat got it ready, those involved felt themselves, in their own small way, responsible for restoring a vital piece of baseball's past. It didn't matter that it marked the game's darkest moment. Superstition has always been part of baseball, but nobody expressed reservations. The last thought in anyone's mind, in fact, was that it's best, sometimes, to leave well enough alone.

Chapman, after all, was the most famous example of the damage a baseball can do. On August 16, 1920, the Indians' popular short-stop—29 years old, newly married, mulling retirement—was carried off the field at New York's Polo Grounds after being hit in the left temple by a fastball fired by Yankees pitcher Carl Mays. He died the next morning—the first and last man ever killed on a major league field. Some good came out of the incident: Cleveland won its first World Series that year in honor of "Chappie," and since Mays was suspected of doctoring the ball, professional baseball responded by banning the spitball and enacting a rule requiring umpires to police and replace dirty balls. "This tablet is erected by lovers of clean sport" began one passage on Chapman's plaque. His name was invoked often over the following decades whenever there came a push for the use of batting helmets and, really, anytime baseball suffered another scare.

They weren't all that rare. Although Chapman was the only death on the major league level, according to researcher Bob Gorman—who, along with co-author David Weeks, wrote the definitive account of baseball fatalities, *Death at the Ballpark*—since the advent of the modern minor league system in 1883, 9 other pro players and 90 amateurs have died as a result of beanings by pitchers. Ninety more were killed by a ball thrown from other parts of the field. The first such beaning occurred in 1887, and the last pro fatality occurred in 1951, when Dothan (Alabama) Browns outfielder Ottis Johnson took a ball to the temple, remained unconscious for eight days, and then expired. Later that same month, a catcher for the Twin Falls (Idaho) Cowboys named Richard Conway fell dead from a throw that hit him just below the heart. More commonly, players in that era suffered and survived injuries from thrown and batted balls that their familes talked about for generations. In 1941, for example, Jack Stephens, who later became a billionaire financier in Little Rock and chairman of the Augusta National Golf Club and the Masters Tournament, got knocked out by a line drive while playing third base at Columbia Military Academy in Tennessee.

"That was the end of his career," says Jack's son, Warren. "He hung it up.

"And it's funny: The few times I've been to, say, Yankee Stadium? We're on the third base side—just past third base but down really low—and the first time I took my kids there I was a nervous wreck. I wouldn't take my eyes off of any pitch because I was scared we were getting ready to get hammered."

The skill level never mattered; even the best athletes were vulnerable. In 1957 Indians left-hander Herb Score, a supremely gifted pitcher who had struck out 508 batters his first two seasons to lead the American League, was nearly blinded when Gil McDougald's liner hit him in the right eye. His retina damaged, Score then developed elbow trouble and never came close to being the same dominating presence. In July 1962, Minnesota pitcher and 16-time Gold Glove winner Jim

Kaat lost three front teeth to a Bubba Morton one-hopper. After he cleaned up his bloodied mouth and wiped the bits of tooth off his glove, legend has Kaat greeting his startled host at a post-game party with the words, "I was invited, wasn't I?"

Still, nothing approached Ray Chapman's tragic import until 1967, when Red Sox right fielder Tony Conigliaro, a homegrown superstar on Boston's "Impossible Dream" team, had his left cheekbone pulverized by a rising fastball from the hand of California Angels pitcher Jack Hamilton. Before the night of August 18, Conigliaro seemed on a sure path to the Hall of Fame: After making the majors one year after signing his contract, Tony C. homered in his first Fenway Park at-bat in 1964, hit 32 homers in his second season to become, at 20, the youngest home run champ in American League history, and midway through the '67 season had become, at 22, then the youngest player ever to hit 100 home runs.

Conigliaro always crowded the plate. He was wearing a batting helmet when he faced Hamilton, but not one with a protective earflap, and the impact felt like something coring his skull—"as if," he later told *Sports Illustrated,* "the ball would go in one side of my head and come out the other." But more shocking than the sight of the batter dropping was what happened to his face as he fell. By the time Conigliaro hit the dirt, his left eye, the retina permanently damaged, had already swollen to the size of a purpling handball. Home plate umpire Bill Valentine had been manning games for 16 years then, and he left the game two years later without ever seeing anyone hit so hard, to such instant and horrific effect. Full-color photos of Conigliaro's face, his left eye peering through a puffy slit, circulated nationwide, showing the carnage in a way that few sports photos had ever shown before. Two inches higher, the doctor told him, and you would have been dead.

"The look was what was so damaging," Valentine says. "His whole face, his whole eye, in seconds was swelling up, blood rushing in there. The thing that sticks with me is that when he hit the ground his eye was completely shut. It was closed. A doctor told me your body does that to protect, but I'm talking in seconds. It was unbelievable. That was bad."

Conigliaro was carried off the field on a stretcher. Hamilton stayed in the game. Led by captain Carl Yastrzemski, the Red Sox players in the dugout pointed their bats at Hamilton, fingering and warning him at the same time. Hamilton was known for his spit-ball, and Conigliaro later maintained that the ball had moved un-like any legal pitch. But Hamilton, who had never hit anyone in the head before, has always said that he wasn't throwing at Conigliaro; he blames the shadows, his own incompetence. "I had no reason what-soever to throw at him," he says. "The pitch got away from me, in the middle of the afternoon." He tried visiting Conigliaro in the hospital that night, but was turned away. The two men never spoke. Hamilton insists that the beaning never affected his pitching. "It didn't bother me any; I still had trouble getting 'em out," he says. "Half-assed ball-player."

Within two years, Hamilton was out of baseball. Within four, Conigliaro would be gone, too. He'd have some sweet moments—Comeback Player of the Year in 1969, 36 homers in 1970—but the trajectory of his life took a tragic arc. His eyesight deteriorated, he got traded to the Angels in 1971 and retired, came back briefly in '75 and then retired for good. Seven years later, Conigliaro was in Boston interviewing for a Red Sox broadcasting job when he suffered a severe heart attack, then a coma-inducing stroke. He spent the next eight years in a vegetative state, dying, at 45, in 1990.

In 1967 umpires didn't throw balls out of the game as casually as they do today. *The pitcher has roughed it up,* they would say, *he's comfortable with it, he can control it better, so maybe it's safer.* After they carried Conigliaro off the field, Valentine picked up the ball and flipped it back to Hamilton. The next batter, Sox shortstop Rico Petrocelli, fouled it back into the stands; a policeman picked it up and took it home. Valentine didn't notice. He had a game to call. It wasn't until 40 summers later, in fact, before he thought about that ball again.

Years later, Bo McLaughlin could speak matter-of-factly about the night that ruined his face, even laugh a bit. He has a tape of the game at his Phoenix, Arizona, home, and every once in a while at parties he has been known to pop it in to liven things up. "It was on WGN," he says of the Chicago satellite TV station. "You could hear the bones break from the microphone hanging from the press box."

But in the months just after the 1981 accident, McLaughlin had little desire to play baseball, much less watch it. The first day he tried going to a ballfield to work out, he jumped into the front seat of his car, put the keys in the ignition, and sat a few minutes before walking back into his house. He tried again the next day, making it out of the driveway and driving around the block before returning home and saying, "Not today." On the third day, McLaughlin made it to the field and was able to play catch, even with his mind racked with doubt. *Do I want to play again? Do I want to do this? Do I want to put my life out there?*

McLaughlin knew: It was a wonder he was even walking. On May 26 of that year, the A's relief pitcher had come in to start the eighth inning of a losing effort against the Chicago White Sox. McLaughlin got the first two batters out, then threw his first pitch, a 91 mph sinker, to Chicago's second-year right fielder, Harold Baines. The ball blasted off Baines's bat at 104 mph, dipping and rising like a knuckleball. McLaughlin, all 6 feet 5 inches of him, rose out of his follow-through to catch it. Baines couldn't have hit it more perfectly. "Sinker down and away? That's where I'm *supposed* to hit the ball: back up the middle," Baines says. "Unfortunately his face was in the way."

The ball pulped McLaughlin's left cheekbone, broke his eye socket in five places, fractured his jaw and nose, spinning him around so that he got a full view of the center fielder before falling on his back. He vomited five towels' worth of blood and went into shock. "That," says Jackie Moore, the A's third base coach at the time, "was as bad as I've ever seen." Baines got his only hit of the night on the play, and the game was delayed for 14 minutes. "It took the ambulance forever to come," says Baines, now a White Sox coach. "Forever could've been five minutes, but it felt much longer than that." Doctors at Oakland's Merritt Hospital weren't sure McLaughlin would survive the night. It took two reconstructive surgeries to rebuild his face. Baines had been hitting over .300 that month, but a call to McLaughlin in the ensuing days did little to ease his mind. He immediately fell into a vicious slump—6 for 42, .142—that only ended 16 days later when the major league players went out on strike.

McLaughlin was 27 at the time. A six-year veteran, he'd spent most of his career with Houston and Oakland in relief, won 10 games and lost 20, was nobody's idea of special. He came back to pitch for Oakland that September, but couldn't get back into shape; the muscles and nerves in his cheek hadn't healed, and when he ran it felt like a hockey puck was sliding around beneath the skin. He appeared in four games, and would seem to be fine until he got two outs; then he'd struggle. A teammate wondered if that was because Baines had hit him with two outs. McLaughlin couldn't say. All he knows is that on September 20 in Chicago, he started the eighth inning, got two quick outs, surrendered three walks, a single, and a wild pitch, then watched Baines come to the plate to face him for the first time since. A's catcher Mike Heath gave the sign for the same pitch—sinker, away—and grinned. McLaughlin actually backed off and started laughing. "I threw him a fastball," McLaughlin says. "I wasn't interested in getting hit again." Baines popped the ball up to end the inning.

After that season, Baines was able to put the accident behind him. He played for 20 more years, had one of his era's great careers, and may yet end up in the Hall of Fame. He never came close to hitting anyone like that again. "It's unfortunate," Baines says, "but it's part of the game."

McLaughlin played one more season with the A's, worked 48⅓ innings for a 4.84 ERA. He bounced around the AAA Pacific Coast League for three more seasons, mostly treating it, he says, "like a beer league." He never recorded another major league win. He married, had three children, started a real estate business and a baseball camp. In 1992 Cubs manager Jim Lefebvre asked him to throw batting practice, and after seven years away it felt okay to be on a mound again. He coached in Chicago's minor league system, moved on to Montreal's, then became the Baltimore Orioles minor league pitching coordinator for three years. When Baines played for the Orioles in '98 and '99, he and McLaughlin talked a bit, no hard feelings. They played golf. In 2003 McLaughlin joined the Colorado Rockies as a pitching coach for the AA Tulsa Drillers.

There aren't many days that he isn't reminded of the accident. McLaughlin's left eye socket is still wired, and his cheekbone too. When he's home in Phoenix and temperatures hit 113, 114 degrees, the metal gets so hot that the whites of his eyes turn red. He's considered a fine coach, committed and communicative, yet hardly exudes a contagious passion. "I'm not a fan of baseball," McLaughlin says softly. "Never was."

With the imposition of mandatory batting helmet use at all levels of professional baseball in 1971, serious injuries from a pitched ball instantly began to decline. One reason the case of Houston shortstop Dickie Thon, whose brilliant career got derailed by a Mike Torrez fastball to his left eye in 1984, seemed so shocking was its relative rarity, a '40s-era story line played out in disco double-knits. But the danger of the batted ball, especially to the men standing just 60 feet, 6 inches away, never faded.

In 1987 Mariners pitcher Steve Shields, who a decade earlier had suffered a seizure and memory loss from a line drive to the face in A-ball, had his cheek broken by a Kirby Puckett rip up the middle. In 1995 Phillies reliever Norm Charlton fielded a Steve Finley comebacker with his face. In 1996 pitcher Mark Gubicza had his farewell season with Kansas City cut short when Minnesota's Paul Molitor broke his left leg with a line drive. In April 1997, Seattle pitcher Josias Manzanillo, not wearing a protective cup, suffered tears in both testicles after Cleveland's Manny Ramirez blasted a shot into his groin. The next month, Detroit pitcher Willie Blair had his jaw broken when another Indian, Julio Franco, cracked a liner up the middle clocked at 107 mph; as Blair lay still on the field, Franco bent down at first base and prayed.

Herb Score, then an Indians broadcaster, sat silent in the booth with play-by-play man Tom Hamilton as the nightmare played out again before him. It had been almost 40 years to the day of his own accident. "You never see the ball," Score said finally into his microphone. "You have no chance. You don't see it."

Surprisingly, no professional player on any level has ever been killed by a batted ball. Of the 76 American deaths caused in that manner—5 of which include batters killed by their own foul tips—all occurred in amateur games. Such injuries in Latin American baseball have received far less scrutiny in El Norte, but in the early 1970s a catcher named Raul Cabrera got struck in the throat by a foul tip during an amateur game in Yauco, Puerto Rico, and died in the hospital hours later. Tino Sanchez's father, Tino Sr., was sitting as close to home plate as possible in Ovidio "Millino" Rodriguez Park that day. Tino Sr. loved watching games from that angle.

"He was moving, trying to breathe," Tino Sr. says of Cabrera. "I thought he was going to be okay, but the next day they told me the player had passed away. That was the first time that had happened in Puerto Rico."

Logic would seem to dictate that coaches, umpires, and other on-field personnel would run less of a risk, if only because they're a step or two removed from the action, and until 2007 the only two pro fatalities were a 13-year-old boy hit in the head while retrieving batting practice balls in Wenatchee, Washington, and major league umpire Cal Drummond, who, a year after being hit in the mask by a foul tip at an Orioles game, died in 1970 from complications related to the injury. Still, any coach with serious tenure in the game has a near-miss tale. In April 2002, Jackie Moore, then the manager of the AA Round Rock (Texas) Express, missed nine games after being laid out by a batting practice line drive in the outfield. Moore suffered a broken cheekbone and a concussion, and required surgery to repair a detached retina. "Someone hollered 'Look out,' and as I turned, it hit me in the side of the face, the eye and everything," Moore says. "I was touch and go there for a while. I still don't have very good vision out of my left eye from it." Perhaps the most famous coaching injury ended well but made for a dubious distinction: In 1999 Yankees bench coach Don Zimmer, who in 1953 had lain unconscious for 13 days after being beaned in the minor leagues as a player, survived a foul ball to the side of his face during a playoff game. For the next day's game, he wore an army helmet.

Still, players and coaches know the risks better than anyone, and in any ballpark are always the most attuned to the ball's every turn. When questioned on the topic, almost to a man they say that their larger concern—rising less out of altruism than the distracted, vulnerable examples they see daily—is about the safety of the fans. Unlike the Japanese ballparks that have protective screens shielding fans from behind the plate all the way to the outfield walls, U.S. parks have screens extending only as far as the dugouts—thus enabling dozens of foul balls to fly into crowds at every game. Since the nineteenth century, 52 fans have been killed by foul balls, two in pro games. In 1960, a 68-year-old man died after getting hit by a foul ball at a minor-league game in Miami. In May 1970, a 14-year-old boy named Alan Fish died five days after getting struck by a Manny Mota foul ball while sitting along the first base line at Dodgers Stadium—the only fatality caused by a batted ball in major league history. After spending 50 years as a singular tragedy, Ray Chapman had company.

Every summer, at major and minor league parks across the country, fans suffer bruises, contusions, broken bones and faces, and sometimes worse. If professional baseball is protected from legal action because of the 145-word warning on the back of each ticket that shifts all responsibility for injury to the fan, it doesn't lessen the players' fears. "Things like that just keep happening in baseball," Jack Hamilton says. "Somebody's going to get hurt. Somebody's going to get hit with one of those broken bats, too, before long, in the stands." First baseman Alan Zinter, who played nearly all of his 19-year career in the minor leagues before retiring in 2007, got to the point that he was telling every fan he could to sit only behind the screen, "because way too many people get hit," he says. "I can't look anymore when I see the ball hit in the stands . . . but I still look. You can't not look. People come there with their little children, eating hot dogs, and they think they can protect their kids? You've got to be kidding me. I couldn't do it.

"I've seen people's noses hit off their faces. I've seen people get hit in the face, just crushed, blood everywhere. The worst thing I saw was the thing I did in Nashville: I was hitting left-handed and I check-swinged and hit a line shot over the Nashville dugout and I hit a six-year-old boy right in the temple. I was with [AAA] New Orleans; I think it was the year I got called up, '02. I hit it right on the barrel, foul along the third base line, and it went straight into the stands. It was slow-motion for me; I'm looking right down the barrel and thinking, *Oh, God,* and it's heading right toward this family and the father's not even watching. The kid was looking into left field so he's not watching and WHACK! right in the head. They carried him out of the stadium.

"I struck out. I couldn't even concentrate after that. I kept calling after the game, kid was in the hospital, and they said he's going to be okay. Had a concussion, stayed that night, I said, 'Give me his number' and I ended up calling him when I made it to the big leagues." Zinter pauses, watching the moment unreel again and again in his mind. "He was okay," he says. "His dad ran him up the steps. . . ."

On the afternoon of Sunday, March 4, 2007, Mike Coolbaugh and one of his closest friends, Jay Maldonado, walked onto the field at Theodore Roosevelt High School in San Antonio. They'd both been baseball stars there in the late 1980s and played together in the Toronto Blue Jays organization, but this was no exercise in nostalgia. After all of Mike's playing options had seemingly dried up, an offer had suddenly come through from a professional team in Tabasco, Mexico: $10,000 just to show up and try out. Mike needed to get ready. And Maldonado, as he had every spring, had come to help. Though thicker than in his playing days, he could still roll out of bed and throw 88 miles per hour, and still loved seeing a power hitter at work. "Come on, Mike," Jay would say every year after grooving dozens of batting practice pitches. "Hit one out." And then he'd put a bit more on the next one, and Mike would launch it high and far.

On this day, Jay had made a point of asking his father, Jesse, to come along. Mike had eaten dinner plenty of times over the years at the Maldonado house, mopping up the juice off another fine plate of Maldonado barbeque, and Jesse always marveled at how much that boy could eat. But this was different: It had been a long time since he had seen his son and Mike on a field together. The two were so close, with a rivalry for bragging rights that made their friendship even stronger. The one time they faced each other as pros, in an intrasquad game during spring training in 1994, Maldonado found himself furiously trying to shake off his catcher's instructions because he just couldn't have Mike beat him. Forced to throw only fastballs, he tricked catcher and batter both by slowing one pitch to batting-practice speed, and a wide-eyed Mike almost corkscrewed himself into the ground swinging and missing. Mike drove the next one straight and deep, but the center fielder didn't need to move a step to make the catch. "He tattooed it, but he was out," Maldonado says. "So we were even."

Like every ballplayer, Mike feared that Mandy or their boys would get hit by a rogue baseball ripped into the stands. "He was more worried about it than anybody I've ever met," Mandy says. "He was so aware of what a foul ball could do." Once, during his 2005 season with the AAA Round Rock Express, Mike was about to settle into his crouch at third base when he noticed Mandy visiting a friend in the seats behind the base, beyond the far edge of the protective netting draped between the batter and the stands fanning out behind. He straightened and, before the pitcher could wind up, walked off the field and insisted that she move somewhere else. He wouldn't return to his position until he made sure Mandy was safe.

In his prime, Maldonado threw a 95 mph fastball. The one time he was hit seriously by a ball came during one of their spring workouts in the mid-'90s, when Mike tagged Jay with a line drive so perfectly square on the tip of the hipbone that it didn't even hurt. That seemed appropriate, somehow: Their early careers had been marked by an odd symmetry. The two men had dated the same women in different minor league towns at different times, without knowing about the other, and both had had fingers on their right hands mangled by a baseball— Mike's thumb mashed by a pitch, Jay's pinkie snapped in a freak run-down. Who better than Mike to hit him?

This would be their second day working together. The two men again set up the protective L-screen in the grass in front of the dirt circle surrounding the pitcher's mound, about 40 feet in front of home plate. Maldonado began to throw—slurves, change-ups, fastballs, mixing location in and out. Jesse stood behind home plate, fingers curling through the backstop fencing. The usual drill went for about 120 pitches, and about halfway through, the right-handed Maldonado fired an 87 mph fastball and got a bit lazy, stopping on his follow-through so that his head didn't dip behind the high part of the screen. Mike swung. The ball blazed just over the crotch of the L. Maldonado saw a flash of white in time to turn his head, and felt a crack behind his right ear. He dropped to the ground like a sack of stones; the ball stopped rolling somewhere in left field.

At first, Jesse thought his son was gone. Finally Jay sat up, fighting to stay conscious by fixing his eyes on the fence, the bat, Mike's stricken face—anything—and telling himself, *Stay focused. Keep your eyes open.* The two men sat on a bench, their breathing slowly returning to normal. There was no swelling but a sizable bruise, and Maldonado waved off the idea of seeing a doctor. Mike told him not to be such "a fucking Superman," and flew off to Mexico the next day worried. Mandy could tell. Mike always paced when something upset him, and he kept it up most of that first night after telling her what had happened, fighting back tears. "That can kill a guy," Mike said.

6

———

ARE WE BACK IN BASEBALL?

MEXICO DIDN'T FEEL RIGHT, NOT FOR HIM, NOT FOR THE family. Korea, Japan . . . Mike would've considered a foreign gig if the money was right, but this one didn't feel safe. With Mandy pregnant and two young boys? No. He came home at the end of March empty-handed; the team stiffed him on the $10,000. And now it hit hard: He was out of baseball. Spring training was in full swing, each organization had its players and coaches locked in, teams would be breaking camp in Arizona and Florida at the end of the month. Soon his one compelling connection to the game was Joey, refusing to hit off a tee: No, that's for *little* kids, he said. So Mike took the boys to watch the local Double-A club, the San Antonio Missions, work out. "See?" he said. "Even pros practice hitting off a tee."

Inside, though, Mike was beginning to panic. His old teammate Kerry Robinson was right there with him; Robinson retired that May at 33, facing the monster at last. "I was terrified the last three years of my baseball career, thinking of what I was going to do when I was done," Robinson says. "When you're thirty-four, thirty-five, you're behind everyone else, and what are you really qualified to do that pays enough to give you close to the lifestyle you had the last few years? You still make pretty good money in the minors—$60,000, $70,000, $80,000 a year. What can you do when you get out, and be skilled at doing it? That's the reason a lot of guys stick around in the minors when, really, they hate baseball. They're sick of it, but they end up being coaches. They don't know how to get into another industry; they don't know what to do; they don't know what their dreams are. I felt the exact same way. I'm still going through it a little bit."

Coolbaugh kept scrambling. He was taking 24 hours of courses online, a 34-year-old freshman trying to make up for lost time. He tapped his former teammate from Columbus, Mike Frank, who had moved on to a job as a mortgage officer with a developer in Sacramento and had pretty much lined up a position for him there. The plan now was for Mike to finish up his courses and move the family out to California in the summer. Mandy was working as a substitute teacher to bring in some cash; it seemed like they could relax. The couple started to get excited. Stability . . . no travel . . . a job in which, if you put up the numbers, a man couldn't help but advance . . . a fresh start . . . an entirely new career! They were just waiting for the green light. "We would've been gone," Mandy says, "in a heartbeat." But when Mike called Sacramento at the end of May to set up a start date, the job had disappeared.

Now all that leisure time began to wear. Mike made a fine Mr. Mom, but he believed that a man's role was to provide. Mandy wanted to stay home, and now all his on-the-fly attempts to find what he wanted to do, what he was qualified to do, how much money he needed, took on urgency. Coolbaugh's sisters and mother noticed him becoming increasingly snappish, reacting to slights when none were intended, and they'd phone each other asking, "What's the matter with Mike?" But they knew. He felt boxed in, restless, less because he was out of the game than because he was *in* nothing else. "It was life," Mary Lu says. "He had two kids and a baby on the way and he was frustrated—more than I'd ever seen him."

Jay Maldonado worked in San Antonio installing air conditioners, was handy with plumbing and electrical. Maybe they could start something together, buy houses, fix them up, flip them. "He was lost, man," Maldonado says. "He was out of ball. He didn't have a job. He was trying to cling onto anything, any idea: *What are we going to do, Jay? What are we going to do to make some money? Give me something.*"

The last time Jay was at his house, Mike climbed up into the garage attic and hauled down dozens of his bats and gloves and began handing them over. For Joey, this was like watching a magician sort through his trunk; the boy had caught the baseball bug bad. He couldn't ever keep his hands off his dad's old equipment, and the garage and attic were a wonderland of muddied spikes, old jerseys and socks and batting gloves. Joey trailed Mike as he went up and down the foldaway steps. He kept eyeing one piece in particular, the big black bat with a piece of masking tape and some words scribbled on it. But it wasn't the scrawl that got him—"July 16, 2001, first major league hit." The bat just looked powerful, so cool and sleek and dark.

"I'm done with ball," Mike said to Jay. He nodded his head at the pile: "Take it. For softball, your friends . . . whatever." The cluster of equipment was worth close to $3,000. Mike even threw in the bat he used to hit his first professional home run: Medicine Hat, 1990.

"Mike, you can sell these," Maldonado said. "I'll sell them for you. Or save them for Joey and Jake. . . ."

"You sell them and make some money," Mike said. "Just get rid of them. I don't want them."

He did keep the black bat, though. He wasn't looking to jettison the past completely. Mike started calling high school friends he hadn't spoken to in years, spending hours on the phone with people Mandy hadn't ever heard of. They talked, too, about what to name the new baby, but Mike would make that decision. He always had a plan. He had named Joey and Jake, but he just knew this one would be a girl and wanted to honor Mandy's mom, Anne, who had died after her long bout with cancer in 2003. Mike insisted: Somehow, first or middle, the baby would bear her name. This touched Mandy, of course, but his feelings went deeper than mere gesture. Something kept troubling him. Mike had been her rock throughout Anne's illness, practical and steady, but for the first time he wanted to know details about the pain Anne endured, the moment she passed.

Mike was sure of an afterlife, and rarely indulged ghoulish questions about life and death. But now, says Katie Pavlovsky, Mandy's sister, "he was scared of it." The looming arrival of a new child is always a time to take stock, and both Mike and Mandy had made wills when Joey was born. But now he talked about the two of them getting burial plots to "know where we're going to be." He had handled all the family finances, to the point that Mandy never knew his exact salary. But now he insisted that Mandy learn how to handle the household accounts and bills, just in case. "It was never 'If something happens to you,'" Mandy says. "It was 'If something happens to me, I want you to know what I want for the kids.'"

In early June, Mike sat with Mandy watching a newsmagazine show, a segment about the wives of American soldiers who had had their sperm frozen before deploying to Iraq. The men died there, and their widows had used the sperm to get pregnant.

Mandy turned to Mike. "I can't believe they have the courage to do that," she said. "There's no way, knowing you were not coming back, that I would intentionally impregnate myself with your kids."

She figured he'd agree. But by the time Mandy finished speaking Mike was visibly shaken.

"I can't believe you wouldn't want to have my babies if I was gone," he said.

"Mike, why would I make things harder on myself? Knowing they're not coming home, knowing these kids would never know their father? Why would you do that to a child?"

Mike took Mandy's hand and looked at her squarely. *This is weird,* Mandy thought.

"I would really hope if that was me," he said, "we would've thought to do that."

That month, Mike drove the family to Colleyville for a weekend to see Scott's family. Scott was gone for the season, of course, but with her mother in the hospital and her 14-year-old son, Tyler, playing that weekend in a baseball tournament, Susan needed the help. One night they were all sitting on the couch, and Mike kept tossing Tyler and his sister, Chandler, brain-teasers; finally he asked if anyone wanted to hear a joke. He knew the answer. Tyler loved hearing Mike's baseball jokes.

"There are these two old men who love baseball, Moe and Joe," Mike began. "Joe's really sick and dying and Moe says to him, 'If you get to heaven before me, come back and let me know if there's baseball in heaven.' Well, that night Joe died, and the next day his spirit came down to see Moe. Moe saw Joe and couldn't believe his eyes.

"Joe says, 'I've got good news and bad news.'

"Moe says, 'Give me the good news first.'

"And Joe says, 'There *is* baseball in heaven and the fields are beautiful and you play all day and all night and never get tired.'

"That's awesome, thought Moe. Then he asked, 'What's the bad news?'

"And Joe said, 'You're pitching tomorrow!'"

Everybody laughed. But at times it could get to be a bit much. Usually when Mike would take the boys out front and throw pitches, adjust their swings, Mandy would use it as her chance to relax, run an errand, get away for an hour or two. "That's your time," she would say. But now Mike insisted she sit in a chair and watch, to listen as he poured all he'd learned from 5,860 professional at-bats, from 17 years of hitting, into his sons. Nobody wanted him as a coach? At least the boys would know.

"If something ever happens to me," he told Mandy, "I want you to remember how to teach them to hit."

Finally she snapped. "Mike, you're not in baseball anymore," she said. "We're home. Nothing's going to happen to us."

It's not that they didn't want to hire him. But the same quality that made Mike Coolbaugh an attractive commodity as a coach—his long playing tenure in the minors—had also tripped him up with the Houston Astros brass in the winter of 2007. He had just retired the previous fall, and farm system bosses are always wary of the newly sprung: No matter how good a soldier, the years of disappointment and its resulting tone—that ring of resignation or anger—can make an indelible impression. It's not common for a player's personality to soften once the pressure of performing fades. But Houston couldn't wait. Its coaching opening was in rookie ball, and the Astros hardly wanted to present its fresh-faced talent with firsthand evidence of how the system can break a man. Instead, Houston hired Stubby Clapp, whose name sounded like a dirty joke and whose signature move as a player was an ebullient backflip each time he took the field. "Coolie wasn't the guy who was always smiling," Purpura says. "He wasn't negative, but he took it all seriously. That wasn't the personality we were looking for at that level. We were looking for more of a lighthearted guy, a pat-on-the-back kind of guy. I thought he'd be perfect at Double-A or Triple-A."

In late May, the lines began humming for Mike with the AA Tulsa Drillers and its parent organization, the Colorado Rockies. The week before, Drillers hitting coach Orlando Merced, weeping, had declared that he had to quit because of what manager Stu Cole calls "family issues." When Tulsa arrived outside Dallas for a three-game road set against the Frisco RoughRiders, Scott Coolbaugh, the Frisco hitting coach, buttonholed Cole. They had played against each other once. "I got a brother at home and he's not doing anything and he wants to get into coaching," Scott said. "If you could drop his name, I would appreciate it." In early June, a Colorado cross-checker walked into Marc Gustafson's office in Denver to say that Mike was available.

Gustafson called Mike, liked his attitude, called people who'd played or coached with him, and liked what he heard even more. He called Mike again.

Fit was a problem, though. Coolbaugh's demeanor might well work better in Tulsa, but it didn't make immediate sense to send him there. First-year coaches rarely begin careers at the Double-A level and Merced's disruptive exit made a radical departure from the norm even more sketchy. Many of the Drillers had worked with Dave Hajek, the hitting coach of Colorado's Single-A affiliate in Modesto; one logically calming move would be to elevate Hajek to Tulsa. When Scott approached Stu Cole, he assumed such a shuffle was in the offing and that Mike's only shot would be at rookie level. Mike didn't dare tell Mandy about such conversations; they were still debating whether she'd go back to teaching so he could stay home as Mr. Mom. He didn't want to jinx it. "It felt like we were always being jinxed in his career: just in the wrong place at the wrong time," she says.

This time? Just the opposite. The numbers game actually worked to Mike's advantage. It made no sense to Gustafson to move Hajek up to Tulsa and hire Mike for Modesto; that would mean that two teams and two coaches would have to adjust to each other in mid-season. Meanwhile, Cole and McLaughlin were experienced hands, and Tino could help as a de facto player-coach. Putting Mike in Tulsa would be radical, but less disruptive than the alternative. Gustafson pulled the trigger. But to give himself wiggle room, he told Mike to look at the rest of the 2007 season as an extended tryout. If he did a good job in Tulsa, blended in and showed he could effectively embrace the job, he'd get a full-time coaching position in the organization—but not in Double-A Tulsa. Next year, crisis averted, the norm would kick back in. Mike could expect to start in rookie ball and work his way up the chain.

Sure, Mike said: Whatever you need. He was puttering around the family's backyard pool the third week in June, clearly preoccupied, when he finally told Mandy. "I don't know if you're going to like this . . ." he began.

"Awww," she cut him off. "Are we back in baseball?"

"Yeah," he said, "we are."

He had hesitated because he knew: Mandy had gotten used to having him around. What Mike didn't know is that her mixed feelings were complicated; a coaching job meant, definitively, that his playing days were over, and in one sense that depressed her more than it did him. In truth, a part of Mike couldn't have been more relieved to have the pressure of performing gone: no more waiting for his hopes to get crushed. Mandy? She knew that part of his job, but she had never lived it. And she couldn't help herself; she loved seeing Mike in uniform, hearing his name announced, watching him club home runs like a circus strongman. She loved how other fans treated her when they found out she was Mike Coolbaugh's wife. It didn't matter that he was minor league; in a minor league town, Mike Coolbaugh was someone special. "It was sad knowing my husband wasn't going to be the best on the team anymore," Mandy says. "It was a fun life. I'll be honest: I liked him being the star. It was nice to have people come up and say, 'Oooh, your husband's good, your husband hits.' I loved Mike for Mike; if he was a garbageman I would've married him. But there was just that added, special quality to him." She laughs. "But being a coach? You're the old guy on the team. You're the dried-up player."

And, as a woman with a keen radar for portents, she couldn't tell what hooking up with the Rockies organization *meant*. The first year they had been serious with each other, when they knew they would be together for good, Mike had played his one Triple-A season for the Rockies organization in Colorado Springs. When, ten years later, "he said, 'the Rockies,' I thought, *We've looped around*," Mandy says. "*Is this a good sign or a bad sign?*"

Scott was less conflicted than stunned: The game usually didn't work like this, not for Coolbaughs, anyway. After retiring as a player in 1999, he had slowly climbed up the chain, bouncing between A- and Double-A ball, spending two years as a manager in AA El Paso, then joining Frisco in 2006 as a hitting coach. Now here was Mike, in his first job, hitting a quick jackpot. Not only that, but Tulsa was close to Dallas, to San Antonio, to the whole family, and with both of them working in the Texas League they'd get to see each other a couple times a summer. *Good*, Scott thought. *If anyone deserves it . . .*

It had been nearly two years since Mike had felt at all secure about his place in baseball. Even in Round Rock in 2005 he was a minor league player hoping, at best, for the vagaries of a September call-up. Now? He couldn't ask for a better start. In his best moments Mike even dared imagine that maybe all his bad karma had dissolved with his playing career. Perhaps that's how it worked, cosmically. Maybe his life as a coach would be charmed as much as his life as a player was cursed. Maybe this was just the beginning.

Mike was set to join the Drillers on July 4, after they arrived in San Antonio for a three-game series against the Missions. The day before, he got a call from Rockies manager Clint Hurdle. That was a surprise. The two didn't know each other well, but Hurdle remembered

Mike from his one season with the Rockies organization in 1998. He knew the brothers' reputations and wanted to welcome Mike back, congratulate him on this opportunity. Soon, though, the conversation segued from coaching to family to kids, to the coming sacrifices and strains. Hurdle has three children, two of them then under ten, and one diagnosed with epilepsy. For nearly 30 minutes, the two men measured each other.

"We talked about the common fabric we had," Hurdle says. "We talked a lot about family and the challenges and opportunities this was going to bring for his family and his boys. His wife being pregnant . . . and Mandy—all of it. There were just a lot of similarities in our lives, as far as having young families and being good husbands and being good daddies." It was a good start, good to hear Hurdle use that word so much, but even better it felt right, backing up everything Mike had heard. The Rockies had that reputation; everyone in baseball knew it. They treated their people like family.

THE ROCKIES ASSIGNED TINO SANCHEZ to Tulsa for the 2007 season, his fourth stint with the AA Drillers, but this time there was no mistaking where he stood. For the first time he spent opening day as a "phantom"—a perfectly healthy player assigned to the disabled list, drawing a paycheck but unable to play, squirreled away until the team deigned to summon him. Another player would have to go, or get hurt, for Tino to gain a spot. He was 28. It stung. Indeed, phantoms often read their status as the signal to retire. But Tino wasn't about to squawk. "Don't worry," he told Marc Gustafson. "I'll stay in shape and

stay sharp. When you need me, I'll be ready." But he wasn't playing
the sap. Tino was trying to map out his next step; now he wanted all
those years, the reputation and the connections he'd made, to pay off.
Weeks passed and he kept sitting, but he helped the younger players
with their questions, adjusted their swings, chatted up the pitchers.
"He's the nicest, happiest guy," says Drillers pitcher Jon Asahina. "The
coolest guy ever."

On April 23, Colorado promoted infielder Tim Olson to its Triple-A club in Colorado Springs, throwing the switch that brought
Tino back to life. Tulsa activated him for that night's game, the Drillers' first appearance in the Arkansas Travelers' sparkling new stadium:
Dickey-Stephens Park in North Little Rock. In the eighth inning,
manager Stu Cole sent Tino to the plate for his first at-bat of the
season, pinch-hitting for second baseman Duke Sardinha with two
out and the score tied 2–2. He drew a walk to keep Tulsa's rally alive,
setting up the next batter, Tommy Duenas, for the two-run double
that won the game. Three nights later, Tino got his first start of '07, at
designated hitter. He went hitless. Tulsa lost 7–0. None of that ended
up mattering.

With one out in the bottom of the fifth and the count 1–1, Asahina tried to fire a sinker away past Travelers left fielder Aaron Peel.
Asahina, a 26-year-old right-hander, had come into the game with
a 2–0 record, but was distracted in a way he hadn't been all spring.
His girlfriend, Jenny Hamilton, had just arrived from back home in
Fresno, and Asahina hadn't seen her in months. He found himself
instantly besieged; by the time Peel stepped in, Asahina had already
given up six runs on nine hits. "My focus wasn't on the game and that's
why, I felt, certain things happened: because I disrespected the game,"

Asahina says. "I was so happy to see her and I was thinking about how much fun we were going to have after." He'd all but given up on winning, in fact, thinking, *Well, I'm just going to pitch these innings, throw strikes, and move on to the next one.*

Now a strike, traveling somewhere between 88 and 91 miles per hour, drifted over the center of the plate. Peel jumped on it. Whenever a ball is hit squarely, it invariably picks up speed; this one hurtled back up the middle at 101 mph. Asahina had no time to react. He felt a sharp, stabbing pain near the upper rim of his left ear. The icy crack of a projectile striking, of a skull buckling, echoed into the stands.

"The ball got on top of me," Asahina says. "It gets on top of you so fast you can't even see it."

Bo McLaughlin, the Drillers' pitching coach, was standing on the steps of the Drillers dugout, and thought instantly, *I hope it's not as bad as mine.* Asahina recoiled over the mound, dipped a knee to the grass. Like McLaughlin 26 years before, Asahina never lost consciousness. He landed on his hands, and with years of training honed into instinct, began looking for the ball. It had ricocheted far to his left: First baseman Duke Sardinha needed only a few steps to field the ball and step on the bag for the out.

Manager Stu Cole, trainer Austin O'Shea, and some teammates rushed the mound. Asahina grew dizzy but tried to tough it out. He walked back to the rubber. He didn't know that the concentrated impact had fractured his skull, with the break actually occurring behind and below the point where the ball struck, and ruptured his eardrum. Fluid poured out of his left ear. Blood trickled down the side of his head, seeped into his gunmetal blue jersey. He was led off the field to the dugout, where a doctor peppered him with basic questions.

Asahina answered each one, carefully, reminding himself to breathe. It was oddly urgent to him that the doctor know he was okay. He felt a hand on his shoulder, rubbing softly, and turned to see that it belonged to the normally cool and stern Cole. Asahina had played for him three years. For the first time, he understood that the man actually cared.

Asahina spent six days in a Little Rock hospital. During his second day, two neurosurgeons studied his CAT scans. The bruising, or hematoma, seemed limited to the area between his skin and skull with no deeper damage to the brain. "You're a very lucky man," one of the doctors said. "Very, very lucky. Two inches this way or an inch and a half this way? We don't know."

Asahina had been hit by comeback balls before, mostly in the legs. He had never been shy about hitting batters with his 92 mph fastball, if a message needed to be sent; that's baseball, part of the code. Asahina starred at Fresno's Edison High, and after a short stint at Wake Forest served as the ace for junior college powerhouse Fresno City. He had been playing pro ball since 2001, rising as high as Triple-A in '06, had appeared in 150 career games. He remembers countless times when a line drive rocketed just past him and into the outfield; Asahina saw them all coming. But Peel's liner was different. There was nothing in his angle that should have cut off Asahina's view of the ball, and he believes in one sense that he may well have seen it all along. But it's as if, faced with imminent and perhaps deadly danger, his brain or nervous system flashed a protective order for an instant, preemptive amnesia, obliterating that horrifying moment, making it irretrievable.

"I don't recall seeing the ball off the bat or anything else, and it wasn't because I lost consciousness," Asahina says. "I think it's something different. I'm a pretty spiritual person, not affiliated with any kind of organized religion. But here's the only way I can relate this: My friend is a pilot who was skydiving. He jumped out of the plane, and something went wrong and the next thing he knew he was on the ground and they came up to him and said, 'Well, your parachute works'—and that's all he remembered. It's like something in your deep subconscious says, *No, you're not supposed to see this*. I can remember every pitch I threw in the game, I remember exactly how I felt, I remember exactly what I did immediately afterward, I remember all the days in the hospital and the people I talked to. But for that split second? I've seen so many balls off the bat and I've always been able to react to them, either catch 'em or get out of the way. But I didn't see it. I almost feel like it was supposed to happen to me. I don't know why."

Asahina left the team, headed home to Fresno. Tino played two more weeks, got shut down to make room for another player, was placed again on the phantom disabled list. Then Merced quit, leaving Cole shorthanded, and everything changed. Though players revolve in and out, minor league coaching staffs rarely turn over in mid-season. Cole suddenly found himself tutoring hitters, throwing hours every day in the batting cage—along with his usual duties of writing game reports, managing games, evaluating talent, and riding herd on 25 emotional, high-strung, egocentric personalities. Tino, meanwhile, got called up to Triple-A for the first time in his career on June 11 as an emergency fill-in and went 2 for 3 with a double, an RBI, and a run scored in his debut with Colorado Springs. He was only there to hold the spot for injured catcher Edwin Bellorin, but who's to say what would've happened if Bellorin had stayed on the disabled list longer? Tino went 2 for 3 in his second appearance, too, far from overwhelmed. . . .

It wasn't enough. Bellorin came back, and Tino returned to Tulsa on June 22—the latest sign that, no matter how well he played, the Rockies didn't envision a future for him as a player. But Stu Cole was still swamped. Tino saw his new chance. He made himself available to any hitter in a jam, worked as first base coach, hit fungoes, kept the "situational hitting card"—an organization-wide standardized charting of how well each player moved runners, executed a sacrifice bunt or the hit-and-run, or led off an inning—and called in the post-game report nightly to the Rockies' minor league hitting coordinator. Cole says he "was taking him under my wing," giving Tino a feel for the daily mechanics of coaching, but the manager wasn't being charitable. He needed a hitting coach, and when Tino was reactivated to play for good in June, he kept right on coaching, in game and out, and phoning in the card afterward, too. Everyone in the organization knew his ambition; the players kept hearing rumors that the Rockies might just make the job permanent. Enough people kept telling him: Do good work here, and who knows?

But Tino had one problem. During batting practice, he couldn't get the ball over the plate. Day after day, he would go out with a group of hitters—all just looking to take their cuts—and plunk them one by one in the back or the arm; each time, Stu would have to step in and relieve him. It became a team joke, one of those opportunities seized upon by a pack of males to relieve tension. Cole and Gustafson say Tino wouldn't have been hired anyway—too inexperienced—but he's sure of one thing: It didn't help. What kind of hitting coach can't throw BP? He tried to laugh along; the worst thing a guy can do in that environment is reveal himself as sensitive or soft. "But I wanted so bad to throw a strike," Tino says. "I put so much pressure on myself; I *wanted* to throw BP. I wanted that coaching job.

"I think that's why they never hired me. All my life I had thrown batting practice and I always threw strikes. I don't know why, but suddenly I couldn't."

Competitors, the great ones anyway, learn early the virtues of tunnel vision and mercilessness. So you could say that Drillers pitcher Jon Asahina grew up with something to overcome, raised as he was in a household centered on endless questioning and compassion: His mother, Roberta, teaches advertising and mass communications at Fresno State, and his dad, Bernie, an orthotist, goes to hospitals and clamps halos around the heads of frightened patients. But Jon also grew up agile and strong—6 feet 1, 190 pounds—and conditioned by constant success to carry the young athlete's perspective: *This body will never die. This sport, this game, this inning is where I live.* He got sent home from Wake Forest after one semester in 1999, his grades a mess, his coaches and parents convinced he needed to grow up. After two years at Fresno City, Louisiana State offered a scholarship and the Florida Marlins offered a $550,000 bonus. Jon went for the money. "Any way you can get on the fast track," he told the *Fresno Bee* then, "is a good reason to get going."

He was going to be a star; he was sure of it. A part of him still is. "I've always thought, even now," Asahina says, "that all-around I can be the best player of any team I play on." And he knew what it took. He had been teammates with Royals pitcher Ryan Braun in high school—hell, he had basically cajoled, shamed, dragged Ryan back into the game after he had quit his freshman year—and the two work out together every off-season. Braun still calls Asahina one of the best athletes in professional baseball, his dedication and innovative work-out methods an inspiration. "I have no doubt about him at all," Braun says of Asahina's ability to play on the major league level. "He just needs the opportunity."

But when Asahina went home to Fresno in April 2007, he had a fresh ridge behind his ear where his skull was slowly mending. He could barely remember a summer when he didn't play something. For 17 years he'd been going, going, going: Now his doctor was warning him to move no faster than a walk. Now, for more than two and a half months, he was forced to rest. He found himself too quiet, too alone, too idle with too much time to think.

Asahina tried to keep things light; he's always quick to smile. Those who didn't know him called him "happy-go-lucky"; those who do speak of his positive energy. "A control pitcher with no fear," McLaughlin says. "He was just so aggressive and had so much self-confidence. He doesn't back off." But Asahina's cockiness wasn't ironclad. There's a school of thought in sports that, Bill Bradley, Bill Russell, and Ken Dryden aside, you can be "too smart" to be a great athlete. It's an inexact theory, because what it actually criticizes is not brainpower but overthinking, the inability to shut the mind down and let the body do its job. If not a student, Asahina had always been thoughtful, quick to analyze situations and people in a way his fellow jocks rarely bothered. Early success as a power pitcher allowed him to blow past any second-guessing, but after a shoulder injury forced him to rely more on guile and placement, his mind became more of a factor. Asahina dwelled on his outings, good or bad, and found it hard to be, as Zen-sportsters like to put it, "in the now"; if his pitches didn't place, it sparked a mental as well as physical sorting. He found it harder to move on to the next start, and as the stakes mounted, it showed. After breaking out in 2005 with Tulsa, becoming a Texas League All Star by going 12–10 with a 4.19 ERA, Asahina's ERA ballooned in Tulsa and Colorado Springs in 2006. He couldn't get out of his own way. It didn't help any that, by the spring of 2007, he'd lost velocity and in overcompensating took some bite out of his best pitch, the sinker. The Rockies cooled on him. The organization boasted some of the best pitching prospects in baseball, and he'd had to battle to earn a spot in Tulsa.

Such slippage alone would have softened Asahina up for a bout of soul-searching. But getting hit in the head that night in North Little Rock sent him spinning. For months he couldn't put his finger on how, exactly. The process of skirting death felt anything but logical, and his first impulse was to roll with the mystery instead of overanalyzing and destroying the good it could do. For the first two weeks, he managed a cool detachment, a casualness about cracking his skull that shattered when, happening upon a TV show highlighting sports accidents and watching one athletic collision after another, it finally hit. "I freaked out," Asahina says. "I wasn't crying but I was getting super-excited and pretty much could feel how close I was to dying, and what that meant and all my beliefs—all the things I think I believed in—I'm questioning: *What if there's nothing? What if there's just lights-out, that's it, it's over?* All within five minutes I'm freaking out, jumping around the room."

Asahina called his father. "I've been waiting for this to happen," Bernie said. "I can't believe you lasted this long.'"

Bernie, after all, had been whipsawed on the same emotional ride himself once. When Jon Asahina's dad was 12, he had walked outside his Salt Lake City home to find his 5-year-old brother, Jonathan, lying in a pool of blood. Two small neighbor kids, fiddling around with their parents' Oldsmobile, had disengaged the parking brake. The car had rolled across the street, slammed over Jonathan as he stood on a sidewalk, smashed into a neighbor's house, then rolled backward over him again. Within three hours, the boy was dead. It made no sense, of course. Bernie began to see the universe as a random, illogical place, each day as a gift. He later named his only son for his little brother, to remember, but by then had boiled his philosophy down to the utmost simplicity: *I wake up in the morning, I'm happy I'm alive, and I start from there.*

Hearing that again helped Jon for a while. He went to the mountains, sometimes twice a week, sometimes with Jenny or his parents, sometimes alone. He found himself, when watching baseball on TV, seeing more clearly, reading the game better than ever: feeling a tug in his gut and thinking "double play right here, this pitch," only to watch it happen a moment later. He'd talk to friends, parents, teammates, and nearly vibrated with a perception he'd never had: He knew where the conversation was going, picked up on moods and shifts almost before they occurred. He felt fully awake, stronger, as if for the first time in his life, mind and gut were working in sync instead of at odds. Asahina found himself letting it all flow through him—life, experience, relationships—like a stream, and he followed the flow: *Let instinct take over. Let that decide what to do next.*

"I just feel free," he said in August. "Do I really care now how I do? No: I'm going to do the best I can. We try to be great, and I've always focused on achievements—getting to this place, then the next place. Finally I understand: Everyone talks about enjoying the process, but I don't really have a choice. I'm happy the ride's still going. I smell things better. I look at the sun. Sometimes the sun shines so bright now, it's like a movie."

Far from downplaying a pitcher's worst nightmare, Asahina almost embraced the line drive that sent him to his knees. "A lot of times he'll *want* to talk about it, about how he thinks this had to happen because of 'these changes in me now. I'm better because of them,'" Braun says. "How do you explain that? That's what's weird."

Asahina knew it was a cliche: Man nearly dies, and the searing experience alters everything. But he didn't care. For ten weeks, he knocked around home, fighting off sleep and wondering, "Why am I here?" in senses both pedestrian and cosmic. What sent me home? Why am I alive? "I went to the depths of my belief system and what I believe is my soul, asked myself what I want to do," Asahina said. "And I realized that I'm still as passionate, if not more, about a few things in my life—my family, my beliefs, baseball, and the people that I love. The whole situation made me realize how much I appreciate everything: every single moment, every single day. Every ballplayer says, 'Take it a day at a time, take it a pitch at a time.' Now I feel like there's no choice. I embrace that. I'm tasting my food better, I'm sleeping better, I feel like I talk better, I love better, and I absolutely love coming out to the field. It feels like Little League again."

On July 13, Asahina flew back to Tulsa to rejoin his team. He went first to Drillers Stadium, reunited with his teammates and Bo

McLaughlin, welcoming him now into that unique pitching subset: survivors. Then Asahina noticed a strange face, the new hitting coach. He shook hands with Mike Coolbaugh and noticed his presence— "very strong," Asahina says. "You just felt him. He had that warrior energy, very stoic." But hitting wasn't his department, and besides, Asahina had plenty to think about: He knew Cole, his teammates, the fans, and McLaughlin especially would be watching his every move to see if he was gun-shy. Bo was never reticent to speak of how he had flinched, trying to pitch again after his face was shattered by Baines's liner back in 1981. *That's your problem*, Asahina thought. *It's not going to be mine.* He felt ready. He just wanted to unpack, get in step again with the baseball rhythm.

That afternoon, Asahina checked into the Tulsa hotel where the team put up its personnel. By midsummer, most players and coaches had landed apartments or rooms in sponsor housing, so he figured on seeing few familiar faces. The woman at the front desk became confused about his payment method, and Asahina, his voice growing emphatic, was intently explaining that he was a member of the Tulsa Drillers baseball club when he heard the door open off to his right. He didn't look to see who lined up behind him, didn't think much of it at all, and kept right on explaining until he felt that presence again, pulling him up short. Asahina lowered his voice. He found himself choosing his words carefully. He tried not to sound like some entitled ballplayer; it seemed very important suddenly not to sound like a jerk.

Asahina settled with the woman, wheeled, and headed out the door. But something made him look over his left shoulder at the last second; he needed to see who had thrown him off, forced him to alter his tone. It was the new hitting coach.

Mike didn't say a word. He looked Asahina in the eye, cocked his head, and lifted his eyebrows. He waved a hand. Not passing judgment: letting Asahina know he'd been seen and recognized. Just saying hello.

When Mike Coolbaugh introduced himself to the Drillers nine days before, most of the team knew little about him. Some players had heard that it was his first coaching job; some knew that his brother, Scott, was a hitting coach for their Texas League rivals, the Frisco RoughRiders; some pieced together that he'd had a long minor league career. But Coolbaugh had just turned 35 and looked younger, and the fact that he'd racked up 1,600 hits and 256 minor league home runs made him, for this team, as attractive as the lone female at a Boy Scout jamboree. The Drillers needed a hitting coach. Now here he was, and on the Fourth of July, no less. The fact that Coolbaugh could laugh at himself was gravy. Upper lip stiffened above a grin, he stood in the batting cage at San Antonio's Wolff Municipal Stadium and blamed his hard-luck journey on bad reflexes. "I always had trouble," Mike said of all those hand and wrist injuries, "getting away from inside pitches."

He was not a yapper. He didn't cheerlead. But Coolbaugh didn't work his way in slowly either; his love for the craft of hitting, an obvious determination to make the most of this chance, pushed him past any natural reticence. "You could see that passion from the start," says Drillers outfielder Matt Miller. "You could tell from the way he approached the team, the way he talked: He was not scared. He didn't tiptoe into our clubhouse; he went after it and did his job. And he definitely clicked with the team. Everyone liked him right away. He gave good advice. He had had a tremendously lengthy career and knew how to hit, but there's a communication, an X-factor involved, too. To be a hitting coach is a tremendous job, but we were hitting well shortly after he joined the team. A lot of guys really took off, right away."

Something else: Baseball may be a fame game at its highest level, a commercial property with too-loud talking heads and endless fluffy talk about "marketing" and "entertainment," but its lifers are hyper-vigilant for any sign of fraudulence. They possess what Ernest Hemingway called "a built in, shock-proof, shit detector" and can sense when someone is shining his own badge or politicking for promotion. Drillers manager Stu Cole is one of those terse types with little use for cameras or notepads; he doesn't suffer fools. Each day Coolbaugh would pop his head into Cole's office and say, "What can I do today to make these guys better?" or "I'm here for you. If you need anything, I'm here to help you out." Cole liked that, but he listened more to Mike as he talked with other coaches and players, watched how he'd sit for hours talking hitting if anyone gave him the time.

"And he meant it," Cole says. "You could see it in his eyes, you could see in his face, that he wasn't just saying it. This was something he really wanted to get involved in, put his heart and soul into helping these kids get better, helping me, doing whatever he can to make the team and organization better. It wasn't a phony thing, eyewash. Whatever he said, he meant it."

The Drillers played three games in San Antonio, Mike's first series as a coach. Mandy and Mary Lu couldn't get over how young Mike looked compared to the other coaches; after his first game they told him he looked like some kid. "Thanks a lot," he said. After the second,

Mandy took the boys home and Mike drove Mary Lu, and on the dark highway he spoke of how strange it was, seeing what he'd lived for 17 years from the other side. "There's twenty-five guys there, Mom, but they're really only looking at three," Mike said. "If I report on a guy and he's not the one they're looking at, they really don't care."

But he seemed content enough, and took to the job quicker than anyone expected. Mike had always had trouble sitting still and watching Scott play; he once asked Mandy how she could take just *watching* for four hours at a stretch. Now, though, he found himself engrossed by the sight of hitters hitting, by the challenge of picking apart each player's approach and, of course, giving his opinion; he was Bob's son, after all, and there was an entire team of professionals eager to listen. Mandy couldn't believe how excited Mike seemed, and so soon. "I love this," he told her.

The team left San Antonio for a three-game set against the Corpus Christi Hooks. Mandy came down with the boys for the weekend, an extended send-off for his new career. Each day, before Mike left for the ballpark, the family would go to the edge of the Gulf of Mexico. Mike wasn't a beach guy; he liked water-skiing but blanched at the thought of dirty low water, didn't like splashing in the surf. But the last day, a Monday, July 9, he insisted that Mandy bring a camera and he tossed and swam with Joey and Jake as much as they wanted, made her snap picture after picture. Then he suggested a stroll. "He hated sand between his toes, but he wanted to take a long walk," Mandy says. They ambled about an hour hand-in-hand, waves lapping on the shore, the kids running in front and laughing—one of those moments you'd swear you saw in a movie.

"Isn't this nice?" Mike said.

They packed the car. Mandy dropped him at the field. That night, Mike had his first breakthrough: He took catcher Tommy Duenas aside for a stint of one-on-one batting practice before the finale, and Duenas went on to hit two home runs. "And it was like *he* got a hit," Tino Sanchez says. The team left on the bus that night for Tulsa, but the next day, Tuesday, would be a day off. Mike stayed with the family at a cousin's house in Corpus, drove the family home to San Antonio the next morning, then worked there a few hours, finishing an English paper. He packed, gathered his gear, kissed his family goodbye. It was about 8 p.m.

Mike split the drive to Tulsa that Tuesday evening in half, stopping to sleep at Scott's home in Colleyville. The two brothers sat in the living room for an hour or so, near midnight, talking baseball. Mike wanted to know the best way to get through to his new players; he needed to make an impression, quick, show some results.

"How should I address the team?" Mike said. "I don't want to come off as a guy who acts like he knows everything."

"Be yourself," Scott said. "The players will get to know you. It's all about trying to help the player. It's not about you anymore. Your career isn't relevant; they don't want to hear that you hit 30 home runs and got screwed. They want to hear what's going to help them out."

Scott asked Mike about Stu Cole and how he'd received him, and they talked about their game some more. Scott loved seeing Mike fired up, rewarded; he'd lived with uncertainty for too long. Now they both had something solid: coaching in the same league, being close to home, and soon their next meeting, when the Drillers would play in Frisco on August 8. The two spoke of how cool it would be, facing each other on the field again. The whole family was coming in for that one—Mom, Dad, sisters, Mandy and the kids. "I'm looking forward to seeing you," Mike said.

Mike left early the next morning, Wednesday, and Scott slept in, missing him. The two spoke by phone once more, five or six days later. "It's really starting to click," Mike said. And so soon. Wasn't he supposed to feel some hangover, a lingering itch to still play before he could embrace coaching? The hitters really seemed to be buying in, listening and actually putting into practice what he had to say. He called Kerry Robinson, and his old teammate could feel it coming through the phone: Mike wasn't one of those bitter lifers hanging around the game even though he hated it. He seemed stunned by the satisfaction that bubbled inside when a kid took what he was teaching, made the proper adjustment during a game, and actually lashed the ball for a hit. "It's like the best feeling ever, Robbie," Mike told him. "It's awesome."

Tino didn't know anything about those calls. He didn't know about Mike's career or family. Still, he found himself watching the Drillers' new coach. Tino had wanted that job, yes, and he might've been hurt by the snub if he had been younger. But he knew the game and one of its key unspoken rules: *Don't expect anything.* Understanding that doesn't make a man a pushover, yet as the days passed in Tulsa Tino found himself feeling happier for Coolbaugh than he expected. Part of it was what Stu and the players saw: Mike cared. Mike wasn't trying to impose his own compact swing on the hitters, but tailoring his approach to get the best out of each player's individual stroke. But he was tough, too, or at least gave off the impression he could be, a mix of P. J. Carey and Dave Collins. Tino sensed the other players' respect for Mike—his career, his short but very real stint in the majors—and knew that it's a prize grudgingly given, and usually a good gauge of character. "I was very careful," Jon Asahina says of his attitude around Mike. "I would only ask him crisp questions. I wanted to let him know I'm not here talking about last night or women in the stands. No: It's baseball."

And then there was the lifer shorthand, understood best by the lifer himself: If you're in the minors for 17 years like Mike, or 11 years like Tino, by virtue of time served you've proven yourself a "team guy." "That's how you survive," Tino says. He sensed instantly that Mike was no complainer. That Mike kept playing after his dream died because he had a family to feed. That Mike had a passion tempered—inflamed, even—by rejection and pain. For Tino, seeing Mike wasn't like looking in a mirror. It was a telescope: That's me, a few years down the road.

"It's amazing to me how similar Mike and Tino were," Marc Gustafson says. "For both, it was: How can I serve? How can I help? Is there anything more to fit in? They put their careers to the side, if you will. For Tino, it wasn't about him showing: I can do this, I can do that. It was, How can I help?"

So Tino showed Mike the ropes, easing himself out of the job he wanted, training the man that the organization liked better. He told Mike how to fill out the situational hitting card, how to call it in to the minor league coordinator after games. He streamlined a process that could've taken weeks for Mike to figure out alone, broke down the roster hitter by hitter: The strengths and weaknesses of Christian Colonel and Matt Miller and Tommy Duenas, the buttons to push on Duke Sardinha, whether to stroke or challenge Aaron Rifkin. He told Coolbaugh to keep it simple, not to assume that these kids would understand veteran lingo or even the concept Tino prized most: respect for the game. "We have to find a way to reach them," Tino said, and that "we" meant plenty. By mid-July, Mike spoke with his mother about how quickly the guys were responding. Just before the Drillers left home on July 19 on an 11-game road trip starting in Little Rock, Mike told Bo McLaughlin that he hoped the Rockies would renew his contract for the following season.

The Drillers lost their first two games in Little Rock. For weeks Mike had been pestering Tino: He wanted to buy him lunch, payback for all the help. Tino kept putting him off; it's not necessary, he said. Finally, on Saturday, July 21, Tino agreed. Mike insisted Tino pick the place. They went to a Mexican restaurant in Little Rock, and for a while the conversation was all about players and coaches they knew, hitting, their combined 28 years of stories bubbling up over the chips and salsa. "All about baseball," Tino says. "We couldn't stop talking about baseball."

But then Tino mentioned that Angie was going to have a baby, his first, and Mike's face changed. Male banter, with its cool laughter and casually tough judgments, has a can-you-top-this quality that makes any chat a competition, but all edge drained out of his eyes now. Mike's voice went soft. He spoke of his own boys and the new baby coming. He told Tino how his life would forever change, and "that it's the most beautiful experience I would go through," Tino says. "That's when I knew how much he really loved his family."

On the afternoon of Sunday, July 22, Mandy Coolbaugh sat in the living room of her home on Apricot Drive in San Antonio, clicking through channels for the boys on the TV remote. Nearly six months pregnant, more and more fatigued, she needed Joey and Jake to gear down. She also needed to finish packing. The following day, she would start a convoluted trip: Drive up with the kids to meet Mike in Little Rock, leave him there to go to a family reunion in Atlanta, fly back to meet him again in Little Rock when the Drillers returned there on the 26th. Together, then, all of them would drive down to Tulsa and find a place to live.

She jabbed the remote, and there on the screen was a baseball field and players: perfect. Joey and Jake could always be enticed by a baseball movie, and this one, *Angels in the Outfield*, had the added advantage of the supernatural. The boys had heard about angels in church, of course, but this was the first time they'd actually seen some, and now angels were helping baseball players win games, too. They couldn't take their eyes off the screen.

In North Little Rock, it was getaway day. The Drillers had lost a contentious game the night before, 4–3, their third in a row, and after tonight's 6 p.m. contest would hit the road for the 449-mile trip to Wichita for a three-game series. Mike checked out of his room at the La Quinta Inn, and about 1 p.m. boarded the bus for Dickey-Stephens Park. He sat up front reading a two-day-old *USA Today*, and broke out laughing: One of the editorial cartoons featured Falcons quarterback and notorious dog tormentor Michael Vick reading *Old Yeller* and saying, "I just love a happy ending." The other showed Osama bin Laden holed up in a cave. "Who writes these things?" he said.

Drillers play-by-play broadcaster Mark Neely, in the row behind, leaned forward. Mike craned his head around and said, "Whoever writes them is ingenious." When the two got off the bus at the park, Coolbaugh handed Neely the newspaper. "Keep it," he said. "I'm done."

Neely slipped the paper into his shoulder bag. He hadn't interviewed Coolbaugh since he'd been hired.

"Mike, I haven't had you on the pre-game show yet," Neely said. "You got time later so we can record something?"

"Sure."

But when Neely ducked into the clubhouse before batting practice, recorder in hand, the Drillers were staging Kangaroo Court. One of those time-honored baseball traditions—like making major league rookies dress up like fools on the final road trip—designed to ease tension and build camaraderie, Kangaroo Court gives players and coaches a chance to call each other out for stupid mistakes, silly infractions, and just about anything else that embarrasses the guilty party and gives the clubhouse a laugh. Stu Cole sat at a table near the door with Bo McLaughlin, hanging judges doling out justice to the players arranged before their lockers in a rough circle. "Neely: Late for court!" Stu declared when he saw the broadcaster. "Guilty," Neely admitted, accepting his $2 fine. He sat down in the far corner of the room. Four feet away, Mike stood leaning against a wall.

Sometimes, a Kangaroo Court doesn't work. Someone gets mad, or a slumping player isn't in the mood to joke. But this was one of those bizarre days when every violation and sanction seemed to only lift the level of hilarity. Second baseman Corey Wimberly recalled that, earlier in the season, he had walked out of a shower and Tino Sanchez said, "Man, Corey, you look fabulous naked!"

The room broke up. The player-jury yelled, "Tino, did you say that?"

"Yeah," Tino replied. "Take your clothes off, Corey! He'll show you!"

That earned a fine. Coolbaugh's turn came near the end. A couple nights before, he had lost track of the innings and started shaking hands with his counterparts on the Travelers at the end of the eighth; by the time he realized his mistake it was too late. Busted. The players were laughing uproariously now, some so hard that it hurt, and Mike chuckled and took his fine, knowing that there could be no clearer sign that he had arrived. *They don't give you shit unless they like you.* Neely was struck by it: Not just how quickly the team had accepted him, but how much Mike enjoyed the players too. No, not just enjoyed, Neely thought, more than that. It's affection. It's real.

Neely had first met Mike 11 years before, when the 24-year-old had jumped to Tulsa, then a Texas affiliate, and driven in nine runs in seven games during his one season in the Rangers organization. He remembered him, if only because that had been his first year as the Drillers play-by-play man; you never forget that first nerve-racking year. Coolbaugh was less reserved now, and there's always that question when a player first becomes a coach: When will he stop identifying with the former and think like the latter? But Mike was making the transition look easy. Watching him stand there, grinning, Neely had a sudden flash: *He's going to do really well at this job.*

Not long after Kangaroo Court ended, some players conducted a fantasy football mock draft. Mike noticed and walked over. "I want to get in on this," he said. "You know that, right?"

"For sure," the players answered. "Right!" Mike checked in with Tino, the designated hitter on the night's lineup card. Sanchez was hitting just .163, had been uneasy with his swing of late. Now he told Mike, "You know, I'm starting to feel better."

All of that provided a needed tonic. With a 47–51 record, Tulsa had been trying—and failing—to shake the 46–53 Travelers all season in a run for the North Division wild-card playoff slot. Worse, the Travelers had beaten the Drillers at nearly every turn, winning 11 out of the last 13 and, after the previous horrible night, five in a row. In Saturday's fifth inning, Tulsa led 3–1 with one out and two men on when Matt Miller ran down a warning-track fly ball. He seemed to catch it over his shoulder, but dropped the ball as he turned to throw it to second base. Umpire Tyler Funneman, working third base, ruled that Miller never made the catch, scoring the play as an RBI single. That's when Cole bolted the dugout: Miller, he argued, had made the catch for the out—then dropped the ball. Funneman held his ground, but when Cole raised a finger to make his point, a line got crossed. Umpires expect arguments, profanity-filled and heated, but the ump's side of "respect the game" demands that players and managers don't show *them* up with gestures that could incite the crowd. A batter can mutter all he wants facing the pitcher, but if he looks back at the ump during an at-bat, pantomiming his question, he's asking for trouble.

Funneman told Cole to speak without pointing. "Don't tell me what to do," Cole yelled, closing the gap between himself and Funneman, butting the umpire's forehead with the bill of his cap. "I am a fucking man!"

"Stu, watch the hat," Funneman said.

"You're not going to tell me what to do!"

Funneman ejected Cole, sparking more "fuckings" that served to modify Miller's great catch, Funneman's horrid mistake, bullshit itself, and Cole's elemental manhood. The next batter smacked a two-run double past Miller off the left field wall, and the Travelers took a lead they never relinquished.

It's standard procedure for the managers to present the night's lineup card to the umpires. But Cole, still livid some 18 hours later, feared that if he took the Drillers' lineup to home plate Sunday evening, he'd blow up again. So after the pre-game routine, after the Travelers made do with an instrumental recording because their anthem singer no-showed and the crowd stood in silence, he sent Mike out to do the honors. For the first time as a coach, then, Coolbaugh trotted up out of the dugout and onto the field, lineup card in hand, and what was expected to be a tense exchange became something else altogether. Mike gathered in around the plate with the three-man umpiring crew of Brian Sinclair, Steve Barga, and Funneman, the 24-year old crew chief, and Travelers manager Bobby Magallanes.

"So, Mike," Magallanes asked with a smile, "how do you like it so far?"

"I really needed this," Mike replied. "I love it. The one thing that's hard is that I miss my family; they're back in San Antonio."

"You got family in San Antonio?" Funneman asked. "Do you get to see them a lot?"

"I'll see them in a couple of weeks."

A train whistle wailed in the distance. The wind blowing out of the northeast at 10 miles per hour, clouds blocking the sun, 82 degrees and not too humid: perfect for baseball. It was nearing 6 p.m.

7

THE FOUL BALL

ONLY ONE OTHER AMERICAN CITY—BUFFALO, WHICH HAS had the Bisons since 1886—has had a more enduring relationship with minor league baseball than Little Rock and its Travelers. Given the nickname at the team's inception in 1895, Little Rock's minor league club has borne it steadily despite changing affiliations, levels, and fortunes, despite league shutdowns and a franchise move and return. When one incarnation bolted for Shreveport in 1959, the town's baseball eminence, Ray Winder, maneuvered to create another by selling stock to the public at $5 a share. After raising enough to buy the New Orleans team, Winder moved it to Little Rock in 1960 and went on that season to win the Southern Association title. The Travs have been a fan-owned franchise ever since, one of a handful in the minors, with some 1,400 shareholders and a six-member executive committee. Such a homespun operation fit hand in glove, for 74 years, in the charmingly crusty confines of what came to be called Ray Winder Field. Time, however, eventually made the place less an asset than a threat.

"It was one of those classic ballparks from the '30s and '40s, one of the only ones left, so it was special," says Travs play-by-play man Phil Elson. "I did six years at Ray Winder, grew up there and met my wife there, and a lot of people in central Arkansas grew up and fell in love there just like I did. But there was no way we could continue there. We had to get waivers every year on stuff like the height of the lights, and the dugouts were like concrete pillboxes. There was a concrete platform at the front of the dugout and at the back there was nothing to keep a player from falling down four to five feet. A guy could've been killed, knocked over by some first baseman who falls into the dugout and bowls him over and next thing you know they're in the back of the dugout and one's dead. I'm shocked that never happened. Ray Winder Field was a fairly dangerous place, I felt, to play baseball."

Even worse, it had every chance of killing baseball in Little Rock outright. Since Round Rock's move into a new park in 2000, the Texas League had been on a stadium-building binge, with modern, spacious mini sports palaces opening in Midland, Frisco, Corpus Christi, and Springfield, Missouri. The competition for minor league teams among small towns may be even more intense than that between their big-city brethren; franchise movement is far more common, with the lure to major league organizations nearly always a promise of sparkling, state-of-the-art facilities. Travs executive vice-president/general manager Bill Valentine began sounding the alarm that Little Rock either had to upgrade Ray Winder, build a new ballpark, or watch its team fade into irrelevance. The publicly owned Travelers wouldn't necessarily move, but the prospect of losing its current affiliation with the Los Angeles Angels—and any hope of a future with any major league organization—was real and nearly as harrowing. The only option then would be to continue life as an independent team, cut out of the major league pipeline of players, and when Little Rock's billionaire financier, Warren Stephens, heard that, he knew something had to be done. "You lose your affiliation," Stephens says, "and you *have* lost your team."

Located in an office building looming over the Arkansas River, Stephens, Inc., is one of the world's largest brokerage firms outside of Wall Street. A vital Little Rock helps Stephens attract and retain talent. But the firm built by Warren's father and uncle, Jack and Witt Stephens, also prides itself on being a state institution—one that helped launch powerhouses like Wal-Mart and Tyson Foods—just as shrewd and cutting-edge as any in New York, and its stewards know that any civic hit reflects on the company. "You can't let a baseball team leave, particularly a minor league team," Stephens says. "You lose your minor league team, it sends the wrong message to the community and the world that there's something wrong with the town: It's not supporting organizations; It's not a good place to live."

But if the idea of being the kind of good corporate citizen, the man who could help bring 4,000 to 5,000 loose-walleted baseball fans downtown 70 nights a year, appealed to Stephens, there was one other consideration, unquantifiable but perhaps even more central: His father loved baseball. The sports world knew Jack Stephens only as a golf guy, the chairman of the Augusta National Golf Club and the Masters Tournament from 1991 to '98, or, perhaps, as the man who'd personally given $5 million to spur youth golf programs, and why not? Jack Stephens didn't play much baseball after that ball knocked him out at third base in high school in Columbia, Tennessee. But the game lived on with him on a daily basis, through the four-pointed friendship involving Witt and Jack and brothers Bill and Skeeter Dickey. Bill, of course, was the former Traveler who went on to a Hall of Fame career as catcher with the New York Yankees, roomed with Lou Gehrig, and wrote the foreword to *The Pride of the Yankees*. But Warren knew Bill Dickey more as the man who took him to his first big league baseball game, and who worked for Stephens after he retired. Skeeter Dickey, also a catcher but no Hall of Famer, played three seasons with the White Sox in the '40s, finished playing in 1948, and became a vice-president at Stephens. He and Warren's dad were closest of all, best friends, and when Skeeter died of a heart attack in 1976 something in Jack died, too. Even ten years later, when Warren came upon his usually reserved father after one wearying afternoon, the old man peered up from his desk and sighed and said, "You know, I really miss Skeeter."

Jack had a stroke in 1998. Early in 2004, after meeting with community leaders about a possible ballpark site in downtown Little Rock, Warren led them up to the 25th floor of his offices, to the Stephens boardroom. There they walked out on the balcony on the northeast corner, and Warren pointed out three different spots across the Arkansas River, in North Little Rock. On one of them sat a branch of a local bank, operating out of a double-wide trailer. Later that year, Warren bought the 11-acre parcel for $5.8 million and announced his intention to donate it, with one stipulation: that he control the naming rights. He told almost no one his plan, not until the day in 2005 when he took his father up to that same 25th-floor boardroom and pointed out the site and told Jack he was going to name the new ballpark after both sets of brothers, the Dickeys and the Stephenses. And his dad gave him a look he won't soon forget: a big grin crossing his dying face, enough for Warren to know he'd done the right thing.

Jack Stephens died that summer, at 81. Financed by a taxpayer-approved 1-cent sales tax, construction on Dickey-Stephens Park began with a nice piece of urban lore: During the original excavation, workers dug up a child-sized coffin, finding inside the skeletal remains of what was apparently a canine. Residents couldn't really ask for a more appropriate sign of Dogtown's rise, and when the ballpark opened on April 12, 2007, a perfect balmy spring evening, cars jammed the Broadway Bridge linking Little Rock to North Little Rock for hours before. As Warren walked in and saw the packed-in crowd of 7,943 fans and the name on the building itself, he tried not to think too much of how his dad would have loved it, because he knew he would never make it through without crying. He had never been involved in a project that resonated so. "And I probably never will again," says Stephens. "That's one of the reasons you work hard and try to build a company and be as successful as you can be. Because every once in a while you get to do something like that."

Warren gave a speech before the game, speaking of unity and building metaphorical bridges, drawing some warm applause. Even better, during the game a foul ball came rocketing into his suite and bounced off the ceiling before Warren grabbed it rolling on the floor, the billionaire caught up suddenly in a pure baseball moment, scrambling like some $5 fan. Warren held the ball up to show the crowd, and Little Rock cheered the hero and his prize.

Now, 101 days later, on July 22, Stephens arrived at Dickey-Stephens Park for the first time since the opener. The decision to come had been one of those sudden impulses, an intuitive flash: Warren had flown into Little Rock from New York late in the afternoon, bringing with him a friend from Manhattan. The man had never been to a minor league game, wasn't even a baseball fan, but the idea had occurred to Stephens and that was that. "Come on," he said on the way into town from the airport. "Let's kill some time and catch a few innings."

Maybe he wanted to show off some, and who could blame him? Without Stephens there probably wouldn't have been an Arkansas Travelers game in a sparkling new $40.4 million ballpark in North Little Rock that Sunday evening. If he had stung some civic egos by effectively moving a team that had played in Little Rock for 111 years to its stepsister city, so be it. He had helped save the team, hadn't he?

It was the second inning. The Travelers led 2–0. Stephens's seats were located in the upper deck just behind home plate, shaded a bit up the third base line, affording a clear panorama: the Main Street Bridge and the Little Rock skyline and that dominating and sun-splashed "Stephens Inc." tower; the signs for "Doublebees" and "Pipe & Tube Supply Inc." along the right field fence; the pitcher, first base, the opponents' dugout. Really, his friend couldn't have asked for better for his first minor league game. You could see everything.

One flight below, a bristle-haired force with a Foghorn Leghorn voice, a deep love and gift for profanity, his flashy suspenders as much a signature as anything he ever set to paper, sat on a folding chair on the main concourse behind the stands. It wasn't the particulars of the ballgame that interested him; he'd seen enough of those. It was the stadium. His stadium. If anyone has a stronger claim on Dickey-Stephens Park than Warren Stephens, it's Bill Valentine. For more than three decades the 75-year-old former major league umpire had been the face of the Arkansas Travelers—which, notwithstanding the Dickey brothers, means that he'd long been the face of baseball in the state—and from its eponymous upscale eatery (officially "Bill Valentine's Ballpark Restaurant" but everyone calls it simply Valentine's) to its railroad-themed architecture and details, Dickey-Stephens is a daily validation of Valentine's sensibility, if not his ego. He loves it, no surprise: The place is a monument to his victory, his revenge, and his childhood all at once, and after it opened he found himself one of its biggest draws. It wasn't uncommon for folks to call the restaurant on game days to see if Bill would be there. Hearing only "maybe," they'd cancel their reservations.

"You got to understand: Arkansas is a very small state," Valentine says. "I'm very visible; people think they *know* me. But it's amazing how I became . . . a kind of icon."

Still, no one can say he hasn't worked for it. Valentine's daddy was a railroad man, working for the Missouri Pacific painting diesel engines, and Bill was born the same year Travelers Park—later Ray Winder Field—opened and grew up three blocks away. Just before World War II, the family bought a two-room house in North Little Rock, but at nine Bill started crossing back over the river for Travs home stands, staying with his grandmother and chasing down foul balls. Ballparks were happy to set kids to work then, collecting discarded deposit bottles, sacking peanuts, picking up rented seat cushions for a dime apiece. At 14, Bill umpired Midget League games, three a day, four days a week, $3 a game: $36 a week at a time when men were raising families on $40. He landed a scholarship to study journalism at a nearby college, then got a better offer: His grandmother offered to pay for "empire" school if he wanted it. Valentine shipped off to Bill McGowan's Umpire School in Daytona Beach, and upon graduating worked the Ohio-Indiana League—at the dewy age of 18 both the newly minted husband of Ellouise Pefferly and the youngest umpire in the history of the professional game. "Baseball was crumbling bad," Valentine says. "That's when baseball started to fall apart: '51."

He doesn't laugh as he says this, so whether Valentine is taking responsibility isn't clear. He's not shy about mocking himself—the restaurant features an unusually large collection of photos of Valentine flying ass-over-teacup in various collisions—but during his minor league climb he built a reputation for imperiousness, independence, and a quick trigger. Valentine called in two policemen to enforce his ejection of Houston manager Harry "The Hat" Walker during the first inning of a 1958 Texas League game, and he hardly mellowed when he rose to the major leagues in 1963. On October 1, 1964, Valentine tossed Detroit's Dave Wickersham, never mind that the pitcher was going for his 20th win, after Wickersham tried getting his attention by grabbing his shoulder. Valentine also happily ignored any star standard when it came to calling balls and strikes, and he was only one of two umps to ever eject Mickey Mantle. "We had a love-hate relationship," Valentine says. "I called him out on strikes and he went to the dugout and threw his helmet out and called me a sonuvabitch and I ran him."

But Valentine's most memorable run-in with history remains 1967, that game in Fenway Park, serving as home plate umpire and seeing Conigliaro's face when he hit the ground. For those keyed into Boston's heartbreak past, Conigliaro's post-beaning plummet made him one of the franchise's tragic figures. Forty years later, people still talked about Tony C., and someone called the Travelers vice-president to have him authenticate the ball. In the summer of 2007, Valentine remembered for the first time that he had watched it fly foul, into the stands.

In 1968, American League president Joe Cronin fired Valentine and fellow ump Al Salerno, who had been organizing a union for American League umpires, for supposed "incompetency." Valentine insists that Cronin eventually offered both men their jobs back, but a 1971 National Labor Relations Board ruling found no evidence of a deal, and Valentine was out of umpiring. In retrospect, it's just as well. If he'd remained an ump? At best, Valentine would have been no more than a major league footnote. But after 18 years, he had the sense to go home.

Valentine returned to Little Rock, worked as a sportscaster, play-by-play man for Travelers games, even temporary director of the state Republican Party. In 1976, Travs president Max Moses made him general manager, and on opening day of that year Valentine sent a midget named Roscoe Stedman to the plate as an attention-grabbing gimmick—and never looked back. His gate-goosing promotions—wire-walkers, a $9,000 cemetery plot giveaway, guaranteed-win nights, and the twice-yearly appearance of Captain Dynamite, a stuntman who lay down in a coffin on-field during Saturday's doubleheader and blew himself up with four sticks of dynamite—earned Valentine Executive of the Year awards three years running and five times over the next 24 years. Attendance soared. He called his team "The Greatest Show on Dirt" and became a minor league legend mostly because, it seemed, there was almost nothing he *wouldn't* do.

If Valentine did become a state "icon," though, it wasn't only because of the circus he produced. It's because of what he said and how he said it, even as the country around him kept changing. With its ultra-local signage, idiosyncratic owners, and time-capsule confines, minor league ball had carved out its place in American life by serving, town by second- or third- or fourth-tier town, as a mirror—sometimes the funhouse kind—of small-town tastes and cares. But over the last few decades, the minors began to follow the same cookie-cutter wave that swept over filling stations and roadside eateries, its stadiums cleaner and more family-friendly, its executives more polished and dull. Not the Travelers, though: not yet. At a time when even New York accents were being sanded down by television's leveling monotone, Valentine's squawking Southern drawl seemed only to gain in cartoonish distinction. He used it as a devastating public weapon, railing against the players' lack of discipline and fundamentals, the "abortion" of the $8 beer sold in major league ballparks, his own parent club's priority of developing players instead of winning. He could be as rude as he was charming, and offended many. In 2001 Valentine feuded with his own Texas League winning manager, Mike Brumley, over Brumley's well-founded complaints about Ray Winder Field. Valentine has always despised pitchers—especially relievers—whom he considers gutless, so it was no shock, in 2000, for the crowd to see him heckling his own reliever, John Ambrose, as the pitcher exited the field after a disastrous outing. "You're garbage, Ambrose!" Valentine shouted. "G-A-R-B-A-G-E!"

The Arkansas players? "They hate him," Phil Elson says. "The players have hated Valentine for a long time." Elson doesn't blame them, but he knows how singular a figure Valentine is. "He's one of those big personalities," Elson explains. "There are still some around, but they seem contrived; they're *trying* to be different. But that *is* Bill; that's exactly what he's always been. I love him, and he's bitched me out. He's the kind of person who could leave you the nastiest, most fuck-filled voice mail you've ever heard in your life, and the next time you see him, it's like, 'What are you doing?' Like it never happened."

Still, in 2007 Valentine would win his sixth Texas League executive of the year award for opening what some rank as the best minor league stadium in America. But his delight derives less from the building than in the maneuverings it took to get it done, from forging alliances with North Little Rock mayor Pat Hayes and Stephens, to—best of all—outpointing his nemesis, former St. Louis Cardinals general manager Walt Jocketty. Bring up the subject in the most benign way and Valentine will proceed to call Jocketty, who moved on to Cincinnati in 2008, "two-faced," a "jackass," and various other unprintables. The Cardinals, after all, had been the Travs' parent club and a secondhand Little Rock institution since 1966, and figured to remain that way forever. But then, Valentine says, Jocketty started making demands about Little Rock needing to build a new stadium—high-handedly ignoring, in his eyes, any effort to upgrade Ray Winder Field. In 2000, with the St. Louis–Arkansas development contract due to expire, Valentine heard that Jocketty was negotiating with at least one other AA town to take his affiliation elsewhere. Jocketty admits to pushing for a new ballpark, but flatly denies ever talking to another club behind the Travelers' back.

The problem, Jocketty says, is that even getting Valentine to provide adequate working conditions for the players—from stall dividers in the bathroom to enough balls for batting practice—was "a constant struggle," and the Cardinals never got a sense that the situation, or the Travs impresario, would improve. "He was hard to deal with, and he obviously was very vindictive," Jocketty says. "The bottom line is that Bill Valentine really is the reason the Cardinals ended up leaving there."

Within days of hearing the rumors, Valentine locked in a deal with the Angels and, he says, arranged the timing so that, in the usual off-season round of minor league musical franchises, Jocketty could do no better than move his AA team to New Haven, Connecticut—and its refurbished but antiquated facility.

"The worst ballpark in Double-A baseball!" Valentine crows. "The only thing left was New Haven. For me it was the greatest coup in my fifty-six years in baseball, that I have ever done in my life: I gave Walt Jocketty New Haven. He wanted something new? I gave him something new. *New* Haven!"

Never mind that Jocketty says New Haven was better than Little Rock. Never mind that, in 2005—two years before the opening of Dickey-Stephens—the Cardinals moved their AA affiliate into a new ballpark in Springfield, Missouri, and that Jocketty calls it "the best thing that ever happened to the Cardinals. They make a ton of money there." The April opening of Dickey-Stephens Park—the state-of-the-art park Jocketty had demanded and never got—was the final turn of Valentine's screw, and as the day approached he behaved like a man clapping a lifetime of work dust off his hands. On the eve of the 2007 season, Valentine took the title of Vice-President/Chief Operating Officer and surrendered the GM tag and day-to-day responsibility for game-day operations to his assistant general manager, Pete Laven. Toss Mickey Mantle, help start a union, build a stadium: He'd done just about everything you can do in baseball without playing, and in truth, baseball was becoming too buttoned-down, less and less a place for carny barkers like him. Captain Dynamite isn't coming back to Little Rock.

"He died six, seven years ago," Valentine says. "The last couple years he was in a wheelchair so his daughter blew up with her boyfriend. When he died I lost him." But his tone is only slightly wistful. Valentine is grinning as he speaks and his words are coming faster now, because he knows how absurd it sounds and the remembering has got him going because the absurd is *fun*, the absurd is what got people into a baseball park all those summer nights, and BANG! he can still hear it. You just can't beat a good explosion. "I'd blow him up right now," Valentine says.

Houston's decision *not* to hire Coolbaugh, Merced's sudden departure, Mike's unusual elevation to Double-A in his first coaching job, Asahina's harrowing experience on the same field just three months before: Taken alone, each event can be explained as reasonable, random, another moment in life's chaos, seemingly without meaning. But for those close to Mike or the ballpark that night, all of those facts—not to mention the presence of Valentine, Bo McLaughlin, and Warren Stephens, each touched directly or indirectly by the damage a baseball can do—combine to form a kind of fate-spun symmetry, causal lines and connections revealed like a spiderweb after rain. Meaning . . . what, exactly? No one pretends to know. Although if a higher being were looking, through such obvious coincidences, to coldly remind a small swath of the world, "Yes, I am here," the message got through.

"God had a plan for Mike," Mandy says, "and there was nothing we could do to stop it." Now the dozens of swings, hits, pitches, calls, and maneuverings of one obscure baseball game, too, began to nudge the action toward what was to come, each meaningless act a strand for those desperate to see a pattern.

During the fifth inning, in the second row of seats behind the Travelers' dugout along the first base line, John Parke, son of team president Bert Parke and a season-ticket holder, sat talking with two friends, Alex and Cathy Jordan. Prime seats, indeed, Alex was saying, but the guy with whom he shares season tickets doesn't like them. Too close to the hitter: makes him nervous.

"Damn, I'm forty-five years old. I've been coming to these games since I was six," Parke replied. "I can think of two times I've seen somebody seriously get hurt."

Heading into the sixth inning, Bill Valentine meandered down the lower concourse to the elevator, rode it up to the second floor, crossed over the upper-deck concourse into the air-conditioned press box. He hung a right and noticed the open door of the home radio booth, where announcer Phil Elson sat calling the game. Elson waved him in. To his shock, Valentine accepted. Elson had been with the club since 2001 and could recall only two other instances when his boss had donned a headset during a game. He couldn't remember the last time.

Maybe it was because it was a Sunday. The pace at the park is always a bit slower then, especially in July. Too, Valentine's restaurant is closed those nights, and with no place left to hold court, the radio booth offered Valentine his best opportunity to spout off. "I was bored," Valentine says. "It just happened."

Elson introduced his guest to the listeners, but Valentine didn't want to talk baseball yet.

"If I was sitting in Rome right now," Valentine began, "could I go online and hear you?"

"Absolutely, you could," Elson said.

"Anywhere in the world?"

"Anywhere in the world on Travs.com."

"So how would I do it?"

So Elson explained, even though the game was underway, all the links Valentine would need to click onto a game feed while sitting in Rome, Italy—a corny way of promoting the website, but effective.

"Anywhere in the world," Valentine marveled.

"Anywhere. I bet you that they could hear us on the space shuttle," Elson said. "It's an 0–1 pitch to Czarnecki, and that's up high, one ball, one strike."

"Wouldn't it be nice," Valentine rasped, chuckling at the very idea, "if they took a shot of the guys in the space shuttle wearing a Traveler cap and listening to the game?"

Arkansas led, 4–3. Coolbaugh, standing in the first base coaching box, turned to Funneman to ask a question that had been nagging him since last night's game, after Cole was ejected and Funneman had to clarify that McLaughlin had been designated his official replacement. "The pitching coach can't make changes?" Mike asked. "No," Funneman answered, "it has to be the manager."

Tino Sanchez was having a good night at designated hitter, making contact. He had flied out to left field in the second inning, led off the fifth with a line single to right, and scored. In the seventh, Sanchez again led off hacking, and though he got a piece of every strike, still felt slightly off-balance. After slicing off one foul ball, he looked to Mike down in the first base coach's box, widening his eyes with a silent question—*Does this look okay?*—and took a practice swing. Mike put out both his hands and nodded slowly: *You're fine. Right where you need to be.* Tino kept battling. It was, in truth, a superb at-bat, disciplined and tough: With three foul balls in all, Tino did all he could to rattle set-up man Von Stertzbach, stretched him to a 3–2 count before popping out to center field.

Now the Travelers took their one-run lead into the eighth inning. Had that stood up going into the ninth, it would have been logical for Arkansas to bring in its side-arming closer, right-hander Darren O'Day. Instead, the Travelers scored three in the eighth inning to erase the save opportunity. Travelers right-hander Bill Edwards, a more conventional set-up man—a 26-year-old journeyman who, like Tino and Mike, had a wife back home expecting a child—took the mound.

The original crowd of 4,538 fans had thinned mightily, as it does late on a Sunday night, the workweek looming, down to maybe 1,700 diehards. Matt Miller led off the ninth for Tulsa with a single to right. Drillers pitching coach Bo McLaughlin was standing with a leg up on the stairs leading out of the opponent's dugout, along the third base line. Marv Foley, the Rockies' roving catching instructor and a former Drillers manager, sidled up next to him. Twice that night Foley had dodged foul balls that had bounded into the Tulsa dugout and, well, you notice when a guy starts to attract balls like that.

"You'd better take that target off your back," Bo said, chuckling.

"Yeah," Foley replied. "But I'm still quick enough to get out of the way when it's rolling on the ground."

Tino stepped up to the plate, batting left-handed, cocking a 34-inch, 31-ounce bat. Edwards threw three consecutive balls; one more and everyone would have been safe. Now he reared and fired a sinker.

Tino took, and home plate umpire Steve Barga signaled strike. But, says Drillers play-by-play man Mark Neely, it was "a very borderline strike on the outside corner. I'm not blaming this on the umpire. But with all the strange things that had occurred to get to that moment . . . Many times—though umpires would never say this—on a 3–0 count the strike zone does expand. That was a perfect example: a borderline pitch on the outside corner that was called a strike and made it 3–1."

"If it had been an 0–2 count, I don't think a lot of umpires would call that for a strike," Tino says. But unlike batters looking to influence the call, Tino didn't turn to toss his bat away or take a step toward first. "I wanted to hit," he says. "I *wanted* the umpire to call it a strike. I felt good."

It was 8:53 p.m. Mike Coolbaugh, standing a foot or two beyond the far edge of the coach's box, leaned toward Miller standing on first. "We're down a couple runs, so don't get picked off," he told his runner. "Freeze on a line drive. If you're going first to third, you've got to be sure."

He backed up. Miller took his lead. Edwards brought back his arm. Miller took one more step.

It was Coolbaugh's 18th game as a first base coach. In that situation, an experienced coach will watch the hitter first, then the runner, eyes darting back and forth but always weighted toward home plate. From the dugout, Jon Asahina glanced over at Mike. "I could tell: He was just watching Matt Miller's secondary lead," Asahina says. "That's why I think he looked late, because he was focused on the guy on first base." He pauses, then adds, "You can't blame anyone."

The Travelers had a good scouting report on Tino, though, perfect for digging out of a 3–1 hole: *Bites—but can't handle—the inside*

fastball/sinker; he goes for it, but too soon and almost always hooks it foul.
Edwards delivered another sinker, inside and hard. "I was trying to go
middle-in and down and it got a little further in," Edwards says. "It
was down and pretty far in and he dropped his barrel." In other words,
Tino saw the ball coming, spinning, and bit as usual, thinking about
more than just making contact. *A home run gets us back in it.* But Tino
went a fraction of a second too soon, precisely as the Travelers hoped.

"I hit it way out front," Tino says.

"The only thing he could've done with the pitch was hit it foul,"
Edwards says. "For him to hit the pitch where it was located? As hard
as he did? To get the barrel down on it? Pretty unbelievable."

The ball blasted off the bat. "A rocket!" Neely shouted into his
microphone.

"I don't remember," says Valentine, "a ball being hit that hard, that
fast. He really got every bit of it."

Normally, Sanchez never bothers tracking a ball he knows is foul.
But this time he kept watching. The ball flew up the line, hooked just
right of first base. Coolbaugh heard the crack, and out of the corner of
his eye saw something white, coming fast. He threw up his hands, and
tilted his body slightly back.

"It's so crazy," Tino says. "It seemed like the ball *followed* him."

The first noise, the crack of leather hitting wood, was both familiar and
strange—"huge" to Warren Stephens, so he snapped his head away
from the conversation with his New York friend, expecting maybe the
thrill of a titanic home run, only to take his eye off the ball when he
saw it heading foul. The two men were sitting outside Stephens's suite.

A split second later came another sound, "but it wasn't like anything you've ever heard," Stephens says. He shot a glance over at first base, blurting the question.

"What was *that*?"

The skull has evolved to protect the brain, and in that sense the loud impact of a ball can be reassuring; at least something is shielding the vital softness. But in this case, the ball zeroed in on Coolbaugh's most vulnerable spot, the exposed flesh of his neck about a half inch below and behind his left ear. Its report was muffled, moist, like an ax sinking hard into a patch of rotten timber.

"Hit him in the head!" Bill Valentine said on the air, hardly alone in being mistaken. "Hit him in the head! Ohhh, that hurt. . . ."

Within seconds, Valentine began talking about that night 40 years earlier. "I was behind the plate when Tony Conigliaro got hit in Boston, folks," he said. "I can tell you: If that got him near his eye . . . Tony Conig's eye had completely swollen and was sticking out before he hit the dirt. That was the impact of that ball. . . ."

Mike's hands didn't reach his head. "I saw him get hit," Edwards says. "All I could see was him attempting to get his hands up. And it was hit so hard. . . . Before he could get his hands up, it hit him." Mike fell back stiffly, as if frozen, and when he landed on his back the hands rose and fell and flopped limply near his ears. "The instinct is to grab where you've been hit," John Parke says. "He never made it that far." Bo McLaughlin instantly knew Mike's trouble went beyond normal; whenever he'd seen anyone hit before, whenever there'd been pain, the man kicked, rolled, squirmed, *something*. He turned to Marv Foley. "This is not good," he said.

Tino, his body just completing the corkscrew forced by a batter's swing, flinched the instant the ball struck. He watched Mike drop. He threw the bat from his right hand to his left, mouth open, his own hands stopping midway up to his face. He bolted out of the batter's box and up the first base line, so fast that he somehow got to Mike's side before Miller or Travelers first baseman Michael Collins or anyone in the Arkansas dugout, so fast that the fall's force, the weight of a body succumbing to gravity, had just finished rolling Mike over to his right side. Funneman, the young umpire, had been standing six feet behind first base in foul territory, his right foot planted on the foul line. Mike had been just eight feet to his left. But Tino still somehow closed the gap, some 90-odd feet from home plate to Mike, faster than him, too. "He had his hands on his head and he was just screaming," Funneman says. "The look in his eyes was just devastation."

Tino covered the final three steps in a sprint and stood over Mike. He peered down at his face. Mike's eyes were pinballing about, rolling back into his head. His mouth spewed a whitish foam; his body convulsed. He never moved again. Fifteen feet away, the baseball lay near the first base line, a splash of white in the grass.

Tino stood, spun, signaled to the Drillers dugout, dropped to his knees. Stu Cole, Drillers trainer Austin O'Shea, and his Arkansas counterpart, Brian Reinker, rushed onto the field. O'Shea positioned himself in the grass beyond Mike's head, flanked his knees in the space above his shoulders and tried to coolly examine his new friend. Nearly every night since Mike had joined the team, he had cajoled the 29-year-old trainer into taking in a post-game movie, a beer; often strength coach Tyler Christiansen would join them, and they'd chatter for hours about baseball, family. Now O'Shea thumbed open Mike's eyelids to check his consciousness. "Mike, can you hear me?" O'Shea said. "Talk to me. Are you all right? Answer me." O'Shea pushed open the eyelids farther, able now to see the iris and pupils.

"There was just nothing there," he says.

Two doctors had clambered out of the stands from the first base side, including Travelers team physician James Bryan. Bryan pressed his knuckles into Mike's sternum, looking for any kind of voluntary—thus, conscious—response. Two nurses from the stadium's first-aid area rushed over to assist; someone squeezed Mike's hand: nothing back. His pulse was still strong, but within about twenty seconds, O'Shea says, Mike started a half-cough, half-snore—"agonal respiration"—a signal that he'd stopped breathing on his own. Within two minutes of the hit, an off-duty Pulaski County sheriff's deputy working stadium security had called Little Rock Metropolitan Emergency Medical Services (MEMS), which then dispatched an ambulance from its site just a block away, and O'Shea had cut off Mike's jersey; defibrillator paddles had been attached in case the heart stopped. But there was no time to wait. Mike was given mouth-to-mouth, then a bag-valve mask was placed on his mouth. His chest began to rise and fall. The doctors took charge and O'Shea stepped back, thinking, *We're getting oxygen to his blood, his heart's beating. We get the ambulance here, get him to the hospital. Everything will be all right.*

For the trip to the hospital, O'Shea needed his backpack, the one containing all his team paperwork, Social Security numbers, data he'd need at the hospital to check Mike in. It was back in the visitor's clubhouse. He asked Cole to send someone to get it, as well as Mike's cell phone; Mike was constantly calling home. Cole turned and looked across the diamond to the Drillers dugout, where 24 uniforms shuffled and whispered. But he saw only one face.

Stu pointed at Asahina. "Come here!" he said.

The pitcher couldn't be sure, so he looked left and right, pointed at himself questioningly: Me?

"Jon, come here!" Cole said again. Looking back later, he never could figure why he picked Asahina; Cole insists he wasn't thinking at all about what had happened to his pitcher on this same field, three months before. "I can't explain it," Cole says. "Something just moved me to go to him."

Asahina ran. He had been throwing on the side since his return to the club, pitching simulated games. But this was his first time on a field during a game since his own accident. He reached the group. "Go get Austin's trainer's backpack from the locker room," Stu said.

Asahina sprinted back to the dugout, feeling as if he were floating. He found himself oddly calm. The backpack, the teammates asking hushed questions: It all felt familiar, and therefore solvable, a problem he knew better than anyone how to handle. "Such a weird thing," Asahina says. "I don't know how to explain it. But there's a reason he asked me to come out there."

Outfielder Matt Miller put an arm around Tino's shoulder, but it didn't help. Medical people bustled all around Mike now, but Tino was only praying, harder than he ever had in his life, *Please God* for Mike to come to. He begged, *Please don't do this to me*, felt guilty about that, then begged some more. Then he heard someone near Coolbaugh say, "Don't go, Mike! Don't go. Come back . . ."

Four minutes after the ball was hit, sirens could be heard outside the park. But there was a glitch: According to Jon Swanson, Executive Director of MEMS, the original 911 call stated only that "a patient was hit in the head," and emergency personnel, thinking someone in the crowd had been injured, first entered the stadium near the main street entrance. Learning that the injured party was, in fact, lying on-field, the MEMS crew returned to their vehicle and circled around the ballpark in search of the field-level entrance on the right field side of the park. Nearly five minutes after the siren was first heard, the ambulance finally appeared on the field. "I do acknowledge the frustration people at the scene had when the crew demonstrated uncertainty about where they were needed," Swanson says.

Mike was, in the meantime, receiving intensive treatment—paramedics had now inserted an IV tube connected to a plastic bag full of fluid—from the ad hoc collection of medical personnel gathered around him. Travelers' first year general manager, 38-year-old Pete Laven, backed uneasily away from the scrum. Mike's lack of movement wasn't simply a matter of immobility. It was that his body lay so heavily, powerless against gravity's pull. "As if he'd been shot," Laven says.

In the radio booth, Elson was on the air when a call came from someone down on the field near Mike; at first Elson and Valentine thought they'd be getting some news. Elson pulled away from the microphone, but returned to the air after a few seconds. "No additional update," Elson said. "They were just asking that, once they take everybody off the field . . . maybe ask for a small prayer for Mike Coolbaugh."

"You mean it's that serious?" Valentine said.

They lifted Mike onto a gurney, lifted the gurney into the ambulance. Mystified, helpless, the sparse crowd stood and applauded. Asahina felt a rage rising; he wanted to scream, he wanted them all to shut up, go away, fill the air with something other than the same noise that greets every useless base hit. *Oh, is this all just part of the show for you?* he thought. Then he let it go.

Tino sat in the dugout now, on the bench, his teammates awkward, trying to say the right words. Asahina walked over and, remembering Cole's warm hand on his own shoulder after he'd been hit, rubbed Tino's back to try and let him know . . . something . . . everything . . . nothing. But Tino had been made different, separated from the rest of the players by dread, the night's urgent quiet. "Why me?" he asked himself for the first time. "Why him?"

Dr. Bryan climbed into the ambulance, along with the driver and another emergency medical technician. O'Shea rode in back with Mike. The ambulance rolled out the right field gate; it was 9:10 p.m. For a few moments, no one in the park knew what to do. The managers and umpires met and agreed to suspend the game, thinking it would be resumed when the Drillers returned to town the following Thursday. But within a day it was decided that it would end where it ended: with the Travelers taking the win, with all the statistics applying but one.

8

———

GOOD NIGHT
FROM LITTLE ROCK

THERE'S A CERTAIN TONE A WIFE ADOPTS FOR HER HUSBAND in front of other people, especially close female friends, and it's easy to misinterpret. If a woman alone receives a phone call from a husband on the road, say, it likely will be an extension of the endless conversation they've had since they were married: updates, gossip, the day's plan. But a wife seven months pregnant who has just gotten two eternally wired boys—finally!—into bed, a big-as-a-house wife who hasn't had a good night's sleep in months, has a right to a certain theatricality, and if she has gathered three girlfriends for a "Fright Night" and the phone rings, well, who can blame her for exaggerating for effect? The fact is, everyone knows the difference between true exasperation and the mock version that means "You see how much my husband needs me? He's hard at work, surrounded by men who forget their wives once they're on the road, and he still can't help but call."

At 9:20 p.m. on the night of July 22, Mandy Coolbaugh was standing in her kitchen when her cell phone began to ring. She glanced at it, saw the keypad screen identifying Mike as the caller. She put the phone to her ear and, with a glance at her girlfriends and a half-smile, adopted that put-upon tone and said, "Mike, you know I have people over here. . . . What do you *want?*"

And it's no small thing that later, even amid her own fears about money and the new baby and her own confusing shift to the head of the family, Mandy would remember that tone and feel guilty about it. After all, those two sentences stand as the line between past and future, the last moment he was still fully alive in their house on Apricot Drive; these were the last words she meant to say to Mike, the man she adored, before the earthquake hit. It irks her that she couldn't, then, just have been *nicer.* Of course, you can call Mandy's added bit of regret a part of fate's cool meanness. But for those who know it best, that extra twist of the knife seemed almost typical of baseball's cruel hand. Mike Coolbaugh loved baseball and his wife, and now she picked up the phone, frazzled. "This game will step on your neck and keep stepping on it," Astros second baseman Chris Burke says. "But something like this is almost too much to take."

Because it wasn't Mike, who would've understood that tone, on the other end of the phone. It was Austin O'Shea. He had Mike's cell phone, and after watching them roll Mike's body into the emergency room at Baptist Health Medical Center in North Little Rock, after signing a few papers at Admitting, he had pushed "Send" to see the last number Mike had called. The nickname "Gorgeous" flashed up, and he knew, and he hit "Send" again.

When she heard O'Shea's voice, Mandy felt a small flash of fear. Mike always called himself with bad news. "What happened?" she said.

RIGHT Mike Coolbaugh, age two, at home in Binghamton, New York. *(Courtesy of the Coolbaugh family)*

TOP Mike and his mother, Mary Lu, celebrating his fourth birthday. *(Courtesy of the Coolbaugh family)*

RIGHT Mike on the family trampoline in San Antonio, 1983. *(Courtesy of the Coolbaugh family)*

RIGHT Mike, senior quarterback at Roosevelt High School in San Antonio, 1989. *(Courtesy of the Coolbaugh family)*

BELOW Scott; their father, Bob; and Mike Coolbaugh in San Antonio, circa 1990. *(Courtesy of the Coolbaugh family)*

LEFT Mike hits his first major league home run, July 17, 2001. "The most beautiful thing I have ever seen," Bob said. *(AP Images/Morry Gash)*

BELOW Mike, during his Rookie League season with the Blue Jays affiliate in Medicine Hat, Alberta, 1990. *(Ronald C. Modra/Sports Illustrated)*

LEFT Eight-year-old Tino Sanchez, a member of Yauco's Coqui select team. The team won the 1987 Puerto Rican championship and was rewarded with a trip to Disney World. *(Courtesy of the Sanchez family)* RIGHT Thirteen-year-old Tinito in the dugout with his dad and manager, Tino Sr., representing Yauco at the 1992 Junior League World Series in Taylor, Michigan. *(Courtesy of the Sanchez family)* BELOW Tino, sixteen, hitting for Cabo Rojo in the American Legion summer league. *(Courtesy of the Sanchez family)*

Tino, a member of the Single-A Asheville Tourists during the 2000 season, and family. *Clockwise from left to right:* Sister, Hilda Rosa; Tino Sr.; Tino; mother, Rosa Julia Rivera; niece, Priscila Ayala; and nephew, Tony Ayala. In the lower right corner is the son of Tourists manager Joe Mikulik.
(Courtesy of the Sanchez family)

LEFT Tulsa Drillers pitcher Jon Asahina and pitching coach Bo McLaughlin, both victims of a batted ball, August 2007. *(Darren Carroll/Sports Illustrated)*
RIGHT Tino Sanchez, after his return to Tulsa, August 2007. Mike's Drillers jersey hangs behind him. *(Darren Carroll/Sports Illustrated)*

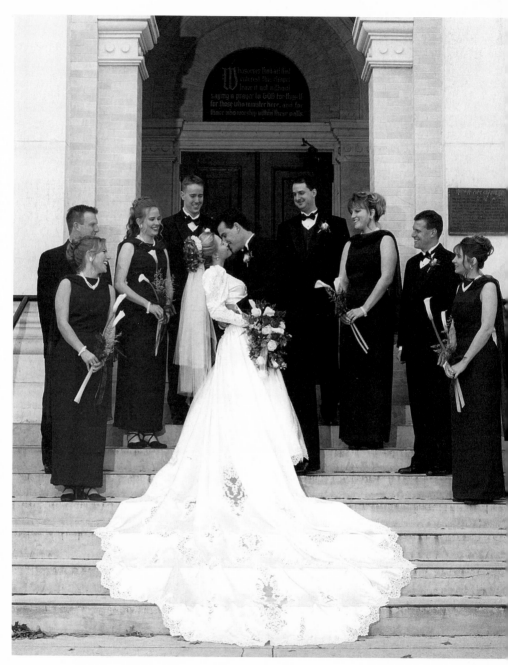

Mike and Mandy's wedding, January 22, 2000. Scott, the best man, stands to the far left, behind Mandy's sister and maid of honor, Katie. "I don't know anybody who wouldn't envy what they had," Katie says.

(Beverly Adams Photography/Courtesy of Mandy Coolbaugh)

ABOVE Mike, Mandy, and Jake, San Antonio, Christmas, 2003. *(Courtesy of Lisa Coolbaugh-Smith)*

RIGHT Mike and Joey at Busch Stadium in St. Louis, 2002. *(Courtesy of Lisa Coolbaugh-Smith)*

BELOW Jake, Mandy, Joey, and Mike, Christmas, 2006. *(Courtesy of Lisa Coolbaugh-Smith)*

RIGHT Joey and Jake throw out the first pitch in Denver, October 6, 2007. (Darren Carroll/Sports Illustrated)

BELOW Joey, Mandy, and Jake, in the boys' bedroom in San Antonio, August 2007. (Darren Carroll/ Sports Illustrated)

RIGHT Mandy and baby Anne Michael, one week old, November 2007. (Courtesy of Mandy Coolbaugh)

"Mike's been hit by a ball on the field, he's unconscious, we've taken him by ambulance to the hospital," O'Shea said. Mandy's voice began to break, so he rushed on. Mike's pulse had been pretty strong in the ambulance, and O'Shea felt optimistic. But a part of him also didn't feel right. If there was to be a crushing phone call, O'Shea didn't want Mandy to receive it unprepared. "He's all right right now," O'Shea said. "He's under good care. I just wanted to let you know."

"How bad is it?" she said. "Do I need to come up there?"

"Yes," O'Shea said. "You probably need to come up here. But don't leave yet. Be calm until we know what's going on. I'll call back as soon as I know."

"I'm putting the kids in the car. It'll take me ten hours, but I'll be there."

They hung up. The movie was forgotten, of course, and Mandy never did watch it: *Premonition,* with Sandra Bullock. It's about a woman whose husband dies in an accident. She spends the movie shuttling between past and present, trying to save his life.

Mandy dialed Mary Lu and Bob, said that Mike had been hit; she'd be leaving for Little Rock soon. "Let me figure this out," Mary Lu said. "I'll call you right back." The two hung up. *Okay,* Mandy thought. *Mike's hurt badly, but he's always pulled through. We can do this: Got to get the kids up. God's not going to let anything bad happen to us.*

That feeling didn't last. If she was going to be in a hospital for hours, she knew she'd have to look presentable; no more of the old shirts, Mike's castoffs, that she'd taken to wearing as her weight ballooned. Mandy went into her bedroom closet, found the only clean maternity dress she had, a black one, and laid it out on the bed. The color sent a chill through her stomach, and it spread out to her chest, her skin. *Please God.* . . . She never could bring herself to pack it.

After hanging up the phone with Mandy, Mary Lu Coolbaugh turned to her husband. "Mike's been hit," she said. "They're taking him to a hospital."

"Jeez," Bob said. "How do you get hit as a coach?"

"Well, we've got to go."

Lisa was visiting, and a quick plan jelled. Mary Lu called Mandy, told her they would come pick up her and the boys in an hour; she would drive in one car with Mandy, and Lisa would drive in another with Bob. Of course they'd done all this before, a sudden all-night road trip to go see Mike, but that Milwaukee jaunt had been pure anticipation, fun. Mary Lu started packing but it seemed senseless to hurry off without knowing more. Scott's team, the Frisco RoughRiders, had just finished up its Sunday night game across town against the San Antonio Missions. A bus was chuffing outside Wolff Stadium, waiting to take the RoughRiders back to their home outside Dallas. Mary Lu reached Scott on his cell phone.

"All we know is that he got hit," she said. "Can you find out from your trainer how bad he is, before we head out?"

The Frisco trainer, Jason Roberts, called O'Shea. Scott called Travelers general manager Pete Laven, and figured the fastest way to get to Little Rock was to ride back to Dallas, then hop in his car and drive there on his own. Scott boarded the team bus and sat in his customary seat in the second row, behind manager Dave Anderson. Word passed among the players that Mike had been hit, was in the hospital. The driver turned off the overhead lights, and they all sat quiet in the dark, only a few murmurs, as the bus pulled out and began winding its way through the streets of San Antonio, their boyhood town, all the way to Highway 35.

At the hospital, O'Shea tried to get back to the emergency room for an update, and was told to wait. He dialed his two bosses with the Rockies, Marc Gustafson and the organization's rehabilitation co-ordinator, Scott Murayama, and was standing in the waiting room updating them when he heard a voice saying, "You can come back here now."

This is good news, O'Shea thought. He had been in baseball five years, had seen bad head injuries like Asahina's, had seen men knocked out at rodeos, saw a guy fall off a scissor lift, 40 feet high, at Colorado State and survive. "Working sports, we're trained and prepared for emergency situations, but I've seen several and everything goes smoothly: You stabilize them, the ambulance gets there, they get 'em to the hospital," O'Shea says. "They fix them. That's the way it goes. They don't die."

O'Shea walked through the doors, expecting nurses, bustling activity. But there was only one man, the neurologist on duty.

"There's nothing we can do," the doctor told O'Shea. "He was dead the moment the ball struck him."

The words didn't seem right. He had been in the ambulance. O'Shea tried batting them away; his mind felt thick suddenly, frozen. "No," he said. "No, we came in here and his heart was beating, his chest was rising, his pulse . . ."

The doctor explained that it's not uncommon: What O'Shea saw were the last faint signals of a system shutting down. The impact of the ball crushed Mike's left vertebral artery—which carries blood from the spinal column to the back of the skull—against the left first cervical vertebra, at the base of his skull. Squeezed almost literally between a rock and a hard place, the artery burst, cutting off the blood supply to the brain and to the vision and balance center in the brain stem, where controls for breathing and heart rate and all reflexes reside. There was no stopping it.

In the hospital, Mike had been pronounced dead at 9:47 p.m. But the official time of death was set at 8:53 p.m., when the ball first struck. "He may have heard the crack of the bat, but that's it," says Mark Malcolm, the Pulaski County coroner at the time. "I think he had no knowledge." Still, explicable as the accident might be, even medical people describe it as "a freak," a one-time occurrence with few analogues. The violence of the moment shifted any analysis from pure diagnosis to the edge of criminal forensics. As Dr. Bryan puts it, "You just can't imagine something like this happening. Strange physics about forces are dispelled when there's impact upon a solid object with a soft center, and it's more of a science of ballistics and very small odds and probabilities than anything we can say is medical." Translation, according to Malcolm: "Man, that's a one-in-bazillion chance. A half a hair in either direction and it wouldn't have killed him."

O'Shea heard the doctor speaking, but a feeling beyond shock had taken hold, making the words near worthless. It was a nightmare, one of those marked by a nearing menace while your arms are pinned and you're helpless to stop it. Who was he? Austin O'Shea, minor league baseball trainer from Red Lodge, Montana, missing suddenly the life on his family's ranch, the calmness there, his brothers and parents. Now he had this awful information; now he knew what almost no one else in Little Rock, San Antonio, Dickey-Stephens Park, Colorado, Binghamton, or anywhere else knew. Worse: He was going to have to tell them.

"Doc, I don't know what to do," O'Shea said. "I'm going to have to call his wife. She doesn't know."

He returned to the waiting room, sat down. His phone burbled with calls from Tino, Stu, Mandy, Scott Coolbaugh. He stood up, went to the desk. "Can I go back there with Mike for a little bit?" he asked.

He went back to the body. He took Mike's hand, stood by him for a while, murmuring more empty words to the still and silent face. He said goodbye. The first wave of guilt washed over him.

"It's my responsibility to take care of these guys," O'Shea says, voice cracking, baseball cap twisted in his hands, 11 months later. "It really is. I'm the only trainer here. Whatever problem they have—whether it's medical, personal, money—it seems like I'm the guy. I take care of them. I take care of everything they need and I take pride in that. To not be able to help somebody?" O'Shea goes silent for 15 seconds, crying in the visitors' dugout at Dickey-Stephens Park. "I never thought I'd work again," he says finally. "I told everybody, I told my parents: No way I'm ever going to put myself in a situation again where I'm *the* guy."

After a few minutes, then, he left Mike's body behind, found the attending emergency room doctor. "Sir," he told the man, "I'm not ready to call Mandy Coolbaugh right now or his brother, Scott. I can't call the family and say their husband or son is dead." And for the second time that night O'Shea felt like he'd let everyone down.

"I guess I wasn't strong enough to do that," O'Shea says. "He did it for me."

Twenty-one minutes after the hit, at 9:14 p.m., Neely spoke into his microphone. "This game will not continue," he told his listeners, voice steady against the fading hiss and hum of Dickey-Stephens Park. "There will be no more baseball here tonight." The players were walking slowly off the field when Neely went to his final break. On came ads for phone service and the electric company, flanking the self-promotion common to American sports-talk stations. "The BUZZ! Sports Network. . . . Feel the POWER of sports! . . . Total Sports Coverage. AM 1430: The BUZZ! If you live sports . . . If you breathe sports. . . . The BUZZ! Sports Network has your back. The BUZZ! Feel the power of sports!"

In the Drillers clubhouse, Stu told the players to stay calm, be strong; everything would be all right. The Travelers filed in, and both teams prayed for Mike and his family together. Teammates walked past Tino whispering don't worry, giving a squeeze, watching him sideways. Neely returned to the air, imploring anyone listening from the Coolbaugh family to call in, asking for listeners to lend their thoughts and prayers to Mike. Finally, with a terse "Good night from North Little Rock," he signed off. The stands were nearly empty.

Neely packed up his mics, mixer board, and cords for the seven-hour trip to Wichita. He took the elevator one flight down, the wheels of his bag rolling scratchily over the rough concourse floor. He caught up there with Laven, talking until the Travs GM got a call on his cell phone from Scott Coolbaugh. Laven told Scott what he knew: There's still a pulse, Baptist Health Medical Center. Neely moved on down to the clubhouse, pushed open the door, and walked past the milling players. In his office, Stu Cole was on the phone. It was Austin O'Shea, making his first tentative call from the hospital.

"Stu," O'Shea said. "You need to come over here, please."

"Why?" Cole answered. "What's going on? Is he all right?"

"Stu, just . . . Would you just please come over here?"

"Is he all right?"

"Please come over here."

"Is he all right?"

"Stu. He's gone."

"Okay, I'm coming over," Cole said, hanging up just as Neely walked into the office. Bo McLaughlin, Marv Foley, and Tyler Christiansen stood around Stu Cole's desk. "Mike . . . He's died," Cole said.

It was close to 9:50 p.m. Cole asked for a prayer, and stood. The other men in the room dropped to one knee or two. All bent their heads, and for what seemed forever the tiny room went silent. Cole spoke at last. "Don't tell the players until I get back from the hospital," he said.

Getaway day has a different set of rules, even more so when the trip ahead is a long one. The plan for Wichita had the bus rolling in there by dawn, so the Drillers had ordered food through the Arkansas clubhouse attendant, a spread usually laid out on a table for everyone to swarm before they shower and dress. The experienced clubbie, though, knows how quickly players can devour a catered tray, and makes allowances for the guys in charge. In Little Rock that night, he dished out individual plates for each coach and left them in front of their lockers. The coaches' dressing room opens off the visiting manager's office; the stunned men filed out of Cole's office to get dressed. In the corner, a flimsy plate sat untouched on the stool before Mike's dangling clothes. A paper napkin covered the food, its underside soaking up the greasy vapor, the stains already grown cold and hard. Suddenly, the players heard something large—a chair, maybe?—crash against a wall in Cole's office.

Neely, the ultimate team observer, now found himself thrust into the action. He knew it was important to get the news to the right people, but not to jeopardize Cole's hope of informing Mike's wife and family first. Neely told Elson by phone, then hurried through the clubhouse with head down to tell Valentine and Laven in person. He told Valentine to call the Wichita front office, to call Texas League president Tom Kayser, and tell them both that the Drillers would not be playing in Wichita Monday night. "We need to go home," he said. The Travs GM wondered if Neely might want to call Scott and tell him, too, and with that Neely knew he had taken on too much. He demurred, went back through the Drillers clubhouse. Some Drillers asked him what he knew. "I can't say anything," Neely repeated, and he realized then that he couldn't bear to hear Cole say those words and watch the players' faces. He had to get out now.

He walked out into the parking lot, the sweet night air. Neely had arranged to drive back to Tulsa with his friend Guy, a Drillers season-ticket holder who somehow could afford the time and money to take in half the Tulsa road games. Now as he approached the car, Neely saw Tino Sanchez speaking with Guy. He heard Tino describing the look on Mike's face. "You heard anything?" Tino said.

"No," Neely lied. "I haven't heard anything."

More than 30 minutes passed after the departures of Cole and Foley. In the meantime, Sanchez called his wife, in Yauco, so much earlier than normal that at first Angie thought he had been released. "No," Tino told her. "It's way worse than that." Tino hung up, asking every teammate who'd just put down a phone or walked through a door if they had any news, a part of him believing that, maybe, all those prayers would work, a miracle might occur. He kept tapping in O'Shea's and Cole's cell phone numbers, but with each passing minute and each unanswered ring, the lie he'd been telling himself dissolved away. *It's bad*, Tino thought. *Something's really wrong.*

He was standing in the street outside the clubhouse, under a hazy spotlight, when Cole and O'Shea and Foley came back. Tino walked toward them. Cole glanced up, saw who it was, and moved past. O'Shea didn't speak. A voice said, "Just come inside." Tino followed them in with it all building inside him now, a fear of the pain to come. Cole walked inside the clubhouse and went into a bathroom and shut the door. *Oh, please don't*, Tino begged again.

Cole emerged. The players gathered. "The doctors did everything they could," Cole said. "But Mike didn't make it."

Shock ricocheted from face to face, leaving behind tears, bowed heads, clenched fists. Tino began flailing, moaning, punching walls and lockers and the very air. He tried to take a step or two to escape, only to find himself dropping to the ground. "I couldn't stop myself," he says. "I went down." He pounded his right fist into the floor, breaking a bone. He tried to catch his breath, gave up. It felt like drowning.

At 10:17 p.m., Mandy's cell phone rang again, this time with a Little Rock exchange flashing in the lighted little window. A voice she didn't know was saying the words, the only way now, bluntly, no mitigating phrases, words raining down like hail: "CPR . . . Your husband . . . He didn't make it." After that, words lost all power and weight, fluttering down and falling away. The house became a wash of colors, blurred, grotesque. The night went on, clocks kept moving, people went in and out the front door. She heard her heart pounding in her ears, heard these voices shifting and shocked and whispering, and Mandy let her boys sleep on because why not give them one last good night of sleep?

Scott's cell phone rang. All talk stopped on the bus, all the ballplayers and coaches and staffers froze. He put the phone to his left ear and a voice on the phone told him his brother was dead, and Scott leaned forward into his hands and wept. He tried to keep it muffled, the sound of a grown man crying. But everybody could hear his misery amid the grinding gears, the hum of rubber on pavement.

The manager, Dave Anderson, stood and pivoted into the seat beside Scott, placing his right arm over the bent back. He didn't move the rest of the ride. No one played cards. No movie was shown on the overhead TVs. Scott cried most of the way, stopping long enough to mark the surrealness of the circumstance, the ridiculous odds against. Scott had been coaching or managing for six years, and only once in that time had a ball hit him: He had been coaching third, preoccupied with his base runner for a split second when a line foul ball crashed into his hip. "No way I could've gotten out of the way," he says. But to die from such a thing? At 35?

Scott had heard stories, of course, about athletes and dumb drinking high schoolers and kids in war zones dying young. But in his bones? Death for a Coolbaugh wasn't this random; death was something that happened when you were wrinkled and at home, surrounded by loving faces. Mike hadn't been driving, hadn't been doing drugs or drinking. Mike was alone on a baseball field, healthy as sin, working a game. "*How?*" Scott kept asking himself. "How can this happen? You play this game, you study the history of this game, you see people getting out of the way of balls. Of course there's some serious injuries that come of it, but here's a guy who played third base all his life, hot corner, and so many scenarios run through your mind: Where was he standing? Where was he looking? Was he not watching the hitter? Was he watching the base runner? Who was pitching? What was the count?"

But each time Scott tried to write it off as a mystery, putting the incident into a compartment in his mind where he could keep it controlled, he would bump up against the other unavoidable conclusion: Here it was, the last and worst war story you ever heard, the final sad proof of how snakebit Mike had been his whole life; how, yes, the game had screwed him beyond all the millions of screwings it had perpetrated on unsuspecting ballplayers for the last 130 years. And Scott would find himself crying all over again.

S. L. PRICE

The trip took five hours. He sat looking out the bus window as it headed north, watching the lights of New Braunfels, San Marcos, and Waco hurtle by, all the lights of cars and houses and businesses filled with people. Scott called his wife, Susan. "He's gone," he said. Scott knew his mother was waiting to hear from him, but he just couldn't take that right now; could she call Mary Lu and talk with her, please?

Susan dialed the number. By then, Bob and Mary Lu and Lisa had finished filling their suitcases, dopp kits, and makeup bags and anything else they could think of; the cars were packed and ready. "We waited and waited and waited," Mary Lu says. When she heard Susan's voice on the phone at first, it was puzzling. Mary Lu expected Mandy, or Scott. Susan tried, but there's no soft way to tell a mother such news. "I'm sorry," she said. Mike was dead. Killed by a baseball. Her son was dead.

Bob was waiting, too, expected some kind of update as soon as Mary Lu hung up. But now she was standing, phone in hand, Susan still there, and the sound of her was like nothing he'd ever heard.

"She was screaming," Bob Coolbaugh says. "Holy shit."

An hour north, it was another baseball birthday for Al LaMacchia. Cake? Candles? He turned 86 on July 22, and celebrated the way he had for near 50 years: at a ballpark with his wife, Annie, watching the talent at a Triple-A game in Round Rock. He had always said that, short of playing, nothing can beat the life of a scout. As long as he can drive, as long as his eyes and memory hold, as long as a team like the

Los Angeles Dodgers is happy to pay him, LaMacchia couldn't imagine anything better than sitting behind home plate.

Late in Round Rock's 5–1 loss to Oklahoma, someone who knew Al's connection to Mike Coolbaugh walked down to him and said that Mike had been killed, hit by a foul ball in Little Rock. Later Al would say that maybe God wanted it that way, Mike dying on a baseball field, deep in the game he loved; why else would that coaching job have ever come open? But at the time, it felt like one final slap. The players he'd signed and liked, they all felt like sons, but Mike was more than that—Al's judgment ignored, a battle lost. LaMacchia had been wrong about other prospects, and was proud to say that, yes, he could always admit it. But not Coolbaugh. All the old arguments, the old names, came streaming back then, as the game went on around him: *Leper . . . Weinke . . . Los Barrios. . . . Pushing him, my ass!* His eyes filled with tears.

"I never gave up on him," LaMacchia says. "To this day, I've never said I was wrong on Mike Coolbaugh. He never got the chance."

The great thing about baseball, fans say, is that at any game you can see a play, a mistake, a hit that you've never seen before. Now, after eight decades, came a first for those who know Al LaMacchia. A game was happening right in front of him and he lost all track of it—the score, the runners, the pitches.

Kid loves the game and it kills him. . . .

Hard to look at it any other way. LaMacchia sat there on his birthday, sagging under the sudden weight. "It killed me," he says. The old scout didn't feel like baseball anymore that night. He needed to get home.

MONDAY MORNING, Mandy Coolbaugh got up before the sun. She had slept a few hours, maybe, and woke for good when the thought hit her: *Mike's dead?* She cried, moved into the living room, sat on the couch and stared out the back window, watching the air above the pool go from black to gray to bleary bright. A pair of cardinals kept flying away and coming back, flying away and coming back to the ledge outside, tapping the windowpane with their beaks. Mandy's father had stayed over. Soon he was awake too. Mandy turned on the computer and there it was, on her AOL homepage: *Mike . . . killed last night by a foul ball . . . Little Rock.* At 7 a.m. the first camera crew knocked on the front door, charged with the day's worst assignment. "Go out to the house at first light," someone in charge had suggested, "and ask the widow if she'd like to say a few words." Closing the door on people with a camera, Mandy knew she wouldn't be able to wait long.

The rest of the day, though, dissolved away. Somehow she ended up in bed, and people kept coming in, whispering. Mandy stared at the walls, the ceiling, through tears, the room with Mike's clothes, their wedding photo.

By the time Joey and Jake woke up on Tuesday, still oblivious, the house was bustling with nearby friends, people showing up from out of town. Mandy emerged in the morning. Mary Lu was there, and before she left, the two women took the boys back to the bedroom they share. The ceiling fan and light shaped like a baseball mitt: Mike had installed that. The personalized baseballs listing Joey and Jake's birth heights and weights, their dad's Milwaukee and St. Louis jerseys on the wall—Mike had wanted those in there, sending a message that even a baby boy would pick up with every breath: *You were born into a baseball family. Work hard like Daddy, and someday maybe you can make the big leagues, too.*

Mandy knew they knew what dying was, or at least had some idea; Mike's insistence on church each Sunday was a big help now. "Daddy's been hurt," Mandy told her sons. "And he's gone up to heaven." She told of how the ball had hit him during a game and how God had taken him away, watching their faces shift with the news, confusion and fear warding off the impact, and it did her some good to see that the hurt wasn't falling on them all at once, like a rock from the sky. Besides, there were uncles in the house, ready to play baseball.

And Mike would be impressed to know that, with Joey anyway, somehow the key minor league lesson had been absorbed. It is, after all, the hard fact of baseball that one man's misfortune is another man's chance, that even your best friend's release may well present you with your best shot. So you mourn, yes; you swallow the bad news and watch your buddy slam his equipment into his dust-caked bag, but then you head to the field and forget it because the only way to survive is to "respect the game" even more when it hurts you, to attack each ball with a fierce kind of love, as if baseball never has and never could do anyone wrong. So when she finished and the room went quiet and Joey asked his first question, it hardly came as shock. Mandy knew her husband, and she knows her sons.

"Well," Joey said, "if Daddy's up in heaven, can I play with his bats?"

For two nights and days, Tino didn't sleep. He'd always prided himself on being tough, cool, mentally strong, but now it was as if a wall inside him had been breached, and all the different streams of emotion that he'd kept behind it, all the sadness and guilt and fear that he'd had under control, came rushing in. The bus rolled west out of Little Rock on I-40. He sent a text to his wife—*sorry for not calling. mike has died*—and turned off his phone. Teammates told him not to blame himself, knowing it was useless. "It doesn't matter what you say," says Drillers outfielder Matt Miller. "It's a burden he's going to have to live with the rest of his life."

On Monday afternoon, July 23, the players and coaches met at Drillers Stadium in Tulsa. The Rockies had brought in grief counselors, plus a minister from Tulsa and the Colorado team chaplain, and they all met together and Stu Cole spoke. When the manager said, "Mike will always be watching us," Tino broke and wept, and from then on found it hard to get right again. He went back to his apartment and decided he was quitting. He had no room in his mind for baseball, for hitting and strategy and pretending some game could matter more than breathing. His father dialed his cell phone more than a hundred times, panicking, finally reaching one of his teammates, Juan Morillo, and begging Tino to answer his phone. If not, Tino Sr. said, I'm coming there now. But his boy still wouldn't answer.

"I didn't want to hear anything," Tino says. "My head was about to explode. At some point I said to myself, *I can't take this. I just can't take it.* It was a continuous flashback in my mind, from the moment I met him to the moment that the ambulance took him away. All the time, my mind was . . . continuous flashback, back and forth, back and forth. And I was like, *How am I going to get through this?* and then the combination of *How is their family going to get through this? His wife. His wife. His wife. His sons, his children*—how are they *going to get through this? What are they thinking about me right now?"*

It wouldn't stop. The chaplain had told him it would be like this, that good and evil would battle inside him now and evil would be pushing him to do something rash, if only to stop the noise. And the thought, yes, would rise then: Maybe I should kill myself? But each time Tino would push that idea away: He had a wife, a baby coming, and he couldn't do that to them. But it was a fight nonetheless. For those two days Tino felt himself inching toward blackness. "Mike is dragging me," he told a friend. "He's taking me with him."

He answered the phone just once. Tino punched the button, and now P. J. Carey's soft voice was in his ear. They spoke for 30 minutes. P. J. wanted Tino to know: "This has nothing to do with baseball. This is life and death now, and it could've happened to Mike in a car, on a ladder. Accidents happen, and there was nothing to do to stop it. You are special. You're a good man. Don't blame yourself."

But, really, it was the warmth behind P. J.'s words that helped steel Tino's nerve. Because Carey's wife, Katherine, was ravaged by stage-4 lung cancer then, had been through 24 rounds of radiation and 6 full sessions of chemotherapy, and yet here P. J. was calling *him*, Tino, to make sure he was okay. "It was so good to hear his voice, knowing that his wife is going through a very bad situation, knowing that a human being is supporting, giving words to anther person while he's supposed to be getting those words himself," Tino says. "It's amazing what P. J. did, reaching out for me. He told me Katherine is doing better. He told me that Katherine is his hero. I was blessed that he called me."

The Rockies sent him home, told Tino to take his time, forever if necessary. Before leaving he wrote a letter to Mandy, and left it with Tommy Duenas to deliver at the funeral. On Tuesday, July 24, Tino flew to Yauco, career seemingly done, body and mind spent. One mean fact remained, and no amount of grace or kind words could change it. "Literally," he says, "I killed a human being."

That night in Wichita, July 24, the Drillers played their first game since Coolbaugh's death. The Coolbaugh family, Scott especially, said that's what Mike would have wanted, would've done: Play on. The team's radio broadcast went over the airwaves without commercial interruption, the buzz of the crowd providing the only breaks between Neely's play-by-play. Mike's jersey, number 29, hung in the dugout. In the top of the first inning, just after the national anthem, Cole turned to Asahina. "Jon," he said, "go coach first base." Asahina stepped out of the dugout and took Mike's place there. The Drillers came to bat. It was a strange place to be for a player, especially one who'd been hit himself, "but I wanted it," Asahina says.

Coolbaugh's death, the run for O'Shea's trainer's kit, the surreal coincidences that everyone kept whispering about—all of it combined to reinforce Asahina's new mind-set. He knew it seemed strange to his teammates for him to be out there; hell, it *was* strange, and he could feel the energy of everyone watching him, wondering how he would react. But it felt right. He could take it all in like no one else, from a cool remove, because he was almost sure that his own accident had laid the psychic groundwork for Mike's, that he was somehow being prepped for the hit and its aftermath. Hadn't he lived it all out once already, on that couch in Fresno? Hadn't he combed through all the implications? He would be the team's rock. Of course Cole picked him to coach first. Who better? How could it be any other way?

For the last two days now, some teammates had asked Asahina: *Do you feel lucky? That could've been you.* And maybe the old Jon would've answered, *Yes, wow, I feel like I dodged a bullet.* But not now. "Man," Asahina answered them, "that could've been *you*. That's the whole point. It could be anyone."

He found himself—and it would last for weeks, this feeling—operating in a state of hyperawareness. Everything seemed new: putting on his socks, pulling on his jersey, tugging down the brim of a baseball cap. Asahina tried to perform his every move deliberately, taking in "the holiness of every act: right now. When you lean over and get your water, when I unwrap my bubble gum," he said not long after. "When I chew my seeds, I make sure I spit each one out perfectly, but I'm not just making sure. I feel like slowing everything down." The idea made him oddly happy. He wondered if he was insane. But he couldn't help it; he was alive. So the Drillers came to the plate that night, one by one, and he bent his knees in the first base box and watched each ball like a hawk but not scared, never scared, and he gave advice to his teammates as they stood at first and watched the balls fly and thought, *This game, this life, is the greatest thing ever.* The Drillers hit a season-high five home runs. They won 12–6, took Mike's jersey onto the field with them to celebrate, touching it together. Asahina would be back on the mound soon. He was sure he was ready.

The questions came at the oddest times: How high is heaven? If Daddy's always looking down on us, can he see through the ceiling? The inner life of three- and four-year-old boys may well be complicated, but when filtered through a new toy—an ever-broadening vocabulary—it can come across as both wonderfully simple and unbearably direct. Mandy Coolbaugh has one of the world's great laughs, easily accessed and thick with joy, but any conversation now about Mike made her cry. Still, the boys needed to know, and who better to ask: Why? Where's Daddy now? Why? She'd try, but sometimes the answers just wouldn't come. It was one thing to have the words whirling in her own mind. But to hear a child ask, with wide eyes and a small voice, left her shattered.

Joey, the oldest, put on all of his dad's equipment that his little body could handle: T-shirts, spikes, gloves. Too quickly, the questions switched from ethereal to earthy: There had been an autopsy on Monday, and that same day people called her asking for Mike's organs, his eyes, his skin. Mike had never checked that box on his driver's license. If she had been with him for his last moments in Little Rock, maybe she would've said yes. But Mike had always said to her: *If I'm in a coma or on life-support, I want to live. Make sure that I'm gone before they do anything.* But now the autopsy had come and gone: She hadn't made sure. She had let him down. Mandy told them all no. "I wanted all of him to come back to me," she says.

And she wanted her Mike, no funereal makeup, no prettying—especially where the ball had struck. Mandy had to call three people in Little Rock, the ones handling the body, before her message got through. "Send Mike to me exactly as he was. I don't want you to clean him up." She needed to study him raw, "to understand," she says, "what his last minute was like." The coroners and embalmers did as told. The body arrived in San Antonio on Wednesday, July 25. Mandy went to see it at the funeral home, Porter Loring Mortuary, spent the afternoon there with Mary Lu and Mike's sister Lisa. She walked into a cool room and there he lay, still in a scanty hospital gown. The coroner in Little Rock had assured her that Mike had died instantly and tutored her in how to look for clues: If he had been alive after the ball hit, his struggle would be written out on the body, made indelible by rigor mortis—tightened muscles, clenched fists, a set jaw. But Mike looked so relaxed. The pain he had feared those last months, all those questions about her mom's death—none of it seemed evident in his face. Mandy reached out. She studied his toes, his hair, his eyebrows. She stared at the left side of his neck, the imprint of baseball seams in his skin.

Mike's chest was raised, swollen from the autopsy. She put her hand under the gown, up on his chest. "I had to feel," she says. "I had to know what they did to him." Her voice breaks at the memory, then drops to a whisper, then rises again. "It crushed me to feel where they cut him open . . . because I could feel it," she says. It wasn't a clean scar, more a crevice in the true center of him, deep and final. She placed her fingers there. "I had to know," she says.

She decided on an open casket for Sunday, the viewing. She wanted the boys to see Daddy's body. She didn't want them to grow up wondering.

In the days after, Mandy tried being strong. Friends, family, strangers: Everyone had a theory on what it all meant, what *Mike* meant, and sometimes in the process of teasing them out all the ideas got tangled. Fellow lifers tapped into his long tenure, and identified.

"His love for the game of baseball is what eventually killed him," says Jackie Moore, Mike's manager in Round Rock. "You love it so much and it gets in your blood, and you can't get it out. But in most cases in professional baseball you end up disappointed. I've had so many people tell me—and I'm the luckiest person in the world, this is my fifty-first year in baseball—'I'd give anything to change spots with you.' And I wouldn't change spots with anybody, but I'm thinking to myself, *There's a lot more behind it than you realize.*

"I was the same type player as Mike: My dream for as long as I can remember was to be a big league baseball player. You love it so much it's tough to give it up. I know Mike tried. But obviously he couldn't stay away from baseball and when he came back, it cost him his life. And what is a mystery to me more than anything: Here's a third base-man who all his career had balls hit at him, from all directions and in all forms. He was tuned to get out of the way or to catch the balls. It had to be a situation where he just wasn't looking. Seventeen years of having balls hit at you in all forms and ways and this happens? I just can't justify that in my mind."

Mandy heard that theory, and dismissed it. She remembered Mike all but chasing her back behind the screen at Round Rock, always so nervous about the danger. That led her down one path. "When people say he was turned the wrong way, I just can't believe it," she says. "God plucked him. There's no way he would've let a foul ball kill him."

But then came moments when her faith seeped away. She'd put on the memorial DVD featuring photos and videos and Mike's favorite songs, and she'd sit through the torment of it and identify the images to strangers as they faded in and out: Mike with his grandfather, Mike and Mandy mugging in a photo booth, Mike and Mandy dancing at their wedding, that last family gathering, Mike walking in the surf with his sons. "Why would God want this to happen to the kids?" she'd ask. "I have no doubt it would've been easier for everybody if it had been me instead of him, because Mike would know where to go from here. He would know what to do."

No real answers came, of course. Tributes from Yankees manager Joe Torre, from Mike's former coaches and former teammates poured over the newswires; old friends e-mailed and called; major leaguers donated cash; minor league teams and leagues reported collecting more than $170,000 for the family—much of it in $1 and $5 bills—from fans, minor league players, strangers. The Drillers retired his jersey. The Windcrest water tower, lit up after every Roosevelt High football win, glowed in Mike's honor the night of his funeral. Maybe all that was a clue. "If he went out any other way, would he have gotten all the respect he has from this?" Mandy says. "If he was in a car crash? By dying on the field, he did."

But that outpouring didn't come solely because of the accident's freakish nature. It wasn't because everybody knew Mike. It was because everybody *was* a Mike or knew a Mike: Coolbaugh had played for so many organizations that, for many, he'd become emblematic of the sport's arbitrary nature, the thin line between perceived success and failure. More than that, during a summer in which one oversized San Francisco Giants slugger broke the all-time home run record while demonstrating just how remote and unlikable a rich athlete could be, Mike's death provided a way for fans and players alike to fully access baseball again, to *feel* what the game is—if only for one mournful moment—at its core.

"He was just a blue-collar individual, out there trying to make a daily living," Scott says. "When you hear stories about Barry Bonds or the big-name player, nobody can relate to that. He doesn't know what it's like to wake up each morning and go out and make concrete."

Still, if Mike's work was the equivalent of working construction, even alive he was a cautionary tale for those who make it to the top of the high-rise. Big leaguers know better than anyone that one broken wrist could've derailed their careers, too, and they respected and feared what Mike stood for. "This baseball game will break our heart," Colorado outfielder Willy Taveras said when he heard the news, and in the end that's what Mike's death represented: heartbreak. He was the guy who always gets a flat tire on the way to a job interview, the one who can never catch a break. He *was* minor league baseball, and if no one grew up wanting to be that, if few wanted to pay to see or televise that, the cold fact of life is that the minor leagues is where most of us live. We aren't going to be stars. We aren't going to make millions. If we're lucky, we might be fortunate enough to discover our own talent; if we're even luckier we might get paid to exercise it. Maybe we'll get a few days to take it to the highest level. Maybe we'll be able to step backstage with the greats for a month or two. But eventually we will sink back, most of us, because we're just not good enough. If we're truly fortunate, though, there will be a partner who cares and a family waiting to cushion the fall.

"Man, I'm so unlucky," Mike would say in his worst moments, puzzled by the "black cloud" that hovered over his career. But looking at his boys and Mandy and, yes, at a job that many American men would gladly seize, missed opportunities and all, his family never let that notion stand. "Mike," his sister Lisa Coolbaugh-Smith would say, "you're so lucky you don't even realize it."

But he did, really. That's why so many of his peers and siblings would remark on how he'd always be holding Joey and Jake, taking them with him on the most routine errand, using his earned clout, his veteran's dispensation, to get the rules loosened so the boys could run about on the clubhouse floor, the field. Coolbaugh knew, and that's one reason he was so desperate to get a coaching job: Joey and Jake wanted to see him in uniform again. It was spring, and the boys wanted to go to a ballpark and run. Mike had raised them to love the game. He needed to work, of course, needed the medical benefits. But he also wanted to keep that flame alive.

On July 30, the funeral was held at Holy Spirit Catholic Church in San Antonio. Some 700 mourners came, including Rockies vice-president Dan O'Dowd, Astros second baseman Chris Burke, and Texas League president Tom Kayser. The Drillers flew down from Little Rock, courtesy of American Airlines and a free memorial charter: Flight No. 29. The umpiring crew that worked Mike's last game drove all night— 633 miles down I-35—from their posting the night before in Wichita. There wasn't an argument: Funneman had made it clear that they'd be going to the funeral and directed his crew to buy new suits during the Wichita series; he found his in a Men's Wearhouse. Funneman wasn't just looking for closure. This was a tip of the mask, lifer to lifer. "We had to pay him that respect," he says. "We had to go."

Jay Maldonado, the teammate from Roosevelt, Hagerstown, and every spring since, was there. "Mike was home for me, and I was home for him," Maldonado says. "That was my best friend and I should've protected him. The smirk on his face, when I saw it at the funeral? I can tell you exactly what was coming out of his mouth: *This is fucking horseshit.*

"You know, people say what they want. Yeah, his life was baseball, but his plan was: Play or coach a couple more years, make some money, finish school, Mandy can go back to work. He had a plan for everything. That's what bugs me most: I know this dude's whole future. I know what he wanted out of life, and he got fucking cheated. I got cheated. Mandy got cheated. Everybody got cheated."

Mandy and Mary Lu and Joey and Jacob placed roses in the casket. Before the service began, some men came and lowered the lid and Mary Lu watched in panicked horror and her chest filled too fast and she broke. "I didn't know they were going to do that," she says. "You can't close the casket in front of your mother. So . . . it ended for me right there. They closed it. And that was the end."

Outside, they loaded the casket into a silver hearse with a black vinyl roof, and the hot Texas light shone in the highlights of Mandy's blond hair. The Cadillac's back door shut with a thud and a click, and three-year-old Jake put his hand on the back of the car as if to stop it. "Mommy," he said. "I want to go with Daddy."

Mandy had her hand out, too. Then the car rolled away slowly toward the fire where they would burn Mike's remains, and his wife and sons were left with the rest of that day and all the days after.

9

BACK AT FIRST

That afternoon, Tino was at a clinic in Ponce, Puerto Rico. Angie's belly had gotten huge with their daughter, 39 weeks and counting, and now the doctor was trying to induce the baby to be born. He knew the funeral was being held in San Antonio just then, and as the doctor put in the IV and measured the cervix and said, 'Try pushing a little more,' the expectant father tried getting into the spirit. But Tino kept thinking of Mike, his family. He wondered if Mandy, pregnant too, ever got his letter. He watched Angie struggle.

His wife wanted the baby, now, but her motives didn't center just on ending the pregnancy. Tino had been home eight days, and different, far quieter than the family had ever known him. "I knew he was suffering," Angie says. "But I didn't know how to start talking about it." For days, his dad would walk by his room, the closed door, and hear weeping. Finally he passed a crisis point; his parents and sister and wife could tell the moment Tinito drove across the island with them up to Yabucoa, east of San Juan, where his nephew Tony was playing in a Little League tournament. The coaches there asked for

Tinito's help, and he went on the field, and hit fungoes and clapped his hands; he didn't shy away from baseball. Everyone watched. They figured he might just make it.

But Angie was scared. She didn't like the idea of Tino being alone, and already he was making noises about going back to rejoin his team. If she could just have the baby, she thought, if he could just see his daughter born, maybe Tino would be soothed and stay home for good. Wasn't he going to retire anyway? The season was almost over. Why go back? So the doctors gave her the Pitocin and poked and prodded. But the cervix wouldn't dilate. The baby wouldn't budge. The doctor said she'd have to wait. And Tino faced another guilty night.

His face. Why did he go up that first base line? Why did God want him to see Mike's expression, to witness that moment? Why does He bring it back to him still? Tino prayed whenever that vision appeared in his mind, but the calm didn't last. "My first thought is to look for an answer," Tino says. "Which I don't think I'm ever going to find."

One thing he was sure of, though: He was going back. Tino knew it made no sense. Yauco was home and he'd already told his dad that he was finished with the game. Yauco was filled with family and friends saying, *Come on, Tino, it wasn't your fault.* He could stay forever and be the town's baseball king, and maybe once in a while someone would whisper or laugh about his lethal bat, but so what? Here they knew him. Here he was loved. Still . . . there was that thing he had been taught: *Respect the game.* The Rockies had taken him back three times over his career, forgiven him his "greenies" bust and the ball he'd popped in Clint Hurdle's face. His team needed him, even if everyone there said to stay away as long as necessary. But the season wasn't over. There were three weeks left, a playoff push to make. "It was his job," Angie says. "He had to finish the job."

They tried to induce one more time the following week, but the baby stayed put. Angie's friends told her: "Don't let him go. Keep him here." She said nothing. He booked a flight. "I had to," Tino says. "I had to give back the support my teammates and the organization gave to me. Simple as that: I *have* to go back."

He got on a plane on August 7, flew from Yauco to San Juan to Dallas to Tulsa, then rode the bus with the team back down to the Dallas suburb of Frisco. Still, he burrowed down so deep in his seat, some teammates didn't know he had returned. Most hadn't known if Tino was ever coming back, not until the moment when they saw him dressing in the clubhouse the next day.

He walked onto the field at Dr Pepper Ballpark, and it all felt wonderfully, stickily familiar: another sun-blasted Texas League afternoon, 98 degrees in the shade. Tino knew the place. He had been there with the rest of the Drillers, in fact, when the stadium officially opened on April 3, 2003, and instantly became one of the slickest models in the ongoing minor league stadium boom. Baseball, with its built-in family appeal, might be Dr Pepper's centerpiece, but the place is sold year-round more as a community center, available for wedding receptions, corporate events, and church services. The building lacks whatever old-timers mean when they mention "character," but players like it. Dr Pepper is new. New equipment makes even the lowest busher feel valued.

A slight breeze stirred the grass, the dust, promising a cool that never came. The Frisco RoughRiders were taking batting practice. On the mound was Frisco's hitting coach, Scott Coolbaugh, beefy, sweat staining his t-shirt a deeper gray, grooving pitch after pitch. The sun pounded down; Scott wore a pair of giant chromed sunglasses, Elvis circa 1972. Scott had just rejoined the RoughRiders himself, after ten games away, when they played in San Antonio the previous weekend. He looked relaxed.

But it had been a battle. The day before Mike's funeral, Scott had told Mary Lu that he wasn't sure how he could return to baseball.

"I don't know if I can go on, Mom," he said. "I can't go on."

Mary Lu was stunned, and not only because Scott usually kept his own counsel. She brought up Scott's son, 13-year-old Tyler, playing on a select baseball team in the midst of the playoffs. "Well, what'd you tell him?" she replied. "You told him to stay and play because Mike would've wanted that. So how can you say 'I'm a quitter' now?"

In the end, her oldest couldn't. "I needed to come back," Scott said in Frisco. "You get to a point where you're just sitting there thinking about it all the time. If I dwell on why and how come he's gone, I'm going to put myself in such a depressed state that I'm never going to want to get off that couch. My brother would never want that. He would say, 'Get back to baseball. Get back to doing what you love to do.' He knows we're not going to forget. But there're going to be days when it's like a dadgum door slamming you in the face: Boom, there it is again—a reminder."

Today was a big one. Today was the day Scott and Mike were to have met for the first time as coaches. His sister, Lisa Coolbaugh-Smith, lives in nearby Plano and would be coming tonight with his wife, Susan, the remnants of what was once going to be a full-bore family celebration.

Now Scott reached into the basket of balls, grabbed one, reared, and threw. There was no music, no crowd yet; the sound of bat hitting ball echoed off the walls. It was 4:42 p.m. Tino had a foot on the steps of the Drillers' dugout along the first base line when the ball arced toward shallow right field, toward a cluster of Drillers.

"Heads up!" someone shouted. Tino started, gut twisting until he saw the ball plop on the grass. His teammates noticed, acting as if they didn't.

"How are you, Tino?" asked one. "Daughter?"

"Not yet," Tino said. "And my wife, she's big. She's forty weeks."

"Well . . . good luck."

A hand flipped the stadium's sound system. The place filled with cheery pop music, the same irresistible sing-alongs played during every batting practice in every pro stadium, major and minor, in America, muffling the grunts, the *pock!* of the bat. For 25 minutes the day seemed almost routine. Tino was the second man up for Drillers batting practice. Hitting right-handed, he bunted twice, ran to first base. The music stopped. Another Driller stepped into the cage. Two teenage girls stood at a microphone and started singing, flawlessly, without a hint of slickness, "The Star-Spangled Banner." They were harmonizing ". . . that our flag was still there . . ." when Tino rounded third. He slowed, jogging toward home, veered off. He picked up a bat. When his turn came, he stepped in again, lefty this time, swung early, and hit his first foul ball, a harmless bouncer to the right of first base and through the coach's box. Everyone tried to ignore that, too.

After batting practice, Tino headed into the clubhouse nestled under the right field stands. Cole called Tino into his office. "You okay?" he said. "Some of the guys saw you flinching back there. . . ."

"You know what?" Tino told his manager. "Every time I hear a ball hit or somebody says, 'Heads up,' my heart is, I don't know . . . splitting."

Cole didn't tell Tino that Scott coached for Frisco, nor that Scott had asked to speak to him; a manager's job is to keep things simple, give players only the most necessary information for the task at hand. Cole didn't start Sanchez, either. In the bottom of the first inning, Tino was sitting on the bench, noting how the base coaches were taking their positions farther back from home plate. The RoughRiders' first base coach turned, and Tino stared at the word—Coolbaugh—on his back. Then he realized.

"Is that Mike's brother?" he asked a teammate.

"Yeah, that's Scott."

Until then, Tino had been holding steady; he'd figured on a bit more time to ease in. But now he felt a panic rise. Up in the stands a volunteer passed around a cowboy boot, asking for donations for the "Mike Coolbaugh Memorial Fund." Tino scanned the faces of the players around him, the thousands of faces in the stands. No answers. In the top of the eighth inning, a Driller got ejected, and Cole told Sanchez to get ready. *How?* In his 11 years, he had played in hundreds of games—some that decided championships, some that seemed vital to his career. But nothing like this.

In the bottom of the eighth, Tino trotted out to first base. He fielded a few grounders. Then he could feel, without seeing, Scott Coolbaugh walk up the line to the coach's box. Tino didn't look over.

But he knew Scott was there now, not 15 feet away. The crowd of 6,853 had dwindled, but the Drillers led 3–2; it was a tight game, and on the surface everyone seemed to be acting normally, playing out the usual roles. In the press box, young men scribbled words, glanced at the stat sheet. In the stands a man ate peanuts, a child slept on his mother's shoulder, someone clapped halfheartedly: Come on, Frisco! Scott took his position in the box. Tino crouched and looked home. In the Tulsa dugout, pitcher Darren Clarke sidled over to Jon Asahina and muttered, "Man, isn't this crazy?"

Asahina didn't know what to say. *This is unreal*, he thought. *This whole thing is just unreal.*

They didn't know the half of it. The Texas League rotates four umpiring crews around its eight-team league on a schedule drawn up the previous February. The three-man crew itself rotates one clockwise turn every game, so that yesterday's home plate umpire is today's third base ump is tomorrow's man shadowing first. Here was but one of the 555 games that the Texas League would stage during the 2007 season, yet on this night the two rotations lined up with the spin of a much larger, more inexplicable third so that there, standing just in foul territory with his right foot on the foul line, Tyler Funneman again found himself just yards away when Tino and a man named Coolbaugh met in extremis near first base. Realizing what he was seeing, Funneman literally backed up a step. "The odds against that," he says, "are astronomical."

Since eighth grade, all the kid from Moweaqua, Illinois, had wanted to be was an umpire. He had skipped college and gone to Harry Wendelstedt's School for Umpires in Daytona Beach, Florida. He happily made a meager $12,500 salary, supplemented with off-season jobs like pasting decals on toolboxes. For six years baseball had given Funneman fun, power, responsibility—all in a controlled environment. Mike's death shattered that sense of control; it had left Funneman weeping that first night in his hotel room. Now it left him grappling, 17 days later, with the human question, large and small: What am I doing here?

"It was . . . chills," Funneman says.

For a moment, Sanchez and Coolbaugh were close enough to hear each other whisper. Scott wanted to tell Tino that the family didn't blame him; that they knew he was innocent, that he could call if he needed support. But the code was too strong. Frisco was trying to win, Tino was trying to concentrate. "A lot of things raced through my mind," Scott says. "But I've always respected the game. I wouldn't want him to be affected by anything I might say."

Tino knew none of that, and he couldn't stop his mind from racing too. He wanted to apologize, grieve, console, be consoled, say something, *anything* to break the tension. He stole a glance at Scott. He fielded the first out, a pop out. The bases loaded up, then Frisco tied the score, but Tino couldn't focus. He prayed no more balls would be hit his way; mostly he stared at the dirt at his feet. The inning ended at last. The two men ran off in different directions without a word.

With no outs and two on in the top of the ninth, Tino came to bat. Mike's sister, Lisa Coolbaugh-Smith, sat with Susan. She watched from the stands, feeling the game edge closer to its end and the reason she had come. The sight of him digging in touched off a jangle in her gut; Lisa had wanted to come support Scott, yes, and to remember Mike. But she also wanted a word with Tino. It felt necessary. Her mom and younger sister, Linda, had told her: "Please. Let him know from us, too." So Lisa had asked Scott to try and set it up beforehand, maybe through the Drillers, but Scott never called and now the game was almost over and Susan was saying, "There's not going to be any formal arrangement. You just need to go down and talk to him."

But as she watched Tino strike out on three pitches, his last swing so weak, so lacking in conviction that it seemed the very picture of surrender, Lisa thought, *I don't know if I can do this.* In the bottom of the inning, Tino headed back out to first. Scott didn't come to the coach's box; the RoughRiders sent one of their infielders instead. At first this was a relief, but then Tino's panic flared again: He wondered if Scott couldn't bear to be near him, if coming back was a mistake. No announcement was made. Lisa turned to Susan. "Why isn't Scott at first?" she said. "Do you think he's having trouble with this?"

The game ended. Tino went into the dugout, began gathering his gear. Susan led the way down to the railing near the field, Lisa trailing behind. "I couldn't breathe," she says. "I didn't know if I could talk."

A teammate tapped Tino, pointed to two women. He walked over just past the on-deck circle. Most of the fans had gone. He didn't know their faces. Susan said her name and said she was Scott's wife. Tino's eyes suddenly stung; he took off his hat and reached out his hand. Susan shook it and Lisa, knowing the attention would shift to her now, felt her throat thicken. Tino turned and put out his hand, but she ignored it and found herself falling through her own tears toward him and the two clutched each other. It was near 10:30 p.m.

Lisa began talking. She told Tino that the family was doing well. That he should feel no guilt. That it's part of baseball, that Mike was proud of how you and he worked together. She cried again, and Tino nodded, two strangers touched by mercy on an obscure Texas ball-field. The stadium lights went dark. For the first time since Mike died, Tino felt lighter.

The next afternoon, Tino was walking toward the batting cage at the ballpark when he heard a voice. He stopped, and Scott walked over and repeated much of what his sister had said, but it was different, less a conversation. Tino said, "I'm sorry," but there were no tears this time and he could feel, past Scott's sadness, the man's struggle. "I'm not angry at you," Scott said. "I know it's not something you meant to do." Then Mike's brother told Tino not to quit, because Mike would want you to keep pushing forward. Scott said that if Tino needed someone to talk to, he could call "because it helps us also talking to you," but he was rushing his words, trying to get it all in, say his piece without cracking. Tino nodded, and nodded again. He knew better than to interrupt.

Mandy would be tougher. She couldn't conceive of facing Tino yet. Intellectually she knew he would be stained; that was unfair. As Scott says, "It's not like Tino went in and robbed a liquor store and shot the clerk just because." But intellect had nothing to do with it: She just couldn't get *there*. Twenty days had passed since Mike died, but she still felt brittle. It didn't matter what anyone said. Something about the accident pushed her grief down past the realm of logic, to a place in the heart where reason holds little sway, and Tino was the explicably human stand-in for the inexplicable; once he was off the hook, all that was left was randomness. And the boys made it even harder to move forward. Lately Jake was waking up with nightmares, asking his older brother, "Joey, are you leaving me?" Out front of the house a few days ago, Joey stood hitting baseballs. Jake stepped into his line of vision.

"Jacob, get out of the way," Joey said. "I don't want you to get killed."

For a week now, Joey had been pestering Mandy about Mike's black bat, the one in the attic. She had no idea what he was talking about, but the night after Scott and Tino first spoke, she finally gave in. She went to the garage, Joey trailing close behind, and climbed up. "There it is!" he cried. "I can see it!" And there the bat lay, sleek and dark amid a pale cluster of other bats, a piece of masking tape on the handle: the bat that produced Mike's first major league hit.

The next morning, Joey, freed at last of the baby aluminum jobs Mike had always insisted he swing, stepped in and raised his father's bat behind his head. It was nearly as long as he was tall. His stance was perfect, upright. His swing was smooth. He lined the first three pitches over the grass. Jake ran them down. When they play and pretend to be grown-up ballplayers, the boys don't choose strangers anymore. "They play Mike now," Mandy said. "Since this happened, they fight over who's going to be Daddy Coolbaugh. It's not 'Mike' up to bat. It's 'Daddy Coolbaugh.'"

She sat on the living room couch, mood shifting from laughter to tears to whispering, a lifetime of emotion played out in minutes. The tribute DVD was playing on the TV; song after song, each invoking some intense slice of the past, filled the air. Shots of their wedding passed over the screen. Mandy spoke of their honeymoon: "That was a surprise," she said. She'd always wanted to go to Hawaii, and Mike had set her up for months, said they couldn't afford it. He told her they'd go skiing, and then she went and bought ski equipment, forcing him to scramble and say, "Plan for a beach"—but they would have to settle for Cancún. She fell for the ruse, of course. Two voices, male and female, crooned as the pictures segued one after another, a country duet by Sammy Kershaw and Terri Clark called "Love of My Life."

> *I spent a lifetime waiting*
> *Always hesitating until you*
> *I was lost so deep inside my shell*
> *'Til you came and saved me from myself*

"This is our wedding song," Mandy said. "He picked it. For our wedding he planned, he went with me to get the cake, he went to pick the music. He was just involved in everything."

> *As we stand together*
> *I promise forever*
> *'Til the day that I die*

"While we were dancing he sang this song to me," she said. "He told me I had to sing the girl parts. I said, 'Riiight.'"

Now came his favorite, Alan Jackson's "Remember When," and photos of Mike with the boys at Corpus Christi beach. "His last day with the kids," she said. Her relatives, the ones who pieced together the DVD in time for the funeral, had edited it with care. A picture appeared then, Mike and Mandy, clutching each other and smiling like young parents catching a break. "That was on the dance floor," she said. "They wouldn't let us dance alone, the kids."

Remember when the sound of little feet
was the music
We danced to week to week

Mike taught the boys to swim, to ride a bike. Now came a picture with the Astros, a shot of him being hit by a pitch. Now the video footage of Mike in a Milwaukee uniform: The White Sox play-by-play man calling it, *Here's Mike Coolbaugh. Been to the plate one time.* . . . On the television, the crowd is howling, sunlight gleaming all over the park. Garland's pitch floats. Mike swings. . . . *High into left field, Carlos going back, back, back . . . at the fence, jumps, he can't get it.* . . . But there's no excitement in the announcer's voice; he's on the White Sox payroll, and a Brewers home run is a hostile act best dispensed of quickly. . . . *And Mike Coolbaugh puts up his first major league homer.* . . .

The Brewers have promised to send a copy of *their* broadcast, Mandy said, with Bob Uecker enthusing like a Milwaukee announcer should.

The screen went black. Jake rushed in one door and out the other, one of Mike's t-shirts hanging down near his ankles.

Mandy confirmed that, yes, she'd be going to Tulsa this week. Frisco and Scott would be there to play the Drillers, and the Tulsa management was going to hold a ceremony and present the family with Mike's retired jersey, number 29. She figured it was time to get out, that she could handle being overwhelmed all over again, publicly this time. Only one prospect daunted her: Tino.

"I'm not ready to sit down and have a conversation with him," she said softly. "I don't know if I could."

Yet of all people, maybe Tino could best understand how she felt.

Because even after friends and family and priests had reassured him, even after Lisa and Scott had reached out to absolve him, even though he felt on a logical level that he had nothing to apologize for, Tino knew it didn't matter. The next morning, August 12, he sat in a dingy hotel lobby in Midland, Texas; the Drillers had bused in from Frisco the day before.

"For nothing in the world, I wouldn't have the thought to harm, to hurt somebody," Tino said, arms folded, shoulders slumping, as if trying to turtle inside a shell. He looked thin, hollowed out by sleeplessness. "Excuse me," he said. He reached for his tin of Copenhagen, shoved a fingerful of dip into his cheek, spat tobacco juice into a white Styrofoam cup. "But if you write it down, I did. I took his life away, and he took a part of my heart with him."

On August 13, Bill Edwards's wife, Mary Beth, gave birth to their first son, Bennett, with mother and child emerging safe and sound. In all, it was the best news the Arkansas Travelers reliever had heard in weeks, and not only because the couple's first try at inducing, on July 31, had failed, and then the due date of August 7 had passed with no action, too. The season had careened downhill since Edwards had turned off the mound to see the ball hit Mike, though he couldn't be sure that precise moment was the cause. Yes, he had found it hard to sleep after hearing the news that night. But guilt wasn't the problem. Edwards had thrown the ball, not hit it, and being one step removed allowed him room enough to consider the moment coolly: With the umpire's calls, Tino's swing, Mike's reaction, it wasn't hard to consider himself blameless.

No, it was the aftermath that left the 26-year-old Memphis native unsettled. The news programs kept repeating the radio play-by-play in the crazy days that followed, and hearing his name repeated over and over, just before he let go of the pitch, felt surreal. Then there was all that distracting uncertainty about the baby. And then there was Bill Valentine.

No one around the Travs can say they're shocked by what happened two weeks after Coolbaugh's death—Valentine, after all, once called his own reliever "G-A-R-B-A-G-E!"—but the old umpire's timing couldn't have been worse. That night back in the booth with Elson on July 22 quickly became a Sunday Travs tradition, and on August 5 Valentine reached into his bag and set off a few verbal fireworks. After blasting the Arkansas bullpen for general ineptitude, he lit specifically into Edwards, who, oddly enough, was in the midst of pitching two scoreless innings. "Somebody ought to sit that guy down at his locker and tell him to pack his bags and go home," the team's chief operating officer told the Travelers listening audience. In essence, the company's top salesman was ridiculing the quality of the product he sells. "Just retire."

Sitting at home in Memphis, Edwards's father heard the broadcast on the Internet. When his son called afterward, he told him, "Don't listen to it. You're just going to get fired up." Edwards's pregnant wife heard it on the radio. When her husband called home, Mary Beth said, "You would not believe what was said on the radio." She added, "But don't worry. You shouldn't listen to it."

So, says Edwards, "Of course I thought, 'I've got to hear what he said now.'"

Father knew best: Bill Edwards got fired up. He called Valentine "unprofessional" and "an embarrassment to a good organization." His teammates were outraged, too; there was talk of a boycott by the players of Travs promotional events, and Edwards considered confronting Valentine personally. But after a few days, the rebellion petered out. The players privately dismissed their local boss as a crazy coot, a loose cannon, a fool. "He has no control over any of us," Edwards says. "His job is to take care of the stadium; he has nothing to do with us."

Still, from the Angels front office on down to Little Rock, no one disagreed with his assessment: Despite his 4–2 record and 3.90 ERA, Edwards was hardly considered major league material. Valentine, unsurprisingly, never backed off. Asked about his comments a day later, he described the quality of his bullpen to the *Arkansas Democrat-Gazette* this way: "You can plow a mule all week, but he's never going to run the Kentucky Derby." And while it's true that he has no control over the players—the parent club's player development department decides where and how to use its talent—reminding Valentine of that fact only irks him further. The mitigating fact that Edwards happened to be the pitcher who threw the ball that hit Mike Coolbaugh? The fact that he might be hurting, discomfited, confused? It still doesn't let him off the hook. "I don't think he could pitch in A-ball," Valentine says, thus beginning a screed on Edwards and most minor league pitchers today.

"You have got to teach the players to win, that it hurts to lose," he says. "We don't do that anymore. You'll have a 5–1 lead and they let a reliever walk three straight guys, give up two hits, throw two wild pitches, tie up the game and leave, and the starter loses seven innings of hard work—and they leave the relief pitcher in because, they say, he has to learn to work himself out of it? Send his ass to Rancho Cucamonga! Send him to Cedar Rapids! You think if you leave him in, he's going to get better? The guy's never going to throw strikes." He points down to his crotch. "They don't have it here. They're afraid to throw the ball over because they don't have enough stuff, they don't have enough command, and when they throw the ball over they get hit. So they try to nibble, they get behind, they do everything wrong. When you get a player like that? Release him."

Mandy arrived in Tulsa on Wednesday afternoon, August 15, riding in from Dallas with the boys and Mary Lu, her brother John David driving. Part of her wanted to see the city, one of the last places Mike had been after he left her. Part of her wanted to get the boys back in a minor league ballpark again: She didn't want them to fear baseball. But part of her didn't want to be there at all. The Coolbaugh family pulled up to Drillers Stadium with just enough time to change. It was nearing 7 p.m.

Mandy walked onto the field with Joey and Jake and Scott, to a spot just behind home plate. A microphone waited. Tino Sanchez and the rest of the Drillers watched from the dugout, stretching, throwing, warming up. Tulsa president Chuck Lamson announced the presentation to the family of Mike's framed jersey, number 29, and Scott stepped to the mic and thanked the teams and the fans. The crowd applauded. The boys ran to the dugout, and by the time Mandy got there she could see them sitting side-by-side, next to one player alone. Tino. She could see her sons talking, but it wasn't a conversation. Did someone lead the boys over? She didn't know. It didn't matter. Tino was weeping, shaking. The boys kept talking.

Mary Lu approached her grandsons, but at the sight of Tino's face her mind froze. She couldn't bring herself to say, "I'm Mike's mother," or even her own name, but a strange momentum kept moving her to him and now she was standing in front of the stricken player. "It's okay," Mary Lu stammered. "It's okay. It's okay. It's okay." She backed away. Tino saw Mandy mingling with some players but she made no move to come his way. "She didn't want to see me yet," he says. The anthem was sung. The Coolbaughs left the field and took their seats in the stands.

The game began, but it kept nagging Mandy, the way she'd acted down there. God knows, she didn't need to talk to the man, but she hated to think he might be suffering because of it, hated to think that somehow she'd acted *small*. Early on, she left her seat behind home plate and went up to the radio booth to see Mark Neely. The Tulsa broadcaster backed up his chair and left the air, asking his backup, Bruce Howard, to fill in. He figured she would need ten minutes. But Mandy wanted to know what it was like all that day and night: how Mike was in the bus on the way over, how he looked when he fell, whether he ever took a breath after. "I didn't talk to Tino down there," she said finally. "I was probably in a daze. . . ." But she sounded ready to try.

After she left, Neely told a Drillers official to make sure Mandy got to see Tino after the game. And though it got very late and the boys were dragging, though it took 12 innings for Frisco to win the slugfest 6–5 (all the time Mandy and Mary Lu taking in the home runs and joking: "Yep, Mike's battling Scott right to the end. . . ."), Mandy stayed. Tino was in the clubhouse when someone said she was outside waiting. He walked toward the door slowly, wanting to stall, to zigzag as he had heading toward an enraged Clint Hurdle that spring—how scared he had been!—but he pushed through and then she was standing there waiting, Mike's wife. And it was as he had feared, far worse than meeting Lisa or Scott or his mom.

Mandy tried. Face smeared with tears, she pushed herself to keep talking because Mike would've wanted that. Tino offered condolences but felt fraudulent, weak, and like a blast of heat coming off the woman, it hit him: her battling so to stave off a breakdown. He cried, but there was no hug; he didn't dare touch her. He didn't speak again.

"I had no words," Tino says. "She wanted to take the blame off me, but she . . . she was destroyed. She could barely look at me. It's hard to be in that situation. You're looking at life, family, people who set goals, dreams, people who think they're going to be together forever. Then all of a sudden? Just . . . gone."

Two nights later, his cell phone rang. It was Angie; her water had broken. Then early morning, August 18, came another call with the news from Yauco: His daughter, Isabella Sophia, had been born healthy, 8 pounds, 2 ounces, and 21 inches long. Tino Sanchez was a father now.

IN MINOR LEAGUE TOWNS across the country, shadows lengthened, the nights became cooler, the baseball season limped to its close. Unlike the big leagues, which crescendo in the fall—rosters expanding, players producing career-making performances, the game's indolent pace adrenalized and transformed by playoff drama—the final weeks of the bush league year most resemble a balloon losing air. There are league championships to decide, but this is the time when the truth of the matter is most starkly spelled out: The minor leagues are never about winning. They're about developing talent. An organization's best players are sucked away now by the parent club, or shut down to prevent injury. High school and college football games kick off, shrinking the weekend crowds. For most lifers, it's the time to begin thinking about next year, or deciding to fade away.

Because that is the usual fate. Unlike their counterparts on the big league level, most players don't get a fond farewell. There's no final tour of opposing ballparks, no final wave to the home crowd, because there's almost never a formal announcement, no *This will be my final season.* Lifers try to make themselves useful to organizations for so long that self-appraisal becomes useless. If, at season's end, the coaches say you can still play, well, then in all likelihood you will play next year. If they don't, you don't. But the decision usually comes in the off-season, signaled not by a cinematic "I'm sorry, son . . ." but by silence. "Nobody calls to offer a contract," says Travis Driskill, the 15-year minor league pitcher who played with Mike in Round Rock in 2005. "They just get pushed aside. They get forgotten."

That's how it happened to Coolbaugh and his playing career, and that's how it would happen for Tino Sanchez, too: Nothing personal. After the 2007 season ended, Alan Zinter finished off his 19th year in the minors with Somerset of the independent Atlantic League. His kids were seven and five years old. It was time. "Last year was very difficult on my family. We didn't make any money; we didn't have any insurance, so I had to pay out of pocket for insurance," Zinter says of his final season. "I could've very easily said, 'I'm in shape, I can still play,' and maybe there was a chance if I kept begging and begging.

But I couldn't do that. I wasn't going to let my playing days get in the way of my coaching career." And like that, without ceremony or even public notice, Zinter began his new life as hitting coach for the Diamondbacks' rookie affiliate in Missoula, Montana.

Every so often, though, lightning strikes. A lifer actually gets to *retire* and, as Coolbaugh once told Mandy, feel that all those years played in the shadows actually mattered. In 2007 it happened to Travis Driskill, at a time when he had no right to think such a thing was possible. Like Tino, the 35-year-old had begun the 2007 season on the phantom disabled list, the 26th player on the 25-man Round Rock Express. Yet he ended up having one of his finest years pitching in relief, made the AAA All-Star team for the first time in his career, even got a final eight-day stint in the majors when Houston called him up in late August. There Driskill saw Craig Biggio and Jeff Bagwell get the official teary-eyed send-off big league teams produce when passing their stars into retirement. He never imagined such a to-do for himself.

But the Round Rock management has a reputation for taking care of its players, and Driskill's intentions were no secret. When the Astros sent him back to AAA for the last series of the year, the Express front office and coaching staff seized on the chance. Driskill had grown up in nearby Austin, had made Round Rock his off-season home for six years. The team made sure his parents attended the final game on September 3 against New Orleans, and told him nothing. Before the eighth inning, Driskill began warming up in the bullpen. That's when it hit him that this was it, he'd never play again; he cried while throwing the ball off the practice mound. He entered the game, pulled himself together, got two quick outs, panicked when he gave up a hit, then struck out the pitcher. Never had one inning left him so emotionally spent. "That's it," Driskill told pitching coach Burt Hooton in the dugout. "I'm done."

"No," Hooton said. "You've got to go one more inning."

"I can't do it."

"You've got to go back out."

Driskill went. He was on the mound, warming up for the ninth, when he looked over to the dugout to see his wife and two sons and manager Jackie Moore walking onto the field to come get him. An amplified voice declared that his career was over. Driskill gave up the ball, walked off surrounded by family, and both dugouts and the entire crowd stood and cheered. Again, he broke into tears. "I lost it for a good five, ten minutes," he recalls. "Heck, I'm crying right now."

It wasn't a perfect ending: The Express lost, 6–2—and afterward, a donation of $24,300 to the Mike Coolbaugh Memorial Fund was announced. But for Driskill, it would do just fine. In return for his 15 years he had appeared in just 57 games in the major leagues, gone 11–14 with a 5.23 ERA; he had seen his highest salary a decade back, $350,000 while playing the 1998 season in Japan. But none of those numbers mattered. In a way, this had been his most gratifying season: Starting out as an afterthought, he had worked his way back, and gone out like a star. Now he was looking forward to coaching, had a job lined up with Houston's Rookie League team in Greeneville, Tennessee.

"I had no regrets; I left everything I had on the baseball field," Driskill says. "I never looked at baseball as owing me anything. I got to make money in Japan, and the times I got called up to the big leagues the minimum salary kept climbing. Baseball has given me everything I've ever wanted. I've got a beautiful home in Round Rock and a beautiful wife and two kids who adore me. I owe baseball for everything that I've got."

Up in Tulsa that Monday, the Drillers were making ready for the playoffs. It had been a draining five weeks. The day before, Tulsa had clinched a post-season spot with an emphatic 11–0 win over Wichita, but even that didn't come easy. Jon Asahina had put together his grittiest outing since his return, fighting off a groin strain to pitch five innings of three-hit ball, but the injury was just one more setback. Between coaching first base, serving as the team's amateur expert on head injuries, and trying to regain his conditioning, he never got right in the second half, going 1–4 with a 5.74 ERA. Worse, the psychic armor Asahina had constructed in the months after his own accident had been dented by time and self-doubt. Jon began to wonder if he'd been lying to himself all along. Maybe he wanted to think like Bernie but couldn't. Maybe that whole "I feel reborn" line and the idea of him "being prepared" for Mike's death by his own accident was so much bullshit. Maybe he just didn't want to admit the worst: that at times he felt emptier than zero, and all his philosophical musings were little more than window dressing on a detachment he couldn't begin to explain.

"To be honest, that's probably how I was justifying myself," Asahina says. "I felt ashamed that I was so numb. I didn't want to come off as being unsympathetic, not sensitive. I felt bad about that, because I wanted to feel something and I couldn't. I really couldn't feel anything. It wasn't just Mike; it was my personal situation as well. It wouldn't have mattered what had happened after. It wouldn't have mattered if I saw . . . anything at that time."

Yes, it could be that beneath the armor, Asahina's mind had constructed another layer to allow him to function after being nearly killed on a baseball field, after witnessing another man dying on that same field, in the same manner, just three months later. Only numbness, perhaps, made it possible for Asahina to return to the game that summer and take the mound again, to see the stray foul ball or a comebacker up the middle and not be constantly paralyzed by the possibilities. "I was scared as hell, though, too," he says. "There's no way that, for a split second here and there, you don't realize what's going on."

Still, Asahina had suffered only one full meltdown, on August 28, when he went out on Drillers Field to start against the Arkansas Travelers. It had been four months since he'd pitched against the team that sent him to the hospital, and for two innings he managed to keep that fact out of his head. But in the third, Asahina found himself suddenly aware that the faces that he saw in April were stepping into the batter's box again. "I started remembering: *Those are the same guys,*" Asahina says. "They'd seen my deal happen, they'd seen what happened with Mike." And from that moment on, he couldn't help it, Asahina started thinking even as he was deciding, pitch by pitch, what to throw next. *These guys are a lot more likely to be hitting balls up the middle, even if they didn't want to. . . . Because that's the image in their minds and that's the image in my mind. Then it's more likely to happen, right? . . . I've got to get my ass in gear. This is serious. . . .*

In other words, he says, "I was mindfucked." Asahina started to try to overpower all of the Arkansas hitters, keep the ball from coming back, "throwing every pitch like it was the last one I'd ever throw," and as is always the case when a pitcher is overthrowing, when a man is trying to force something to *not* happen, it happened. The Travelers ate Asahina alive, hit two home runs, scored six on him in the next three innings. He walked off after five, nerves raw, feeling as if he'd been stripped naked.

Yet even after that disaster, Asahina rebounded. In his next and final start of the year against Wichita, he pulled off that gutty performance to clinch a playoff spot and pick up his first win since his comeback began. But he knew, better than anyone, that it wasn't going to be enough. His future with the Rockies organization was curdling fast. "That's the thing about this game," Bo McLaughlin says. "You've always got younger players coming in, and whether it's because one's more of a prospect or they have more money invested in another, there's just not enough room."

Meanwhile, no amount of winning could erase the obvious. The Drillers beat Wichita again to win their third straight and finish the regular season with a tidy 69–69 record, but it had been a season beyond misfortune, beyond, in the words of the baseball superstitious, being "snakebit." Their sport had killed somebody. They had watched a man die. That sent two messages to sort through the rest of the way, and seemingly contradictory ones at that. Mike's death "put things in perspective," so it made some 0-for-4 day seem less like a tragedy. But when they'd see his photo on the scoreboard or hear announcers exhorting fans to donate money to the Coolbaugh fund, the players would also find themselves running a bit harder, caring even more, because "life is short, and you've got to live every day as if it's your last." It was confusing, and everyone had to sort out his own implications while still trying to perform, excel, impress.

"There are so many cliches I could rattle off," says Matt Miller, the Drillers left fielder who heard Mike's last words. "But what I've taken away is: You've just got to respect what you do. Mike obviously loved baseball and if he wasn't a baseball player he could've done something else and been just as passionate. That's important. That's what I want to incorporate in my life. Whatever you want to do, go after it with passion. Just don't *quit*. I mean, the guy didn't get too many at-bats in the big leagues, but he didn't quit. He played with, like, ten different organizations and he just kept going after it. There's not too many guys like that. *I'm* not like that. I couldn't play that much in the minors. I don't know if anybody on this team could."

Manager Stu Cole had been coaching third base that Sunday in Little Rock, had perhaps the clearest sight line when Tino swung and Mike went down. He didn't tell anyone, but for the rest of the summer he replayed that vision in his mind, and every time he saw a certain swing or foul ball it made his skin go cold. Sometimes during games he found himself daydreaming about Mike, more than he'd have thought about someone he only knew three weeks. "But he was such a great guy," Cole says. When he was alone in his room, Cole would pray for God to take care of Mike and that family. He wanted the cliche, too, to win the Texas League championship in his honor, "to go down and present a ring to Mike's wife."

It didn't happen. The Springfield Cardinals swept Tulsa in its first-round series, three games to none, thrashing the Drillers in the finale. It may have been their worst game of the year. Rain delayed the start 29 minutes, and then Tulsa surrendered a season-high 21 hits and 16 runs. Tino pinch-hit in the seventh inning and ground out, but at least he did it the right way: Matt Miller had been on second base, and Tino lashed the ball to the right side, to the second baseman. He got his teammate over to third, a pro's final act. On paper, of course, his 2007 had been unremarkable: Tino ended up hitting .175 in Double-A, and a late-September stint in Colorado Springs brought his Triple-A average down to .278. But the way Tino responded to setbacks—helping Mike learn the job he didn't get, going back to help the organization, his teammates, facing the family when no one expected it—exemplified what baseball men mean when they talk about facing failure: You get up the next day. You finish the job.

"Tino going back because of his strong need to be with his teammates is going to live forever with those teammates," says P. J. Carey, the Dodgers field coordinator. "It's going to make them better. It's going to make some difficult decision later on in their lives, having to be in two places at the same time, easier because it's going to be clearer to them why they'll make those decisions. He did a tremendous thing in a very tough situation."

In truth, it would've been easier—understandable, even—for the man who hit the killing ball to protect himself by dismissing it as a random event, a freak. What if Tino had been the self-centered prospect he once was? What if he hadn't had a pregnant wife himself, or hadn't known enough about family or time or baseball to *feel* the loss rather than just thinking it? Instead, for 11 years Tino had lived what Mike lived, lost what Mike had lost; his anguish was a lifer's commentary on a lifer gone, a tribute from the heart of the game. It was a step beyond what Carey calls "respect" for baseball: Through his suffering Tino expressed full respect for the man, giving proper due to a life long ignored. That made nothing easier for Mike's family, of course, unless you consider the alternative.

Tino, though, was also fortunate. It's the norm in these litigious days for finger-pointing and ugly posturing to follow disaster, a separation into attorney-advised camps that allows for little contact and less closure. Though immediate and post-mortem analyses by medical personnel agree that Mike's death was unavoidable and nearly instantaneous, it's unclear whether crucial minutes were lost when the MEMS ambulance was delayed trying to make its way onto the field at Dickey-Stephens Park that night—a loophole that an ambitious lawyer could well have tried to exploit. But the Coolbaughs filed no lawsuit. There were no accusations made against the Travelers or the Little Rock emergency response or baseball itself, no cry from Scott or Mandy or anyone else that the game hadn't sufficiently protected its own. And when the call for coaches to wear helmets gained momentum in the months after, the family remained quiet; as Scott says, the ball hit Mike in the neck and there's little reason to think a helmet would've protected him. Mike had signed up for this sport, his family agreed. He knew its dangers.

Still, Tino could have been lost in the aftermath. It would have been easier if, in their dazed condition, Scott and his sisters and mother and Mandy had avoided the player who hit the ball. Their tears when they finally met with him in Frisco and Tulsa say plenty about why it would've been fine to stay away; why subject themselves to a presence that would only bring more pain? Yet they pushed forward. "He needed to hear it straight from us," says Lisa Coolbaugh-Smith. "I know how Mike is, and if that had happened to me he never, ever would've held that person responsible. I had to do it." And in their connection, something started to heal. "It wasn't like I just went up and said, 'Hey, it's okay,'" Lisa says. "It helped me too that I didn't let this go."

It took longer for Tino to sort out what they had done. He didn't expect the Coolbaughs' compassion or comfort. So when they approached him—with bewildering rapidity, one family member after another—it hit with the force of purity, like a straight shot of whiskey or a baby's kiss. "I've not been religious, but when Scott talked to me, when his family talked to me, my life changed," Tino says. "It became a big responsibility when I knew they are going to look out for me." He can't help but think it: They saved him. He wasn't alone. Lisa had hugged him and Scott had said to call and Mandy had stood waiting outside the Tulsa clubhouse, and in all that Tino felt an intimation he can barely articulate. But he tries.

"Everything that's got to do with love is God," he says. "And that was pure love."

On the evening of October 1, 2007, Mandy Coolbaugh turned on the television in her San Antonio home to watch a baseball game. This was a first. She had gone to Drillers Stadium in August, of course, but she barely paid attention that night to the play, to the sensations of a ballpark alive with balls and strikes and men running around base paths. But now she was ready. She wanted to see who was pitching, pay attention to the score, allow herself to get caught up as the Colorado Rockies took on the San Diego Padres, to hear a bat crack and think of it as almost harmless. "I hadn't watched since Mike was killed," Mandy says.

Still, her interest was hardly casual. The Rockies needed to win
that play-in game against the San Diego Padres for the right to move
on to the 2007 National League Division Series, and Mandy needed
them to move on even more. The week before, Colorado assistant general manager Bill Geivett had told Scott that if the Rockies made it
into the playoffs, they wanted Joey and Jake to throw out the ceremo-
nial first pitch for Colorado's first home game. Mandy loved the idea;
the sport was so intertwined with the boys' idea of Mike that it seemed
crucial they take any chance to be part of it. The Rockies, meanwhile,
had unleashed a run that the game's dynamics rarely allow: Winning
13 of their last 14 contests to end the season, they had tied San Diego
for second place in the NL West and forced the one-game playoff for
the wild-card slot.

Because of its hyperpressurized, heartbreaking dynamic, because
it frenziedly runs counter to baseball's usual pace, because of its rarity,
the one-game playoff is one of the great events in American sports.
The Rockies–Padres showdown at Denver's Coors Field, only the seventh in major league history, may well have been the greatest ever. The
teams traded the lead twice before deadlocking, 6–6, after nine innings, sending a one-game playoff into extra innings for the first time.
San Diego took a two-run lead in the top of the 13th on a Scott Hair-
ston home run, then sent in Trevor Hoffman, one of the best relievers
in baseball history, to finish off Colorado. Instead, in the bottom of
the 13th, Hoffman collapsed. He gave up two doubles, a triple, an
intentional walk. The phone was ringing constantly in the Coolbaugh
house; Mandy had told family and friends how much the win could
mean, and every twist brought a new call. Suddenly Mandy realized
she needed this game as much as the kids did; the excitement, the hap-

piness, the mere act of cheering felt good. "It keeps him alive for me," Mandy says.

Then Hoffman gave up a final shallow sacrifice fly to Jamey Carroll, and here came Matt Holliday sliding face-first into home, a delayed call of safe, the replays that never could show for sure whether Holliday had touched the plate. Colorado won 9–8. The boys would get their pitches.

A plan was made. Scott, working fall ball in Hawaii, would fly back on the Rockies' dime and join the boys in Denver. Mandy, expecting the baby at the end of the month, couldn't travel, but Scott's wife, Susan, would accompany them on the plane. Three days later, a reporter called for a reaction to news she hadn't heard: That morning, the Rockies had voted to give the Coolbaugh family a full play-off share—a figure that could reach $362,000 if the Rockies were to win the World Series. Anyone who knows ballplayers couldn't help but be shocked: Even the wealthiest are notoriously stingy with their shares, and baseball lore is full of key late additions and clubhouse personnel who had been stiffed. Mike had never played with the Rockies' major league team. He had only been with the organization three weeks as a coach. He'd had contact with a few current players like first baseman Todd Helton during his year with the organization in 1998, but "really, he was an outsider," Scott says.

"I know all the bad things that are said about players—and we are all selfish. I'll be the first to admit that I'm very selfish when it comes to making money. Your life in the game is very short, so to give money away is tough to do when it's so hard to make it. I couldn't be appreciative enough to the Rockies players for rallying together to say, 'Here's a playoff share.' And it's not as cut-and-dried as it seemed;

they had to jump through a lot of hoops with the players' union to get it approved. But that team was a very special team. They understand what family is. They played like a family and that's why they got in the playoffs. They understand Mike's life and what baseball meant to the boys."

Yet how the share decision came about remains vague. Baseball was gearing into its usual post-season fever that day, with TV and radio commentators and hundreds of writers, bloggers, webcammers dissecting every aspect of every off-day, every play, every human reaction. But no one outside the team knows what the room looked like, where the players sat or stood, if anyone argued or anyone spoke much at all. Like any true act of greatness, this one retains a bit of mystery. After Hurdle broke the news to the press, the players refused to fall into the hands of a media horde desperate to give the story its due. Who first had the idea? Word was that player representative Josh Fogg suggested it, but he wouldn't take credit. Hurdle didn't know or wouldn't say; the players stripped their utterances to the barest bones. "I don't know who brought it up," said Helton at the time. "But once it was brought up, it was a done deal."

"It was a team decision," said Holliday. "It was the right thing to do."

Mandy was stunned. But then, with all Mike's premonitions, with the way the Rockies had won—and would keep on winning, with an unheard-of 21 of 22 victories before finally getting swept by the Boston Red Sox in the '07 World Series—it all made an odd kind of sense. "Turn on the news and all you hear about is people doing hateful things to each other," she says. "Then you hear about these guys taking so much out to give to us, and it reminds you that there's so much good in the world."

On a cold Saturday night, October 6, Joey and Jake stood on the grass at Coors Field. Scott stood beside them, trying not to think of Mike and how much he'd like to be playing in a major league playoff game, trying to focus on the boys' every move and mood because he knew if he didn't, he would surely break down. Before the game, they all had gone to the clubhouse and met the players and Clint Hurdle, and the boys got bags with gear and jackets and Rockies hats. Now play was about to begin; Colorado was holding a two-games-to-none lead on the Philadelphia Phillies. The two stepped and launched a pair of first pitches to Rockies pitchers Jeff Francis and Jason Hirsch. The sellout crowd, who had paid only to see Game 3, who came in expecting only the emotion of winning or losing this night, stood and roared, feeling helpless, tearing up as the two little boys stood in the grass below. Mandy tried watching the moment on television, but the broadcast didn't show it. But there were photos, and video. Joey and Jake got to keep the balls.

Less than a month later, on the morning of November 2, Mandy gave birth to an eight-pound, eight-ounce daughter, just as Mike had predicted. It was 8:29 a.m., the baby had been conceived on January 29, Mike's uniform was number 29; all those 29s Mandy took as a sign. She named the girl Anne Michael, for her mom and husband. "She looks just like him," Mandy says. "She has a dimple like he did, and a certain look—the exact one. He would've really loved her."

Six days later, on November 8, major league baseball's general managers decreed that base coaches would be required to wear protective helmets. By the end of the year, the Rockies' playoff share had been calculated; the Coolbaugh family would receive, before taxes, $233,505.18. Quietly, the team also ordered up a National Championship pendant for baby Anne and National Championship rings for Joey and Jake—just like the ones the players would receive—inscribed with the name "Coolbaugh," sized for Mike's finger. So they'll fit no matter how big the boys may grow.

10

___

ALL THOSE 29s

Six months and two days after he hit the ball, Tino Sanchez is standing next to home plate at Ovidio "Millino" Rodriguez Park, bat over his shoulder. It is a breezy, warm night, the massive but spotty lights above imbuing the field with a ballpark's uniquely inviting glow. Two 15-year-old boys crouch at shortstop. Three man-high piles of dirt loom behind first base, a running oval cuts through the middle of the outfield; a sign in right field declares "Welcome to Yauco." Under the tin roof, sitting in the squat concrete shell built in 1948, Tino's mother, sister, and daughter watch him run his team through drills. His wife, Angie, has just arrived with dinner in a plastic sack; soon she'll realize she locked the keys in the car.

Tino smacks a sharp grounder to short. The ball bounds across grass and dirt, and a boy gathers it in as if it were made of gold.

Tino yells a few words, adjustments. He steps out. "We say in Puerto Rico, in Spanish: *Cru-el,*" he says. "Sometimes the game is; you cannot close your eyes. But you just love it. You find a way. Because sooner or later it gives back. What I'm doing now? I love this.

The other day I was playing on the Puerto Rican team, our first game against Taiwan. It was fifteen years ago that I first put a Puerto Rico uniform on, a long time, and this wasn't a big game, just exhibition. But when they said, 'Play ball!' and started shooting fireworks, I got so excited. After you get to the field at two and work out, you take early work, you take BP, you work hard under that sun, 100 degrees— there's no better feeling than when they say, 'Play ball!' and you run onto the field. Especially when you're home team and you get the field first. Nothing can beat that."

He smiles. Sanchez will soon be 29, and a few months back he informed the Rockies of his plan to retire from pro ball. Everyone knew it was time. His dad, the lone voice—"Give yourself a chance; you never know"—encouraging Tino to go back to Tulsa the last few winters, didn't argue. Tino Sr. didn't even raise the subject. That was strange.

Tinito (in Yauco, anyway; after 11 years he's Tinito again) will still play some—there's a seven-month contract with the Puerto Rican national team waiting to be signed—but he wants to move on. Yauco's mayor has asked him to oversee the city's 40-plus Little Leagues, serve as a roving instructor for its coaches, and he also comes out here two nights a week to work with his dad's old team, the 16- to 18-year-old Yauco Cafeteros. He plans to start college in the fall; the Rockies gave him a $20,000 scholarship when he signed 11 years ago, and Tino intends to collect. He's thinking computers, accounting; with Angie working full-time, selling mattresses at the JC Penney in Ponce, they should be able to get by. If money gets tight, Tino might consider heading back to the bushes, but it would still feel like a lie. He has lost his taste for playing. Mike's death did that.

"Big time," Tino says. "When I went back to play last summer, I didn't have the intensity, that eye of the tiger. I lost a lot."

He hits three grounders, yells *"Vamos!"* to a boy moving too slow. Tino is wearing a t-shirt reading "Play Hard, Pray Hard" that his mother gave him after he came home for good. He has gained back the six pounds he lost last July, his pocked cheeks have filled out, and the rings under his eyes have faded; those first bad days aside, he always could sleep through a hurricane. Still, Sanchez has one of those disconcerting faces given to extremes; like the burlesque symbols of Greek theater, the masks of Comedy and Tragedy, his features are rarely unreadable. When he's grinning, Tino's white teeth and flashing eyes explode on you like a flashbulb. When he's not, he looks as if he's headed to an execution.

"It's amazing," Tino says. "The other day I kind of laughed. Never in my life am I going to laugh about what happened, but this made me feel better. I saw on TV this guy I think in Los Angeles, this Mexican, he fell from a building like forty floors. Nobody believed that this guy was still alive. And then I was happy. That guy wasn't *supposed* to die that day, even though he fell, you know? Then I knew it was God who took Mike, because when you are asked to leave, you're gone."

It's easy, at times like that, to believe that Tino will be fine. But there are times, too, when it flashes through his head again like a high-speed slide show: the lunch with Mike, the pitch. He doesn't talk to Angie or to his mother about it. Who could understand? Soon the feeling passes. Sometimes it takes a beer or two, sometimes a swig of the island's famous Don Q rum. Sometimes it takes crying. But it passes.

And those around Tino know to avoid the topic. This is Yauco, his home, a place where nearly everyone knows Tinito Sanchez though he's been gone these 11 years, where most abide by the code that you don't raise someone's miscarriage or divorce or criminal past unless they raise it first.

Every few weeks, though, he'll meet someone new. Sometimes Tino can feel it coming, sometimes he can't. There will be an introduction, then he'll see a light of recognition flash in their eyes. *Don't say it*, he'll think. *Don't.* . . . But they can't help themselves. It's having that knowledge, wanting it confirmed, thinking somehow that they'll be liked for knowing, that pushes them past the bounds of courtesy or respect.

"Hey," they say, "are you the one who killed that guy?"

Anytime he swings a bat, he can still feel the pinch of the bone he broke punching the concrete floor that day. Anytime a sharp foul ball flies, anytime voices yell, "Heads up!" that sick feeling returns. Such moments would make anyone wonder why Tino goes near a baseball field these days. Why not wash his hands of the game, get himself free, if only for a little while? When he hears the question, Tino's face is closed, dark; boys fire the ball back and forth through the Caribbean night. But as he speaks the light breaks again over his features; the words tumble. He's smiling.

"I think I have to do it—for him," he says. "I have to do good things for people. All the knowledge I learned in baseball, I have to give it back. That's why I'm here. Because as you can see, this is not Yankee Stadium, but I'm happy. I grew up here."

The next afternoon, Tino is sitting in the living room of his parents' house in Yauco, a squat, heavily curtained affair with a spacious patio out back. He and Angie live upstairs; his mother sleeps on the first floor. His sister, Hilda Rosa, who lives in the house Tino grew up in not far away, is here, and her 13-year-old son, Tony Ayala, has flopped on a couch to play a videogame on the large-screen TV. Aside from Tino Sr., off working in Raleigh, North Carolina, for Flextronics, the family is living together for the first time in a decade, if only temporarily. In a week, Tino's mother and sister will fly to the States to be with Tino Sr. Tony will stay here in Yauco. Tinito and Angie will stay, too, with baby Isabella, burbling on the floor now and pulling a blanket over her face.

A duffel bag's worth of baseball gear—gloves, a chest protector, shin guards, cleats, remnants of Tino's career—lies dumped on the floor. Against one wall stands a console table covered with framed photographs, color portraits of uncles, friends, Tony, Tino Sr., a shot from last month when Tino and Angie and the baby made it to Tino's 10-year high school reunion. A Tulsa Drillers souvenir baseball emblazoned with Tino's name and picture teeters along the cluster's edge. Angie points. A memorial lapel button had been carefully set front-and-center: the face of Mike Coolbaugh staring at something far away.

Angie perches on the edge of the couch and speaks of how worried the family became when Tino wouldn't answer his cell phone in the day and a half after the accident, how she agonized over him being so far from home then. His silence made her "crazy," she says. Tino begins translating her words into English, and it becomes apparent that they have never spoken about what happened, not once, in the months since.

After ten minutes, Tino says, "Will you excuse me?" He stands and walks out of the room, as if to go to the bathroom or refill a drink. He returns after a few moments and says, "This is what I've been thinking: God put me in a situation that really makes you appreciate life. Maybe I could take this incident positive or negative, but since it happened I've really enjoyed life. Every time I wake up, I'm a very happy man."

His mother, Rosa Julia Rivera, sits to talk. She is one of those women who looks for any opportunity to laugh, to crack jokes and make those around her comfortable—always supportive, always light. But the instant she starts talking about Tino and Mike, how she couldn't sleep for 36 hours after hearing of the accident and kept crying and calling Tino's phone only to hear it flip to voice mail, that stops: Rosa bursts into tears, drops her face into her hands. Tino is translating again, and it becomes clear that, no, he had never spoken to his mother about any of this either. She's sure that her husband, Tino Sr., is in even worse shape, but "he doesn't let anybody know," she says, struggling to rebuild her smile. "The two of them are exactly alike."

Asked when she began to believe that her son had gotten out of danger, when he finally hit the point where he could live with what he'd done, Rosa doesn't hesitate. "*Nunca*," she says. Never.

"Will you excuse me?" Tino says.

When he comes back, Rosa is saying that she doesn't blame baseball for what happened. "We still love it," she says. "If not, our grandson wouldn't still be playing. We wouldn't still be going to the practices like we do."

The afternoon light has dimmed. Tino suggests taking the conversation out back. His mother and wife and daughter stay inside. Tony follows, picks up a length of white plastic pipe, and as his uncle begins talking, swings it dozens of times on the grass off the patio. Tino mentions again what he said the night before. He wants to make sure he's gotten it right.

"I look back, and I think of Mike and how he encouraged me," Tino says. "How he did that and what God would want me to do. God put us both in that situation; so every time I'm on that field now, God wants me to think about Mike and care about people the way he did. Follow his example. I do appreciate life more and I try to teach that now—not only baseball."

He takes a sip, then hurries inside to spike the drinks with a little Don Q. It's almost dinnertime; the breeze brings a sweet taste from off the Caribbean. When Tino returns, he speaks of the great Puerto Ricans he's played with and how the winter ball scene is deteriorating and how videogames are destroying kids' interest in the game, and how much he wants to coach. He speaks of how, like any player, he just wanted a manager to tell the truth. Then he laughs about how pathetic it was, him hitting all those Tulsa hitters in batting practice last summer. "And my teammates never complained," Tino says. "They always supported me."

His voice softens. Tino apologizes. It's not clear why at first, but then he says, "I had to stop, I had to leave for a minute," and it is then that his abrupt walkouts earlier began to make sense.

"I was feeling this pressure in my head, like I've never had before," Tino says. "I didn't know talking about it would do that. It wasn't a headache, really. . . ." He makes his fingers into claws, lifts them to just above his forehead. "It was like this . . . pressure." He's neither smiling nor frowning now, but something in between, as if his face hasn't settled on how to express a newfound truth. Death lets no one off easy. It just lets you fool yourself a while.

Midway through the fourth inning, as the opposing pitcher warms up, Tino leaves his post along the first base fence, ducks through a gate and out into an alley behind Parque Hermanos Lugo. A rooster high-steps through the dirt, his less cocky brethren crowing through the bushes nearby, just past the makeshift stove squatting a few feet behind the home-team bench. Rosa Julia has been tending this battered steel pot here all game long, and now Tino lifts the lid to reveal dozens of pork chops bubbling in a thick orangy broth. He breathes in deep. "This," he says, "is how we roll."

It's a gorgeous Saturday, 80 degrees and sun-splashed. The Sanchez household had been waiting all week for this morning, when Tino would manage his nephew Tony's team, the Diego Hernandez Indians, in a Little League game against the Mets here at the ballfield nestled in the neighborhood of Barinas. Yauco's green wrinkled hills hover beyond the left field fence; a soft wind blows; the ball stirs a soft cloud of dust every time it smacks into the catcher's mitt. Tino's grandmother and Tony's mom, Hilda Rosa, are also here, and baby Isabella is passed from family to friends to all the women who just have to hold her. Foul balls loop over the covered stands, and everyone listens for the telltale *pock!* as they plummet onto the scattering of parked cars outside. This time, an alarm starts whooping.

"Hijoputa!" Hilda Rosa yells, shuffling to the exit. The 200 people in the stands howl her out the door, and even her own mother couldn't help but giggle.

"She said, 'Motherfucker,'" Rosa Julia whispers in English. Then she laughs some more.

The game is a rout. Tony is 13 but plays much older, beneficiary of having an uncle like Tino, a grandfather like Tino Sr. Hitting left-handed, he lashes an RBI single into right field, racks up an unassisted double play at shortstop, then comes in to pitch in the bottom of the fifth, striking out two and forcing a weak pop-up to short. Tino watches it all, grunting his approval, leaning against the fence and dodging one foul ball that skitters about his feet. He calls out adjustments, encourages the kids who need it: *"Eso es. Don't think so much. Eso es. Bueno."* He tries not to favor Tony; one of his pitchers is battling depression and his second baseman is too small. But sometimes Tino can't help himself.

After all, in a way Tony is his now. The boy's father lives somewhere up north and is not a factor in his life, and with the women moving to North Carolina, Tino knows Tony will be following his lead even more in the next few months. Tino likes this. He has been doing exactly what Tino Sr. did with him, making Tony into a switch-hitter, having him alternate whether the pitcher is right-handed or left-. In the fifth inning, Tony, hitting right-handed, cracked a sacrifice fly high and deep into left to seal the final score, 12–2. With that, Tino walked from the bench to the stands, picked up his baby girl, stared into her eyes, and kissed her on the cheek. When he sat back down, he said to no one in particular, "He hit that ball *hard.*"

The plan is to send Tony, eventually, to the States to join his mother and grandparents, get better schooling, more of a showcase for the scouts. "I think he's going to do it," Tino says. "I really think he's going to make it. He's got the knowledge, he's got the strength. He's twenty times better than I was at that age. I was only an athlete. He's a baseball player."

The players rush off the field. The winners grab plastic plates and forks and wolf down pork chops in the shade. Parents and kids straggle out; Rosa Julia and Hilda and Tony leave, and soon the park empties; the next game won't start until 1 p.m. Tino stays; as a Little League official, he has to show his face and keep an eye on the players and coaches from other teams. But it doesn't feel like work. "Tinito!" someone calls out every few minutes, and maybe he remembers the name behind the voice and maybe not, but the face he always knows. Three steps in front of home plate, a man tosses a baseball to his two-year-old son. The boy bops a nifty pop-up and runs to first, runty legs pumping. The father fields the ball, but the boy doesn't care; he keeps running, kicking up dirt on his way to second, down to third under the noon sun, round the corner and coming home now. He steps on the plate, hard to make sure everyone sees, and cracks no smile as he scores. This is serious.

A thin codger with a bulbous red nose and a Yankees cap walks toward home plate carrying an unruly mass of string, tied at one end to a slender steel stake. No one pays him much attention. He kicks dirt off the once-white plate, drops the stake, untangles the string as he walks it up the third base line. Silently, another man in a Yauco Little League t-shirt appears behind the plate and shoves the stake into the dirt precisely at the plate's pointed rear end. Yet a third man appears carrying a tin coffee can nailed to a broom handle. The can, its bottom reduced by an icepick to hundreds of tiny holes, is filled with powdered white chalk. The third man walks along the third base line tamping the can into the dirt, leaving behind a white blotch exactly every eight inches, his line and distance watched by the hawkeyed Yauco Little League man accompanying him. When the two men reach third, the Yankees stringwalker abruptly departs, describing a slow arc behind the pitcher's mound all the way over to first base. Tin Can and Yauco Little League repeat their promenade, this time up the first base line. Then Tin Can is on his own to tamp out a dotted line around the pitcher's mound, the batter's box.

Now it's 1:07 p.m. A new pair of umpires, shirts puffed with authority by hidden padding, stroll toward home plate. Players loosen up on the side, throwing hard, then harder. Tino is sitting in the stands now, along third base. The game begins, with the level of play a bit higher, the crowd a bit thicker, than the one involving his own team an hour before. Every few minutes, there's a crack and a ball hurtles into the outfield, and one time it spins into the gap and a boy runs very fast and voices cry *VAMOS!* and he beats the throw and baseball's most exciting play—the triple—feels like it always does, a gift for everybody.

Tino is speaking of how those 11 years, that endless pressure and boredom, changed him, how the game changed him, when he notices that everyone on the field has stopped. It's not one of the game's usual pauses, but a rare moment of inaction within the action, when the ball is in play but no one moves. "Look at that," he says. The pitcher has come off the mound holding the ball high, his head on a swivel. One runner dances off first base and another off third, and fans and coaches scream and he's succumbing to panic, you can see it: The kid has forgotten how to back them both down. Tino shakes his head.

"All you got to do is run hard over there, see?" Tino mutters, flinging a hand toward first base. "Then you look at this guy." He points to the runner at third. Somehow, then, the message gets transmitted: The pitcher proceeds to do just that, the base runners back up. Teammates, coaches, parents, relax. Tino spits between his shoes.

"You have no control," he says. "That's the first thing they teach you in baseball: Control the things you can control. Get early to the field, work hard, run the bases hard, make contact with two strikes—things like that. But you cannot control that guy painting two pitches on the black. You can't control that guy diving for the ball and catching it. You can't control other guys moving up to another level even though you're better. The moment when I grew up, when I became a man, is when I took everything upon myself. If I don't play? It's on me. If I don't move up, it's on me."

For him that's it, as deep as baseball gets. The game is hard, and enlightenment within its bounds is reached only when you come to understand that it can be cruel, can be unfair, can destroy marriages, break down pride, morality, hope. And yet the only way to survive intact, to escape a well-justified cynicism, is to ignore all that and assume responsibility. Tino Sanchez didn't get the job he wanted. Another man did, and that man died. Tino was there that night in North Little Rock—not in Denver, not in St. Louis or some other major league city—because he wasn't good enough to be anywhere else. "You have to take all excuses out of yourself," he says. *"I'm struggling because I'm not getting good batting practices; the coach isn't throwing a good BP; I'm not good because the pitching coach doesn't work with me . . .* I say fuck that. A lot of players who don't have success start complaining. Every professional player has a story. But my story is simple: I didn't make it because of me."

Still, the sun is shining and his wife and baby love him, and guess what? His nephew might just be a big leaguer someday. When Tino swears he's going to be fine, you almost believe—you want to believe—that the game can give something back. He loved baseball and got punished, yes. But the game taught him how to be tough on himself—tougher, maybe, than he should be. Mike was an accident but dead is dead, and Tino can't help but think, *It's on me.* That's his motto now, a lifer's guide for life. Without it, Tino knows, he'll be lost. With it, he may find something close to peace.

◯ ◯ ◯

THIS, BOB COOLBAUGH DOESN'T GET. He is sitting at his kitchen table, and Mary Lu has just finished saying how Scott struggled with going back to baseball before the funeral and is about to move on when Bob stops her. "Who?" he says. "Scott said that?" He shakes his head and shrugs: the way people think sometimes. "I can't believe he'd feel like that," he says. "I'm surprised the player who *hit* him quit. If you drove your car and you hit somebody and killed them, I understand you feel bad. But it was an *accident.* Tino had no control; he did absolutely nothing wrong. I don't understand how he lets that affect him so much."

"I think it affected him because it's just . . ." Mary Lu pauses, hunts for the word, finds it: ". . . human."

"It wouldn't affect me."

A late April Tuesday, midday. From the table you can look out back of the squat San Antonio home and see the stretch of backyard where the batting cage used to stand, the spot just shy of where the pool went in and the daughters finally got their way. The phone rings now and then; Scott's in town with the RoughRiders and there are arrangements to make, tickets to line up. Earlier, Mary Lu had walked out of the room and returned with the framed wall hanging plastered with photos of Mike and Scott from '97, in uniform against each other that one time—"Bama Boys," the words up top say—and she was beaming. For that second, you could almost pretend that this is a spring like the previous 35, with the baseball season still young. Even when she or Bob talks about Mike, the two of them can start off so steadily that for a while you'd never know.

"My friend had a two-year-old that drowned," Mary Lu says. "This two-year-old would be fifty years old today. She said, 'You never get over it. One thing you do is, talk about him, but don't think about him.' That's the best advice ever." But then her voice quavers, falls into a whisper, and you're reminded that there has never been a spring like this here.

They're pleased to hear that Tino is getting stronger. But in the family's eyes, reaching out to him felt like no great moral stand. Mary Lu points to the front page of this morning's paper. There's a story about the funeral of 76-year-old Viola Barrios, a renowned local restaurateur who had been killed by her next-door neighbor in a robbery attempt. Viola's son, Louis, who had known Mike since high school and ran the same Mexican restaurant where scout Al LaMacchia last spoke to him, invited the killer's family to the services and offered to pay for his legal defense. "Now *there's* somebody who is really forgiving," Mary Lu says.

But when you mention that, well, it's not the parents' fault, Bob cuts in. "I don't agree," he says. "I blame the parents. Not for the act of killing, but I don't believe they showed enough discipline. You didn't bring the kid up right. Their kid quit school, was in trouble, and you know where that comes from? When he's five, six, seven years old. I was very strict. I tried to teach them the right thing to do. To have your kid murder somebody? You contributed to his upbringing and if you contributed more this wouldn't have happened.

"My own daughter, she has a son. How old is Nicolas?" he says to Mary Lu. "Two? Three? He did something and my daughter said, 'Tell grandpa you're sorry.' He wouldn't. She said, 'If you don't tell grandpa you're sorry I'm not taking you to the zoo.' I told her, 'Lisa, that's psychology that's stupid, because to get him to do something you're giving him a prize. Now when he's sixteen and you say, 'Quit smoking!' he'll say, 'Give me $20 a week and I will.' My philosophy is: If he says no, you take a strap and whack him across his ass. Punish him if he doesn't do it; don't give him a prize if he does. That didn't happen in my house."

At 73, Bob is still loud, *emphatic*, ready to make his case. He suffered a stroke in 2003, Mary Lu bringing him home in a wheelchair, and though limping and lacking much of the grip in his right hand, still attacked problems as furiously as ever: He has just fixed the clothes dryer, built a swing for Lisa's kids. Everyone agrees: The man has barely lost a mental step. But like many with a highly analytic bent, Bob Coolbaugh is made uneasy by the sloppiness of human emotion, its imperviousness to the dictates of numbers and facts. He got a phone call the night Mike died, too, some Tulsa official calling with condolences. "Ahhh, forget it," he whispers now, eyes filling. Better, when someone asks how he's holding up, to try analyzing it away.

"The odds of this?" Bob says. "What's the greatest number there is, beyond trillions? If I took you and stood you in the first base coaching box and had you close your eyes, you wouldn't get hit in the head to kill you if you stood there fifty years. You know how many guys steal second base with their head down and the batter's hitting? The runner from third is coming home; he's even closer. Whether Mike was looking at the runner and he didn't turn his head quick enough . . . maybe he got lackadaisical. I wonder. If you asked me where's the most dangerous place Mike could be? A car, the team bus, airplane rides, anything. I'd say the safest place is the baseball field, unless you were the pitcher or the batter. Aside from them? Forget it.

"The less I talk about it . . . I try to avoid it and then I think about it—and I just wonder. If he'd been killed in a car wreck or a bus wreck, you know? But it was like I was wishing for him to get the job, to get a job in baseball. . . ."

Now Mary Lu is speaking of the moment they told the boys their daddy was dead. Bob stands up, says, "You don't need me anymore. I've got to pack." He walks out to the garage and begins rattling around with the swing, the things he needs to take to Lisa's house up in Plano. When he finishes, half an hour later, Bob pads quietly into the darkened living room next to the kitchen, sits back on the recliner, closes his eyes. Mary Lu keeps talking, but he doesn't interrupt, doesn't call out. He coughs, once, twice, every few minutes or so, a god in this place to four children once. Time crushes every god.

"I don't know if I have the faith," Mary Lu is saying now. "I think that's why I have a lot of trouble. Mandy's so sure she's going to see Mike again, and I'm not sure. I really wish I could believe that he can look down and see all this. I was sitting in Lisa's family room after she had the baby. She's got a fireplace with a spotlight over it, oh my God, it was dark; that's the only light that was on. I was holding the baby, trying to get her to sleep, and I saw him. I know I saw him. She's got these three windows, no curtains or drapes, and he was outside. Her house extends and there's a patio there and it was like he was peeking around but he was huge. Just huge. And it was like he was all in gold, like a brownish gold. He was peeking around and when he saw me look up he was gone. I was crying and Lisa comes out and says, 'What's the matter?' and I said, 'Mike was just here.' My husband would think I was crazy. And then we were both crying. . . ."

Maybe it was just a reflection from the fireplace, the flames, the glass. But if nothing else, Mary Lu is sure of this: Mike wasn't wearing a uniform.

"I never looked at my son as a baseball player," she says. "I never did. Even now, to brag about him like that? I mean, it was happy times, but I always just looked at him as my son. And now I keep thinking he's just away. He'll be back anytime."

Everyone else? They can change the channel or turn off the television, avoid the websites of teams Mike used to be a part of. They can stay away from ballfields for a week or a month, however long it takes to make the memories stop stinging. But Scott Coolbaugh has little choice. Every afternoon in spring, summer, and fall, he's standing behind a screen in front of some pitcher's mound throwing batting practice, and the balls always come back, flying past mostly but sometimes pinging off the black aluminum frame just in front of his face. And every evening, just before the Frisco leadoff man heads to the plate, Scott stands up in the dugout, removes his wool baseball cap, and grabs a batting helmet and sets it on his head. He moves to the dugout steps on the far end, closest to first base, places his left foot up one step as if frozen in the act of climbing. He waits.

Scott doesn't much care for the helmet rule. He sympathizes with those old-school baseball men who think of it as an overreaction; a helmet wouldn't have deflected Tino's foul ball from the killing spot. Still, Scott doesn't squawk. He knows that the general managers who voted in the new rule often think about public relations, and he supposes that if it saves someone from a head injury in the future, that's a good thing. But if a helmet wouldn't have saved Mike, in one sense it's just an inconvenience, one more thing to remember while heading out to the field. It's also the most tangible reminder, inning after inning, that his brother is dead. The first time someone asked his batting helmet size, in spring training, Scott didn't know what the man was talking about; the first time he put one on, it felt strange. All of baseball's customs and rules become second nature with time. But in this, the first season after, Scott always knows when he's putting on a helmet and why.

The leadoff man—today it's outfielder Ben Harrison—hops up the steps with bat in hand. Only then does Scott move. He walks toward the first base coaching box at San Antonio's Wolff Stadium but doesn't stop; he keeps going, passing it on his left, heading a full 10 feet north of the base. Then he veers right, setting himself a full 18 feet east of the foul line. Another new rule has been put in effect for the 2008 season: No coach can break south of the box, toward home plate, until after the ball has been hit. But Scott couldn't even spit to that line, isn't in the box at all. Few, if any, base coaches set up farther away from home plate.

The first pitch flies. Once the game begins, Scott tries to block out stray fears and thoughts, anything that could distract. He used to let his mind drift a bit when in the box, especially when none of his players were on base, but now he pays almost inhuman attention to each pitch and swing, trying to gauge with all he knows of the quirks and history of each hitter and batter—pull hitter? soft-tosser? hard thrower? opposite-field hitter?—the minuscule possibilities of a ball suddenly rocketing his way. "I'm more cautious," he says. "I'll see a foul ball go into the stands or just past the coach, and I get flashbacks. That's the most difficult part. Every time I see a ball hit somebody or something, my first reaction is a flinch: *My gosh, are they all right?* That bothers me."

Still, quitting doesn't seem to be an option. As awkward as it can be these days, being in a clubhouse and on a ballfield "is something that's natural to me, something I've done all my life," he says. "It's my comfort zone."

This is Scott's second year as the RoughRiders hitting coach. After retiring as a player in 1999, he began a climb up the coaching ranks, starting as a AA hitting instructor, then picking up managing stints in A-ball before becoming manager of El Paso for 2003–04. He finished with a managing record of 224–333, which, in the developmentally minded minors, is less underwhelming than it seems. Regardless, he left the Diamondbacks organization, took two years off to start a construction company, then came back to baseball in 2007 with a plan. He wanted to get back to the majors again. But he was sure that if he continued managing, his lack of major league playing or coaching credentials would work against him whenever a big league job opened; he'd spend his career getting bypassed by bigger names. The best way up was by becoming a hitting guru, responsible for 12 players whose improvements would always be quantifiable. When the RoughRiders came to Scott after the '07 season to see if he'd be interested in managing again, he said no. "Bouncing back and forth is not going to be the best thing for me," he says. "I had managed before, but when I got that opportunity to be a hitting coach, I just fell in love with it. Focusing down to one little thing: It really sparked me."

One month into the 2008 season, Frisco is hitting a league-leading .295. Tonight the RoughRiders came back from three runs down to beat the Missions in ten innings. Scott is proud of all that, but a year ago he would've been prouder. He is 41. His son Tyler is 14 and plays select baseball; Scott coaches that team, too, when he's home. When Mike died, one of Scott's first thoughts was to move Mandy and the boys up north to Colleyville so he could help in raising them. Mike, he's sure, would've done the same for him. And though Mandy decided to stay in San Antonio, Scott still felt his days transformed. "It changed my life," he says. "Nothing is taken for granted. You never know when it's going to end. I want to enjoy watching my son play and be a part of his life, and my daughter's in gymnastics and does a lot of activities at eleven years old, and those are the important things. For me it's not so much that we go out and get ten or fifteen hits a night now. It's my relationships with the players, rather than just getting the most out of them. Before I was focused on getting them better; now I'm trying to get to know the players, to know their lives, try to be more supportive and more of a role model as far as life goes, not as far as baseball goes. Because in the long run that's irrelevant. It's what we do for a living. It's not more important than life."

He is standing outside the clubhouse, 45 minutes after the game; the shuffle of freshly showered players to the bus stopped a while ago.

Just 14 years old, Wolff Stadium is one of the senior parks in the Texas League now, its hallways dingy and damp. As he talks, Scott glances up at the wall; a three-inch cockroach scuttles overhead. He blinks, and actually smiles: That's Texas. That's the minor leagues. The clubhouse door swings open, and out comes one last pair of legs and a head flanked by two massive equipment bags: Adam Fox has just gotten the tap. He's on his way to the Rangers' Triple-A affiliate in Oklahoma City, a former tenth-round pick, a third baseman like Scott and Mike, a player who's not quite a prospect and not quite an organizational player, bouncing as he has the last two years between Double- and Triple-A.

"Good luck," Scott says. "Keep it going, and never come back." Fox whirls with the bags on the back, face agleam with excitement and nerves, confidence and fear, youth and energy and the surety that this time everything will work out. "Thanks!" he nearly shouts, and Scott watches as he turns again, until the kid rounds the corner and is gone.

Springtime now, and she's still bargaining. *Send Mike back. Send him just to me and I won't tell the boys, okay? Let me enjoy him for just a day, an hour.* Or: *I should be the one who died. The boys need him more.* Or: *Turn back the clock. Make it so we don't have to have children. I'll trade the family I so wanted to have Mike alive again.* The last one always makes Mandy feel odd, though, because she knows she's not serious. Truth be told, she's not even praying to God. She's praying to Mike. Heaven? She knows that she's supposed to work and live so she can join Jesus someday, but her heaven has nothing to do with what

some priest tells her. "Right now I'm ready to go to heaven to be with
Mike—not God," Mandy says. "I don't cry to God. I cry to Mike."

It's the first day of May, 2008, the afternoon air in San Antonio
already sauna hot. The boys have a baseball game today, but for now
they're at school and the house is quiet; the baby is sleeping. A memorial poster of Mike is propped in front of the fireplace, with a shot of
him from 1998, the year he became hers. High on the living room wall
above the entrance to the kitchen, three green funeral ribbons—the
flimsy remains of wreaths ten months dead—are pinned, their glittery
gold letters sending the same message: "Till We Meet Again," "Beloved Brother," "Your No. 1 Fans Joey and Jacob." Mandy is 33 years
old. She knows she needs to move forward, but . . . forward to what?
She still can't bring herself to clean out Mike's car. She has yet to open
his laptop. At her worst moments, she'll smell him—not his favorite
Dolce&Gabbana cologne, but *him*, the musky scent of Mike's skin.
When it happened again a month ago, the odor was so overwhelming
that she wondered if she might be losing her mind. Then Joey stopped
in his tracks and sniffed too.

Joey is six now, and can go hours and days without showing any
real effect. But during spring training Mandy sat him down to watch
an ESPN segment about the new batting helmet rule, not realizing
there would be clips of coaches dodging foul balls. Joey stared at the
images for a moment, mouth open, then announced, "Mom, Dad had
given me a glove . . ." and began a frantic three-hour search for a glove
Mandy never knew existed. Then on Easter Sunday, he was swinging
his orange aluminum bat when a two-year-old cousin walked into it,
eye first; there was sudden swelling, a trip to the emergency room.
Mandy found her son crying. "Is he going to die?" Joey asked.

Jake, two years younger, has been more direct: Glancing at the baseball images on his Round Rock Express lunchbox and asking, "Is this the field Dad died on?" He notices the coaches in their helmets at a Missions game and says, "They're wearing a hat because Daddy died. Daddy should've worn a hat." Or, in just the past month, repeating casually, "Mommy, I'm ready to die. I really want to go be with Daddy."

But then that stopped. Jake crawled into bed with her one morning. "Mommy, I'm not going to die anytime soon," he said. "Daddy said, 'Jake, you have a lot of good times ahead of you.'" And then he described a conversation with Mike, his father talking to him about baseball and being married someday and eventually joining him and then they'd spend eternity together. "Eternity's a long time, right?" Jake asked.

"It's times like that," Mandy says, "that I think Mike's right there."

He's come to her in dreams, too. The first was a night in September, after she'd heard from too many people that Mike was watching over them, that it would all be okay. She believed none of it, because how could they know? Only Mike knew. And then she dozed off and there he was, wearing the Guess jeans and white shirt that he wore the night she first met him, that blind date set up by his sister Linda. He told Mandy he was waiting for her, he would always wait, and God, she loved how he filled out those jeans. He made her know that he wasn't in anguish. "Then I questioned it: *Well, that's a picture you have in your mind*," Mandy says. "But all I know is that all my senses were alive. I could smell him. I could feel him. He was warm. It was *him*; there's not a doubt in my mind. I know it was. We were together."

That helped. She didn't want to hear that she'd meet someone new after that.

The second time happened around that first Christmas after, when Mandy realized that being faithful to Mike would mean a near-constant loneliness. She thought herself strong enough, but she was scared of the unknown, some vulnerable moment in the future when she might waver. It wasn't so much the idea of sex as the idea of need: of just needing to feel a kiss or a touch from someone who wasn't a friend, a relative, sometime over the next 40 years of her life. Mandy laughs at herself when speaking of this; the subject is embarrassing, of course, and it's one of her good laughs, thick and light. But since that dream, with the two of them even closer than in the first, her fear dissolved. She hasn't felt that need. Somehow, she's sure, Mike is seeing to that. Mandy chuckles again and then stops. Tears roll down her cheeks. Her voice rises to a high moan.

"I want him to come back," she says. "Just let me watch the movie of his life. His: I don't want him watching mine. I know he's watching us, and that's when I think, *Take me*. But if He did, then I know Mike would be in pain and I would never wish this on Mike. He did pick the right person, because I'd never want Mike to have to feel this. . . ."

At 4:30, the boys sit hunched over the dining room table eating noodles, an early dinner before practice. They have no interest in food as food, like all young boys; it's just something to shovel in between babbling and leaning in close and jumping up from their seats every 30 seconds for no reason other than it's good to get up and move. Then it's time to get on their baseball pants, stretch polyester jobs, leaving their half-finished plates behind for a last-minute toilet run and then the gathering of gloves and the bat lying out in the front yard and their blue Rangers hats, and now they're in the backseat stuck in traffic, eyeblack already slashed across their cheeks, not at all concerned because Mommy's up front driving and there's never a sense in a young boy that time is something to be gained or saved.

Joey and Jake are the last to arrive. All the parents have already set up along the first base line at Christ the King church, but there's no urgency: It's a soft-toss, coach-pitch scrimmage, everybody cheering every play, hit or miss, not a hint of pressure. Jake takes up position in right field, the signature glove given him by Rockies third baseman Garrett Atkins in spring training this year on his hand. Now Joey is coming to the plate and his hands look cartoonish, like Mickey Mouse arms in a pair of big white batting gloves. "Willy Taveras gave him those," Mandy says, and you remember: Taveras, the Rockies outfielder, the player who heard of Mike's death and said, "This baseball game will break our heart."

And there's Joey taking his stance with all the big league tics and swivels and confidence of someone who has played for a decade or so, or maybe just a boy who watched his father close. Mike had his routine, digging in: Hold the bat in his left hand, tap the plate, while with his right hand pushing the batting helmet down on his head. Joey does it perfectly, already without thinking, his routine now too. The first time Mary Lu came to a game this spring, she saw Joey warming up, looking so young and so old, taking his hat off, adjusting it, yanking it back on for no good reason other than that's what a ballplayer does, fiddling with his wristbands. "I can't even watch this," Mary Lu told Mandy, but she did. She watched all five innings in tears.

This time, though a natural righty, Joey's hitting left-handed, because Mike already had been teaching his boy at five how to make himself a more valuable player, less easy for some general manager to release someday; a switch-hitter offers you just that little bit *extra*, son. And so Joey is swinging lefty now, though his coaches might want him to concentrate on his natural swing more, because it's Mike's son and they all know it, just as they know that he shouldn't be using a big black wooden bat on this level, but come on now, are you going to be the one to tell that boy to put down the bat he uses to be just like his daddy?

Joey swings, a two-strike roller up the middle, nothing to get excited about, a little kid hit all the way. Except that Joey is chugging. He's racing up the first base line and the fielders are scrambling to get their stubby fingers on the ball, and he's not slowing up, his legs pump and pump until the instant he stamps on first with his right foot. Now he turns, safe, toward the infield as the scattering of parents clap and yell, and Joey puts his hands on his hips, breathing hard but not like a kid—catching it coolly, slowly like he has seen all the pros do all his life, and the back of his head is fully exposed to the crowd. They've all seen it before. Still, it's not something you ever get used to, the stenciling of a dead man's initials and uniform number on the rear of a Little League helmet: "M.C. 29." And that's when you know that Willy Taveras told the truth.

When they get home, the boys rush into the yard and fling the ball back and forth in the dusk, each miss sparking a frantic race into the empty street. Joey gets it in his head that he must put on the catcher's gear; he wants Jake to pitch. But Mandy doesn't have time to help. The baby is tired and she wants to show the quilt some fan made to honor Mike, the photo in the boys' room of Joey and Jake throwing out the first pitch at the Rockies game while Scott watched. She is laughing about how all of Mike's laundry had been dirty when he died, and how strange it was that, for the funeral, the people in charge of dressing him insisted that he be wearing underwear beneath his suit. And Mike, a boxer-brief guy, hated jockey shorts, never let her see him in them, but she had no choice; that's all that there was. "He'll never forgive me," she says. His last outfit: plain white jockeys. . . .

She leads the way into the bedroom, the baby in her arms and crying. Mandy places Anne Michael down on the bed, turns to the bureau opposite the foot of her bed, against the wall. She reaches up to a polished wooden box set atop a soft gray square of fabric, takes it in both hands, turns, and places it on the bed's thick coverlet in the space between the baby and the edge. "Mike would hate me for this," she says. "But it collects so much dust, every two or three days." Her two forefingers wipe the simple grooves, the surface clean. She lays her hands flat upon the elegant rosewood stain, the pianowood finish, the beige inlay offset in the lid. Now her hands start moving, caressing the sides of what funeral directors officiously call an "urn," but what is essentially a small coffin, 11¼ inches wide by 5 inches high by 9 inches front to back, one of the nicer offerings from Batesville Casket Co. of Indiana. Inside, encased in plastic, the last of Mike Coolbaugh gathers together in a loose brick of ash. Mandy turns the box over to show the bolts keeping it sealed. She flips it right side up again, but not without emitting one short, barely perceptible grunt.

"It's heavy," she says. "They told me it was going to be."

The baby is squalling now. But Mandy is staring down at the box, the wood shining under the bedroom light, as if seeing it for the first time. The baby kicks, six months old and hollering, her feet now just grazing the top edge, now drawing back, now just inches from the box that used to be her father. Mandy blinks at last, and lifts the box and turns and places it on the soft cloth set upon the bureau. She turns back to the bed, reaches down with both hands, and picks up her daughter, and the infant curves her back and tucks her limbs to fit into her mother's own. The crying stops. Soon it will be time for a feeding, a bath, and then the house will go dark and one by one they'll drop off to sleep. The last baseball games out west will be finishing late, in stadiums filled with strangers, and by morning all will know who won and who lost.

ACKNOWLEDGMENTS

There's really no way to thank the people at the center of this story, the ones who made this book possible. I can try saying "Thank you," of course, but it rings hollow: Words didn't help those closest to Mike Coolbaugh and Tino Sanchez at the ultimate moment, and I doubt words can express how deeply appreciative I am now.

I don't know if telling a stranger thoughts, memories, and emotions about a departed loved one, enduring a stream of clarifying e-mails and phone calls, can be cathartic. I don't know if repeated conversations with a stranger can somehow ease guilt or despair. What I do know is that, despite many pained moments, the families of Mike Coolbaugh and Tino Sanchez patiently endured my queries, replayed the times that left them devastated or elated—their whole lives, really—and constantly redefined for me the idea of grace under pressure. I'm honored to have known them.

So first, I'd like to thank Amanda Coolbaugh and her sons, Joseph and Jacob, as well as Bob Coolbaugh, Mary Lu Coolbaugh, Scott Coolbaugh, and his wife, Susan; Lisa Coolbaugh-Smith, for both her stirring photographs and constant insight, cousin Susan Andrews, as well as Mandy's sister, Katie Pavlovsky, and father, John Pavlovsky. Their collective strength is astounding.

Yet it's only matched, pound for pound, by the resiliency and dignity of the Sanchez clan of Yauco, Puerto Rico. Time and again, Tino Sanchez Jr. pushed past layers of anguish in order to replay the events of July 22 and, with the bottomless help of his wife, Angie; his father, Tino Sr.; mother, Rosa Julia Rivera; sister, Hilda Rosa; and nephew Tony Ayala Sanchez, welcomed me with great forbearance, hospitality, and perspective.

This book would have been impossible, too, without the help of Mike's friends and colleagues, especially Billy Lee, Jay Maldonado, Mike Frank, Kerry Robinson, Chris Burke, Mark Worley, Reid Ryan of the Round Rock Express, Jackie Moore, and Scott Pose.

With the Tulsa Drillers, eternal thanks go to Stu Cole, Bo McLaughlin, Jon Asahina, Matt Miller, Austin O'Shea, Brian Carroll, and the ever-helpful Mark Neely. With the Arkansas Travelers, Bill Valentine, Pete Laven, Dr. James Bryan, Bill Edwards, John Parke, and the indefatigable Phil Elson helped immeasurably. Jay Jennings's thoughtful and generous tip provided a real boost.

The staffs of the Colorado Rockies—especially Marc Gustafson and Clint Hurdle—Drillers, Travelers, Frisco RoughRiders, Baltimore Orioles, Cincinnati Reds, Toronto Blue Jays—especially Mal Romanin—and Kansas City Royals deserve special mention, as do all the baseball people who took pains to explain Mike, Tino, baseball, and the minor league life: Al LaMacchia, Keith Lieppman, Alan Zinter, Travis Driskill, Tim Purpura, Rob Butcher, Pat O'Conner, Greg Riddoch, Dave Collins, Ryan Braun, Walt Jocketty, Texas League president Tom Kayser, and especially P. J. Carey.

For their time and perspective, I am grateful to Avery Holton, Roberta Asahina, Bernie Asahina, Tyler Funneman, Jon Swanson, Mark Malcolm, Scott Garner, Dennis Higgins, Todd Traub, Warren Stephens, and Frank Thomas.

Two other sources were invaluable to this project. For the chapter on baseball casualties, Bob Gorman—the author, with David Weeks, of *Death at the Ballpark*—provided crucial help and insight personally, and I leaned heavily on the duo's exhaustive research for the statistics and details regarding such accidents. Any errors of fact or interpretation, though, are mine alone.

And in generously providing me with the raw footage of Mike filmed for the documentary *A Player to Be Named Later*, producer Bart Stephens provided an unexpected and unparalleled chance to see Mike whole, not to mention his phone message to Mandy the day he was called up. Both Kirby "Krub" Bradley and Chapman Downes of HBO were instrumental in leading me to such rich material.

Special thanks also go to the Cleveland Indians front office and staff, particularly Bob DiBiasio, Jim Folk, Steve Walters, as well as Bob Knazek. Guys, you did Ray Chapman proud. I'd also like to thank McLaughlin, Harold Baines, Asahina, and Jack Hamilton for painstakingly recounting their own accidents, and the staff of Porter Loring Mortuary in San Antonio for their sensitivity and help.

At *Sports Illustrated*, I'd like to thank Hank Hersch, who first led me to this story and artfully guided the article published in the fall of 2007, and managing editor, Terry McDonell, who allowed me the time and freedom to expand it into a book.

At HarperCollins/Ecco, the eternal faith and skill of Dan Halpern remain a marvel to me. Without the uncanny eye of Ecco's

Virginia Smith, or the exacting diligence and standards of Paul Reyes and Katherine Whitworth, the project didn't stand a chance; without the boundless enthusiasm of agent extraordinaire Andrew Blauner, it never would have seen the light of day. Don Van Natta Jr. as always provided unparalleled suggestions and support.

Lastly, of course, this book does not get written without the boundless patience, love, and stellar copyediting of my wife, Fran Brennan, or the psyche-saving energy and affection provided by our children, Jack, Addie, and Charlie. Strange . . . writing daily about the sport's dangers only made me want to take them out and play catch even more. It's a special game that can so easily turn fun into fear, and vice versa. But that, too, is baseball.